QUICK ESCAPES®

Philadelphia

22 WEEKEND GETAWAYS

FROM THE CITY OF BROTHERLY LOVE

THIRD EDITION

MARILYN ODESSER-TORPEY

The Globe Pequot Press

GUILFORD, CONNECTICUT

To my loves, Daniel, Dana, and Kristen.
We made it home together!

Photo credits: P. 1, photo by Michelle Mykowski; p. 10, courtesy Bethlehem Musikfest Association; p. 21, courtesy Carbon County Tourist Promotion Agency; p. 31, courtesy Pocono Mountains Vacation Bureau; p. 46, courtesy Camelbeach Waterpark; p. 56, photo by Steve Shaluta, courtesy Travel Berkeley Springs, WV; pp. 71, 119, photos by Cindy Turnstall, courtesy Maryland Office of Tourism Development; p. 76, photo by M. P. Myers, courtesy Chamber of Commerce of Greater Cape May; pp. 87, 97, courtesy Delaware Tourism Office; p. 110, photo by Tom Darden, courtesy Maryland Office of Tourism Development; p. 129, photo by Nino Ruisi, courtesy New York State Office of Parks, Recreation and Historic Preservation; pp. 135, 232, courtesy Washington, D.C. Convention and Visitors Association; p. 159, photo by Milton Rutherford, courtesy Bucks County Historical Society; p. 171, courtesy Pennsylvania Dutch Visitors Bureau; p. 201, courtesy Gettysburg Convention and Visitors Bureau; p. 209, courtesy New York Convention and Visitors Bureau; p. 223, photo by Middleton Evans, courtesy Maryland Office of Tourism Development; p. 249, courtesy Virginia Tourism Corporation.

Text design by Nancy Freeborn/Freeborn Design
Maps by M. A. Dubé

ISBN: 0-7627-2755-1
ISSN: 1537-3533

Manufactured in the United States of America
Third Edition/First Printing

CONTENTS

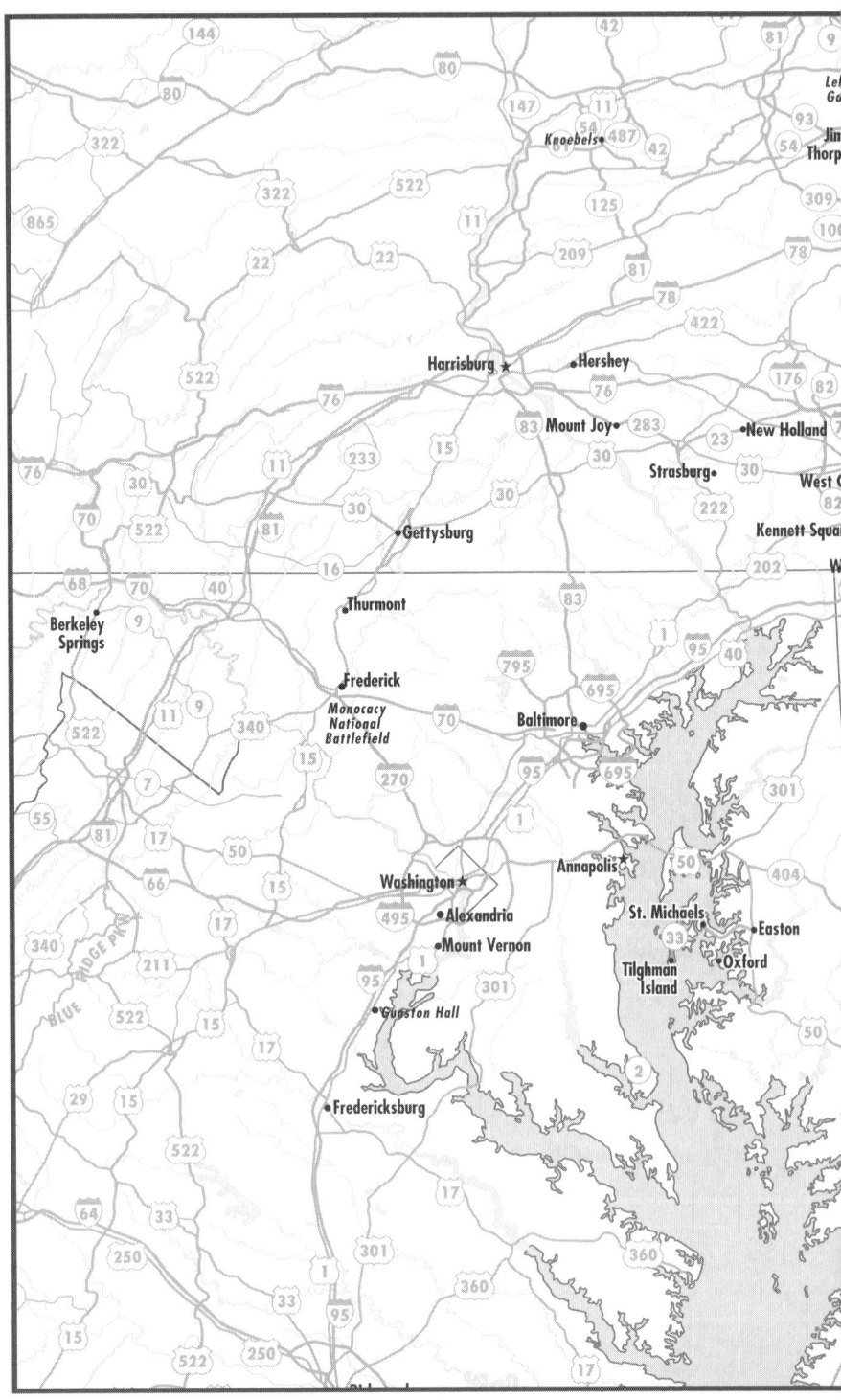

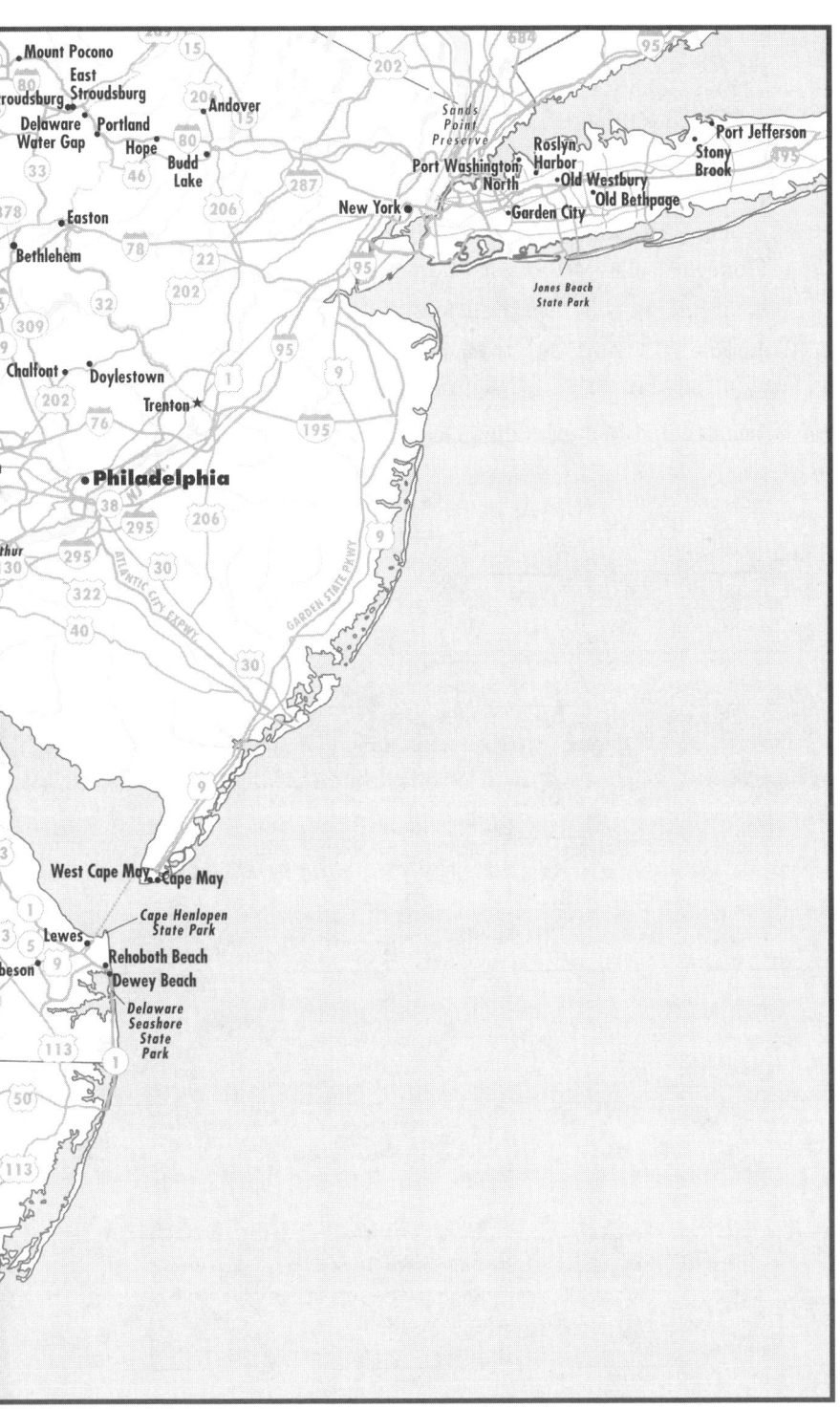

ACKNOWLDGMENTS

As I journeyed up the mountains, down the shore, and between and beyond to research this book, I had a lot of company. There were, of course, my actual traveling companions, namely my beloved Dan and Kristen, and my good friends Mary Ellen Hatch, Michele Lerman, Alonna Smith, and Marie Caldwell. Also crucial to my successful completion of this labor of love was my Dana, for helping to keep the home fires burning. Thanks, also, to my parents, Ben and Connie Odesser, for providing a home away from home for family members of the human and feathered varieties.

I would also like to express a sincere thank-you to the many wonderful professionals I met along the way, especially Mindy Bianca, who has now become a treasured friend. Gratitude also to the many fellow diners, lodgers, travelers, and locals in every town who so generously shared their favorite places, experiences, and local lore with me.

To my wonderful editors, Laura Strom and Shelley Wolf, your support and infinite patience made the experience of writing this book so much easier (and a lot more fun).

And bottom-of-my-heart thanks to Elisabeth Rozin, my friend, role model, and mentor. Your achievements are my inspiration.

INTRODUCTION

L ike most kids, I believed that the place where I lived was the center of the universe. It was kind of hard *not* to think that. After all, I lived in Philadelphia, and what place could have more history, more beauty, more fun things to do? Even our vacation destinations were close by—either "up the mountains" in winter or "down the shore" in summer.

"Up the mountains" generally meant the Poconos, where there were always countless fun ways to make your way down the glistening snow-covered slopes. "Down the shore" meant the beach, specifically any point from Ocean City to Cape May along South Jersey's Ocean Drive.

With age and experience came a broadening of my horizons. I learned that the pristine lakes and woodlands of the mountains make them as wonderful a place to visit in the summer as they are in winter. And I experienced the exhilaration of walking on a deserted windswept beach in the fall. But imagine my surprise when I realized that all mountains weren't part of the Poconos and all bodies of water weren't named Delaware, Schuylkill, or Atlantic!

Although I have lived here all my life, many of the sights, sounds, flavors, and feelings that make up the itineraries of this book were as much a revelation to me as I hope they are to you. I could always point out Philadelphia on a map, but it never really dawned on me how many exciting places and diverse experiences are easily within one to six hours driving time of the city. I hope this book will introduce you to some new ones . . . and, perhaps, put a few different twists on those you may have already discovered for yourself.

Whether your idea of a great time is going "up the mountains," "down the shore," or somewhere in between, whether you feel most comfortable in the lap of luxury or under Mother Nature's stars, and whether you prefer to be in the middle of nowhere or in the middle of everything, these quick escapes are for you. In fact, with so many escape options so close to home, you may well come to suspect, as I have, that Philadelphia really *is* the center of the universe.

UP THE MOUNTAINS
ESCAPES

The Lehigh Valley, Pennsylvania

Forged from Steel, Heart of Gold

2 Nights

Once it was a place of green rolling hills, fertile fields, and sparkling waters ruled by Mother Nature and cared for by a tribe of Native Americans called the Leni-Lenapes (also spelled Lenni-Lenapes). Attracted by the shelter of the surrounding mountains and the promise in the rich soil, the Europeans came and settled in this virtual paradise. By the mid-1700s they had brought with them a diversity of cultures—Scotch-Irish, Moravian, English, and German. In the 1900s another wave of immigrants found their way to the valley, drawn by the hope of employment and a life of prosperity in its shining new cities, the largest of which were called Allentown, Bethlehem, and Easton.

- [ ] Thrills and Chills
- [ ] Family Fun
- [ ] Town and Country
- [ ] Cultural Diversity

Later in the century the steel industry went into a steep decline . . . and so did the fortunes of these cities and their inhabitants. But today the people are fighting back, determined to make their cities shine again. They still have a lot of work ahead of them, but a visit to the Lehigh Valley can yield some delightful surprises, as waterfronts are transformed into vibrant centers for the arts, shopping, and dining; downtown areas are restored to their original charm; and the rich and varied cultural, religious, and historic heritages of its people are showcased.

Bounded on the north and northwest by the Kittatinny (Blue) Mountains, on the east by the Delaware River, and to the south by the Lehigh (South) Mountains, the Lehigh Valley is still a beautiful area. Located only an hour or so north of Philadelphia, it is also an escape for all seasons . . . especially during Christmas, when the valley becomes an old-fashioned winter wonderland of light, tradition, and song. And, after all, what more appropriate place to celebrate the season than in a little town called Bethlehem?

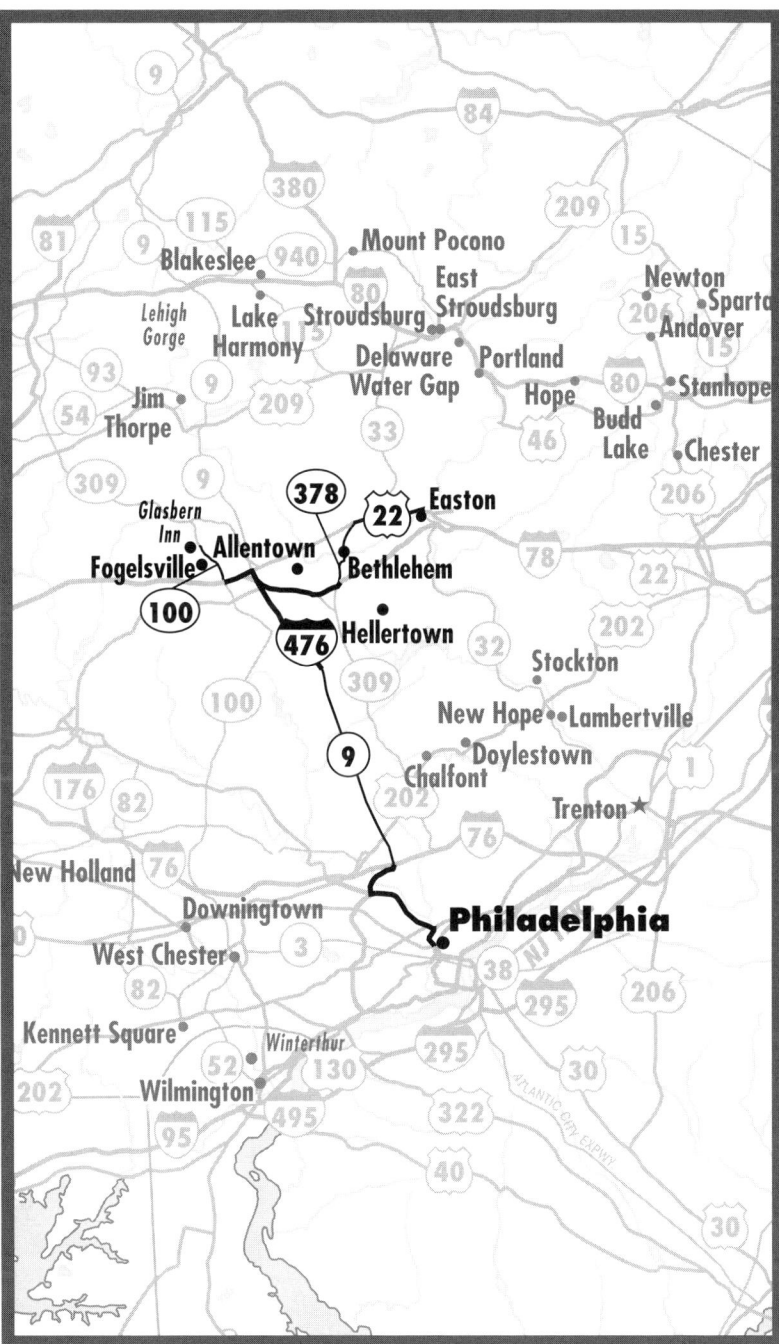

Day 1 / Morning

It's a 55-mile journey from Philadelphia to your first stop, Allentown. To get there, take the Pennsylvania Turnpike to the Lehigh Valley exit, make a right onto Route 22 East and another right onto 309 South and keep going until you see the exit for Cedar Crest Boulevard. Make a left onto Cedar Crest Boulevard and follow it past the light at the hospital. At the next light turn left onto Fish Hatchery Road for a don't-miss stop on the edge of town.

You will be experiencing a variety of different cultures during your visit to the Lehigh Valley. The **Lenni-Lenape Historical Society and Museum of Indian Culture** (2825 Fish Hatchery Road, Allentown, PA 18103; 610–797–2121) documents and celebrates the life and culture of the area's first inhabitants. Through exhibits, programs, historic trails, art, artifacts, and special events, it chronicles their history from the time they arrived in the valley through their early attempts to negotiate peacefully with the early European settlers. Open year-round; Friday through Sunday, noon–4:00 P.M. The museum's gift shop is also a wealth of Indian culture, offering books, music, and other native items. $4.00 for adults and children over twelve; $3.00 for children under twelve, children under three and seniors free.

Next stop: the heart of Allentown's cultural and historic district. To get there, turn left out of the museum parking lot onto Fish Hatchery Road. At the stoplight turn left onto Twenty-fourth Street and continue until you get to Hamilton Boulevard. Park anywhere along Hamilton and you'll be within walking distance of all the major downtown attractions.

If it's Thursday, Friday, or Saturday, it's market day in Allentown. So head to where Seventeenth Street intersects with Hamilton Boulevard and walk 3 blocks north to Chew Street and the **Allentown Fairgrounds Farmers' Market** (610–432–8425). A tradition for more than four decades, the market features sixty-five merchants offering farm-fresh produce, baked goods (the Amish bakery's hot cinnamon buns are to die for), meats and cheeses, herbs, and flowers. Open year-round Thursday 9:00 A.M.–8:00 P.M., Friday 8:00 A.M.–8:00 P.M., Saturday 8:00 A.M.–6:00 P.M.

Then head back to Hamilton and walk over to the **Lehigh County Museum** (501 Hamilton Street, Allentown, PA 18105; 610–435–4664 or 610–435–1704). Currently housed in the circa 1817 Old Courthouse, the Lehigh County Museum (610–435–1074) covers a lot of history, with exhibits that begin with the vertebra of a mastodon that roamed the area in 10,000 to 8,000 B.C. and moves onward to displays of photos and memorabilia depicting agriculture, industry, and life in the valley. By the end of 2004, the museum is scheduled to move to its permanent new location at 432 Walnut Street, Allentown, PA 18101 (phone will remain the same) with expanded exhibits and library facilities. Open Monday through Saturday, 10:00 A.M.–4:00 P.M. Admission is free.

Afternoon

LUNCH: Federal Grill & Cigar Bar, 536 Hamilton Street, Allentown, PA 18101; (610) 776–7600. This spot across the street from the museum is a popular lunchtime hangout for lawyers and other official types from the nearby courthouse. But don't let the profusion of suits deter you; you'll be just as welcome in your jeans, shorts, and polo shirts. Housed in a one-hundred-plus-year-old building, this dining establishment offers a moderately priced lunch menu featuring burgers, wraps, pizzas, and salads. Check out the daily Express Lunch specials ($6.95), which include beer-battered or sweet potato fries. Management credits the absence of cigar smoke in the air to their "state-of-the-art purification system."

Did you know that, during the Revolutionary War, the Liberty Bell "hid out" in Allentown? Fearful that it might come to harm at the hands of the British, the Philadelphia colonists smuggled our pride and joy here for safekeeping. Of course, the real McCoy has been back in Philadelphia for more than two centuries, but the **Liberty Bell Shrine Museum** (622 Hamilton Mall, Allentown, PA 18101; 610–435–4232) still displays an exact replica. Open Monday through Saturday noon–4:00 P.M. (December through February, open Thursday, Friday, and Saturday only). Donations.

The good news is it doesn't take a Rocky-like level of physical fitness to climb the outside steps to the **Allentown Art Museum** at Fifth and Court Streets (610–432–4333; Court runs perpendicular to Hamilton Street). The even-better news is that at the top of these steps is a truly exciting museum. Among the permanent exhibitions are impressive collections of fourteenth- and seventeenth-century European paintings and sculptures, as well as works representing the last 200 years of American art. Open Tuesday through Saturday 11:00 A.M.–5:00 P.M., Sunday noon–5:00 P.M. $5.00 for adults, $3.00 for seniors, $2.00 for students, free for children under twelve. Free on Sunday for all.

The Lehigh Valley is also home to two terrific amusement parks, one in Allentown and one in Easton, each with its own personality and following. If thrills, chills, and heart-stopping plummets are your idea of fun, you'll love **Dorney Park & Wildwater Kingdom** (3830 Dorney Park

Road, Allentown, PA 18104; 610–395–3724), where 200-foot-tall roller coasters, the world's longest elevated water slides, and giant wave pools await. All you have to do is head west on Hamilton Boulevard for about ten minutes and follow the signs. But don't think that the very young (or the older but not very brave) have been forgotten here. Camp Snoopy offers an array of rides scaled for wee ones, including Woodstock's Express roller coaster and Flying Ace, a mini swinging ship. Kids can also meet and greet Peanuts characters. The park also offers live entertainment for the whole family. Both parks are open May through early September; Dorney Park alone remains open until mid-October. Prices for both parks are seasonal, ranging from $26.00 to $33.50 for adults, $12.00 for children four and older, free for children three and under. Adult admission to Dorney Park alone is $21.00. Parking is $7.00.

Evening

LODGING: Glasbern Inn, 2141 Pack House Road, Fogelsville, PA 18051; (610) 285–4723. The inn where you will be dining and lodging this evening is about 10 miles west of Allentown. From Dorney Park follow Route 22/78 west to the Fogelsville exit (exit 14B). Turn left at the first traffic light; go ³/₁₀ mile and make a right onto Church Street. Proceed ⁶/₁₀ mile and make a right onto Pack House Road; continue for about ⁸/₁₀ mile. The entrance to the inn will be on your right.

In 1985 Beth and Al Granger began their transformation of "sixteen acres and the very tired farm buildings" known as Glasbern (Middle English for glass barn). The nineteenth-century bank barn for which the property is named now boasts a soaring 28-foot cathedral ceiling, stacked slate and shale walls, and ten two-story windows, creating a lovely setting for twelve elegantly rustic guest rooms and a restaurant serving gourmet fare. Mountain bikes, a video library, and an on-site fitness center are also available. Double-occupancy room rates in the Barn range from $143 to $176 (for fireplace and whirlpool) weekdays, $150 to $193 or $205 to $264 (depending on season) weekends. Accommodations are also available in the Farmhouse, Gatehouse, Garden Cottage, Carriage House, Pack House, and Stables.

Outside there are lovely trails to stroll, romantic views to share, and a heated pool.

DINNER: Glasbern Inn. Rustic wooden posts and crossed beams and ladders that climb to the hayloft provide a dramatic contrast to the gleaming cherry tables and sideboards set with pewter, silver, and crystal in the

Glasbern's candlelit dining room. It's the perfect place for enjoying expertly prepared classics with a twist, such as risotto with braised lamb, wild Alaskan king salmon with ragout of lobster, and pan-seared sea scallops and foie gras. Menu selections change seasonally. Expensive, but worth it—especially the four-course $50 prix fixe menu available on Saturday.

Day 2 / Morning

BREAKFAST: Glasbern Inn. Bask in the morning sunlight in the same room in which you dined by candlelight the night before. The inn serves a bountiful eye-opener (included with the room) that begins with a buffet of oven-fresh muffins, fresh fruit, granola, and yogurt. Country-style entrees include fragrant fruited pancakes, waffles, and assorted egg dishes and accompaniments.

After breakfast it's on to Bethlehem. Take Route 22 going east for about 20 miles. Stay on Route 22 until you get to Route 512; take 512 going south until it turns into Center Street. Keep going south until Center intersects Broad Street, one of the main streets of Bethlehem. Turn right onto Broad and go 2 blocks down to Main Street. Park your car in the public lot at Broad and Main Streets (free evenings, Saturday, and Sunday) and forget about it for the day. This town is extremely walkable.

Bethlehem is a town of startling contrasts. In the course of a 2-block walk between Broad and Church Streets, you will pass back and forth through three centuries as rustic buildings of hand-hewn logs and limestone mingle with modern structures of steel, glass, and brick, and original colonial and Victorian facades peacefully coexist next to twentieth-century chic. The majority of the town was built by members of the Moravian Church, who founded Bethlehem when they immigrated from Europe in 1741 to do missionary work among the Native Americans in the area.

To get a glimpse of early Moravian religious traditions, start at the **Moravian Museum of Bethlehem,** also known as **Gemeinhaus** (Community House), located at 66 West Church Street, Bethlehem, PA 18108 (610–867–0173), right around the corner from Main Street. Built in 1741, it was home to the town's entire population while other buildings were being constructed, and it remained the center of worship and daily life. Today exhibits explain the ideals, arts, and culture of the early Moravians. The gift shop offers deliciously scented beeswax candles and other handmade items reflecting traditional early Moravian arts and crafts.

Open February through December, Tuesday through Saturday 1:00–4:00 P.M. Admission is $6.00 for adults, $3.00 for children six and under. Whether or not you join a tour, some of the key sites you should check out are:

- The **Central Moravian Church.** Constructed in 1806 when the total population of Bethlehem numbered only 580, this structure is designed to seat 1,500 because the Moravians planned to share their house of worship with the converted Indians and friendly colonists in the area.

- **God's Acre,** off Market Street between Heckewelder Place and New Street. All the grave sites at this 1742–1912 Moravian cemetery are marked with identical flat stones to symbolize the Moravians' belief in equality in death as well as in life. One of these graves belongs to Tshoop, a member of the Mohican tribe who was immortalized as Uncas in James Fenimore Cooper's novel *Last of the Mohicans.*

- **Nain House,** at Heckewelder Place. This small 1758 log house is the only structure along the Delaware and Lehigh Heritage Corridor that was built by and lived in by Native Americans. Open by appointment; call the Moravian Museum. Admission is free.

After your walking tour, head for 427 North New Street, where you'll find 250 years of folk art, furnishings, paintings, and fine art at the **Kemerer Museum of Decorative Arts** (427 North New Street, Bethlehem, PA 18018; 610–868–6868). The collections of Bohemian glass and regionally made tall case clocks are particularly dazzling. Open year-round Tuesday through Sunday noon–5:00 P.M.; daily during December. $6.00 for adults, $3.00 for children six and under.

Afternoon

LUNCH: Bethlehem Brew Works, 569 Main Street, Bethlehem, PA 18018; (610) 882–1300. It's only a 1½-block walk from the Kemerer Museum to this fun spot that serves great food in a dramatic setting. The interior is all steel pipe, diamond plate, and copper tanks, attesting to Bethlehem's industrial heritage and the presence of a working brewery on the premises. The moderately priced menu includes salads, burgers, and sandwiches, along with some uniquely "spirited" offerings such as beer and cheese soup, porter beer chicken, diamond plate pork (medallions marinated in beer), and sweet golden ale salmon. Kids' meals—of the nonspirited variety, of course—range from $3.00 to $6.00.

For the first part of the day you've been immersed in Bethlehem's early history. Now it's time to sample some of its more modern attractions . . . like shopping. One of the best places to do that is on the 1-mile strip of Main Street that connects the north and south campuses of Moravian College, a location that has earned it the nickname "the Moravian Mile."

A shining star in Bethlehem is **Main Street Commons,** two floors of mom-and-pop owned and –operated shops at the corner of Broad and Main Streets. Some particularly interesting tenants include **Bone Appetit Bakery** (610–332–BONE), which offers all-natural, preservative-free, no salt or sugar-added treats for your best friend—the one named Spot or Fluffy. Since you deserve a treat, too, indulge in one of owner Barbara Garrison's super-premium concoctions at the **Heavenly Hedgehog Ice Cream Company** (610–332–1600).

Wonder what ever happened to the part of town where the steel mills once dominated the landscape as well as the economy? Bethlehem's SouthSide is being revived, rejuvenated—actually reinvented—into a lively, energetic center for arts and culture. From downtown New Street to the heart of the SouthSide is a quick 1½-mile trip south and across the Fahy Bridge. At the **Banana Factory** (211 Plymouth Street, Bethlehem, PA 18015; 610–332–1300), so named because it is housed in an old banana warehouse and distribution center, you can visit the studios of twenty-five emerging artists who work in a wide range of media. There's also a unique gift shop and two art galleries that exhibit local and national works. Open Monday through Thursday 8:30 A.M.–9:00 P.M., Friday until 7:00 P.M., and Saturday 9:00 A.M.–noon.

SouthSide Bethlehem also has some great shops such as **Cleo's Silversmith Studio and Gallery** at 21 East Third Street, Bethlehem, PA 18015; (610) 868–7200; **Home & Planet** at 26 East Third Street, Bethlehem, PA 18015; (610) 866–7370 (5,000 square feet of home furnishings crafted by more than 300 artisans and small companies out of recycled materials); and **Monsoon**, 11 East Third Street (between the Banana Factory and Cleo's), Bethlehem, PA 18015; (610) 866–6600 (original oil paintings, limited-edition serigraphs, and glass sculptures).

Evening

DINNER: Sun Inn, 564 Main Street, Bethlehem, PA 18018; (610) 874–9451. George Washington slept here . . . so did Martha, separated by three years and a set of stairs. John Adams called it "the best inn I ever saw." Since 1758 when the Moravians first constructed it as their first

At the Banana Factory, you can visit the studios of emerging artists.

official *Gasthaus* for travelers, this building has been a place of gracious welcome and bountiful repasts. Today the first floor of the Sun Inn, furnished in eighteenth-century style with antiques and period reproductions, looks very much as it did back then. On the upper level are the dining rooms, including the particularly pretty Tile Room, named in honor of the composition of its centerpiece stove. The moderately priced menu, with selections such as Martha Washington Pecan Salmon and Marquis de Lafayette's Vegetable Napoleon, is a tribute to traditional and contemporary cuisine as well as to the illustrious clientele the inn has hosted over the years.

Rather than steel, higher education is probably the Lehigh Valley's most prized product today. Almost a dozen colleges and universities prosper here, bringing with them an indefatigable energy and a wealth of cultural activities. One example is the **Zoellner Arts Center** at Lehigh University (420 East Packer Street, Bethlehem, PA 18015; 610–758–2787), which offers performances year-round in its three theaters, ranging from Broadway to Shakespeare, from country music to concertos and ballet to Irish dancing. While you're there, be sure to visit the center's galleries featuring exhibitions of painting, photography, sculpture, and other visual arts.

LODGING: Glasbern Inn.

Day 3 / Morning

BREAKFAST: Glasbern Inn.

Later today, you will be heading for the last of the trio of the Lehigh Valley's "big cities," Easton. But first a little side trip to Hellertown. Take Route 78 east to exit 21 (Hellertown/Bethlehem). Turn left at the bottom of the exit onto Route 412 south. Continue $1\frac{2}{10}$ miles to Penn Street; turn left. Go ½ mile. On your right-hand side will be **Lost River Caverns** (726 Durham Street, Hellertown, PA 18055; 610–838–8767). Formed sometime within the last 2,500 years and discovered in 1883, these natural limestone caverns are so beautiful that one, called the Crystal Chapel, was a popular ballroom in the late 1880s and is still used today as a wedding and christening chapel. During Prohibition, bootleggers also used the caverns for their illegal operations. On the walls, crystal formations become strange and dazzling jewels, and minerals suddenly erupt in blazes of color under the illumination of an ultraviolet light. At the gift shop, rock, mineral, and crystal specimens, jewelry, and other related items range from 27 cents to hundreds of dollars. Open year-round; Memorial Day through Labor Day 9:00 A.M.–6:00 P.M., remainder of year 9:00 A.M.–5:00 P.M. $7.50 for adults, $3.75 for children three to twelve.

To get to Easton, take Route 412 north to Route 378 north until you come to Route 22 east. Get off at the Fourth Street exit and follow signs for EASTON ATTRACTIONS. One of the most popular attractions is **Two Rivers Landing** and its focal point, the **Crayola FACTORY** (30 Centre Square, Easton, PA 18040; 610–515–8000). The fun-filled tour includes a crayon-making demonstration (complete with free samples) and many opportunities to let the artist in you go wild. And remember, old crayon colors never die; they retire to the Crayon Hall of Fame. Hours vary seasonally. Admission is $9.00, $8.50 seniors, children under two free, and includes both the Crayola FACTORY and the National Canal Museum.

The **National Canal Museum** (610–555–8000), located on the third floor of Two Rivers Landing, takes you on a journey back to a time before railroads, highways, and airplanes through photographs, artifacts, and audiovisual and interactive exhibits.

Now that you know what canal travel looked like, why not experience it firsthand on the **Josiah White II**, a real mule-drawn canal boat located right around the corner? Days and hours vary seasonally. The ticket ($6.00 adults, $4.00 children, under two free) also entitles you to visit the **Locktender's House Museum** in nearby **Hugh Moore Historical Park**, where you'll also find trails, picnic areas, and rental boats.

Afternoon

LUNCH: Pearly Baker's Ale House, 11 Centre Square, Easton, PA 18042; (610) 253–9949. A huge crystal chandelier, brought here from Czechoslovakia in the 1940s, is the centerpiece of this razzle-dazzle pre-Prohibition–style restaurant/bar right across from Two Rivers Landing. One signature recipe on the moderately priced lunch menu is Brooklyn Brown Ale Onion Soup, regular or "boulder style" (baked with mozzarella and blue cheese). Some interesting entrees are grilled chicken and papaya quesadillas; mushroom ravioli; and flat breads (pizza toppings served on a hand-rolled whole-wheat crust). Children's selections are also available.

Bushkill Park (2100 Bushkill Park Drive, Easton, PA 18040; 610–258–6941) is the second of the great Lehigh Valley amusement parks mentioned earlier. This one's for individuals and families who long for the good old days before bigger, faster, and scarier were the standard. Pay by the ride or purchase an unlimited ride pass to enjoy the seventeen classic old-fashioned delights, including a 1926 Allan Herschell carousel with Grand Wurlitzer band organ, and walk-through fun houses. Picnic grounds and free parking. Open weekends Memorial Day through June 15; open Wednesday through Sunday, June 17 through Labor Day. An all-day ride pass costs $15, $10 on Wednesday.

To return to Philadelphia, take Route 22 west until you get to Route 476 (northeast extension of Pennsylvania Turnpike). Drive south on 476 until you get to the Schuylkill Expressway. The trip home should take you a little more than an hour.

There's More

Haines Mill Museum, 3600 Dorney Park Road, Allentown, PA 18104; (610) 435–1074. Learn about farming and milling techniques during colonial times at this working gristmill built in 1760 and restored in 1909. Open May through September, Saturday and Sunday 1:00–4:00 P.M. Admission charge.

Allentown Symphony Hall, 23 North Sixth Street, Allentown, PA 18101; (610) 432–6715. Home of the Allentown Symphony Orchestra and other performances for all ages from musical theater to professional concerts and lectures.

Easton Museum of Pez Dispensers, 15–19 South Bank Street, Easton, PA 18042; (800) THE–PEZ1. Whether you're a collector or just have an appreciation for these whimsical wonders of the candy world, 500-plus Pez dispensers on one wall can be quite impressive! Open daily 10:00 A.M.–6:00 P.M. Admission is $5.00 for adults, $3.00 for children under five.

Bethlehem Walking Tours, Bethlehem Visitors Center, 52 West Broad Street, Bethlehem, PA 18018; (610) 868–1513. Year-round one-hour tours. Call for times and rates.

1810 Goundie House, 501 Main Street, Bethlehem, PA 18018; (610) 691–5300. A Federal-style brick town house built in 1810 by a successful brewer and former mayor of Bethlehem. Peek into this 1810 brick town house and see a restored period kitchen, dining room, parlor, and bedroom. Free. Open year-round; Monday through Saturday 10:00 A.M.–5:00 P.M., and also Sunday from April through December, noon–4:00 P.M.

Touchstone Theatre, 321 East Fourth Street, Bethlehem, PA 18015; (610) 867–1689. An intimate theater in a restored 1875 firehouse where original and classic dramas are performed by a resident professional acting ensemble and distinguished guest artists. September through May. Tickets are $16 ($20 Friday and Saturday).

Dutch Springs, 4733 Hanoverville Road, Bethlehem, PA 18020; (610) 759–2270. Scuba diving in the Lehigh Valley? That's right, in a forty-seven-acre freshwater lake that has been especially designed for maximum sightseeing of submerged vehicles, aircraft, and plenty of fish. There are also facilities for picnicking, boating, swimming, and snorkeling. Open April through mid-December weekends and summer holidays, 8:00 A.M.–6:00

P.M.; Memorial Day through September 30, weekdays 10:00 A.M.–6:00 P.M. No admission after 4:00 P.M. Only certified divers are permitted to scuba dive. Admission is $22.00 for divers, $10.00 for nondivers, $5.00 for children (nondivers).

Godfrey Daniels, 7 East Fourth Street, Bethlehem, PA 18015; (610) 867–2390. An intimate coffeehouse/listening club featuring folk, jazz, blues, Celtic, and Cajun music; poetry; and children's programs. Light menu featuring homemade vegetarian chili or soup and desserts. Performances are scheduled every Thursday through Sunday beginning at 8:00 P.M. Jams and special shows are often featured on Tuesday and Wednesday. Advance ticket prices range from about $12.50 to $17.50, depending on the performers.

Discovery Center of Science & Technology, 511 East Third Street, Bethlehem, PA 18015; (610) 865–5010. Science and technology come down to earth with interactive exhibits demonstrating how basic principles apply to our everyday lives. Open Monday through Saturday 9:30 A.M.–4:30 P.M. from second Monday in June through Saturday after Labor Day; Saturday only, 9:30 A.M.–4:30 P.M. during school year. Adults $7.50, seniors $6.50, children three and under free.

Passport to Color Fun, Easton; (610) 555–8000. This program bundles admission to a number of Easton's major attractions into one economical ticket price.

State Theatre, Center for the Arts, 435 Northampton Street, Easton, PA 18042; (610) 252–3132 or (800) 999–STATE. Year-round live performances including comedians, headliners, drama, musicals, and children's shows.

Special Events

March. Bach Choir of Bethlehem, 423 Heckewelder Place, Bethlehem, PA 18018; (610) 866–4382. Annual concert by America's oldest Bach Choir (its centennial birthday was celebrated in 1998). One hundred ten voices, the Bach Festival Orchestra, and distinguished soloists.

Late July to August. Philadelphia Eagles Training Camp at Lehigh University, Bethlehem, PA 18015; (610) 463–2500.

August. Bethlehem Musikfest, Bethlehem, PA 18015; (610) 322–1350. More than 1,000 free performances from Bach to bluegrass at an outdoor festival that also features ethnic foods, crafts, children's activities, and fireworks.

Late August/early September. The Great Allentown Fair, 302 North Seventeenth Street, Bethlehem, PA 18014; (610) 433–7541. A weeklong extravaganza featuring agriculture, horticulture, domestic and fine arts, top-name musical performing artists, carnival rides and games, and "every food and gadget imaginable." Nominal admission.

September. Celtic Classic Highland Games & Festival, 437 Main Street, Bethlehem, PA 18018; (610) 868–9599. A celebration of the cultures of Ireland, Scotland, and Wales with Highland athletic, dance, and bagpipe competitions; Irish step dance; children's activities; food and wares from the Celtic isles; and continuous music. Free.

November through mid-December. Christkindlmarkt Bethlehem, Main and Hill Streets (under the Hill-to-Hill Bridge), Bethlehem, PA 18018; (610) 868–1513. A Yuletide family tradition modeled after European holiday markets. Features include juried crafts, holiday and specialty items, food, St. Nicholas, and entertainment. Three consecutive weekends (Thursday through Sunday) starting the Friday after Thanksgiving. Nominal admission.

December. Live Christmas Pageant, Community Arts Pavilion, Bethlehem, PA 10817; (800) 360–8687 or (610) 868–1513. The Nativity story is reenacted in an outdoor setting by a large cast of costumed adults and children as well as live animals. Second weekend in December, one-hour program. Free.

Other Recommended Restaurants and Lodgings

Allentown

King George Inn, Cedar Crest and Hamilton Boulevards, Allentown, PA 18103; (610) 435–1723. A National Historic Site built in 1756, this pretty dining place serves veal, seafood, steaks, and pasta. Wine list offers more than one hundred selections. Seasonal outdoor dining. Moderate to expensive.

Yocco's "The Hot Dog King," 625 Liberty Street, Allentown, PA 18102 (610–433–1950) and 2128 Hamilton Street, Allentown, PA 18104 (610–821–8488). With or without chili sauce. Try the pierogies, too. Inexpensive.

Bethlehem

Morningstar Inn, 72 East Market Street, Bethlehem, PA 10818; (610) 867–2300. Located in the heart of downtown Bethlehem's historic district. Rates, which include full breakfast, range from $130 to $160 weekdays, $145 to $165 weekends and holidays.

Starfish Brasserie, 51 West Broad Street, Bethlehem, PA 18018; (610) 332–8888. Fresh seasonal seafood is the star here. So are the house-made desserts. Expensive.

Confetti Cafe, 462 Main Street, Bethlehem, PA 18018; (610) 861–7484. This popular casual dining spot offers everything from cappuccino to full lunches and dinners. Sunday brunch also serves up live acoustic jazz. Definitely don't skip the homemade ice cream, even if you can't handle the house specialty, a monstrous masterpiece served in a real kitchen sink! Inexpensive to moderate.

Sayre Mansion Inn, 250 Wyandotte Street, Bethlehem, PA 18015; (610) 882–2100. Grace and luxury in an antiques-filled restored 1850s mansion. Room rates range from $110 to $190.

Easton

Lafayette Inn, 525 West Monroe Street, Easton, PA 18042; (610) 253–4500. A fully restored 1895 brick mansion with Old World style and modern-day amenities. Room rates range from $110 to $165.

For More Information

Easton Visitor Trolley, Center Square in front of the Crayola FACTORY at Two Rivers Landing, Easton, PA 18040. A seasonal resource for brochures and other information.

Lehigh Valley Convention and Visitors Bureau, 2200 Avenue A, LVIP I, Bethlehem, PA 18002; (800) 747–0561 or (610) 882–9200; www.lehigh valleypa.org.

Jim Thorpe, Pennsylvania

America's Little Switzerland

1 Night

At first glance, Jim Thorpe looks like a movie set, Mary Poppins's England come to life with rows of ornately trimmed Victorian homes and quaint little shops lining the winding, gently sloping streets. Brooding majestically from a high hilltop overlooking the town are two mansions that look as if they could have come straight from the pages of a gothic novel. And at the center of it all stands a bustling train station from which the clanging of the bell of an old-fashioned locomotive echoes cheerfully throughout the town.

☐ Fairy-tale Town

☐ Mountain Majesty

☐ Downhill Biking

☐ Art-full Diversions

Far from a fairy tale come to life, this is a town that has been known by a number of names and has had just as many personalities during its two-century-long history of fortune and misfortune. Called Coalville in the early nineteenth century, it was an important transportation center for the booming coal-mining industry. Later in the century, the arrival of the railroad made the town, which by then had been renamed Mauch Chunk (Lenape for Bear Mountain), a popular tourist destination often referred to as "America's Switzerland" because of its glorious mountain surroundings.

Mauch Chunk's glory days abruptly ended with the collapse of the coal-mining industry and the onset of the Great Depression in the 1920s, followed by years of hard economic times. In 1954 the town got a new name, Jim Thorpe, along with a new spirit and new hope. Jim Thorpe was a Native American athlete who had won glory and two gold medals at the 1912 Olympics in Stockholm, Sweden, only to be stripped of them later because he had earned a little bit of money playing semipro baseball in his younger years. Although the Olympic Committee eventually restored his medalist status (and copies of the gold medals themselves) after Thorpe's death, his widow thought the man once regarded as "the greatest athlete

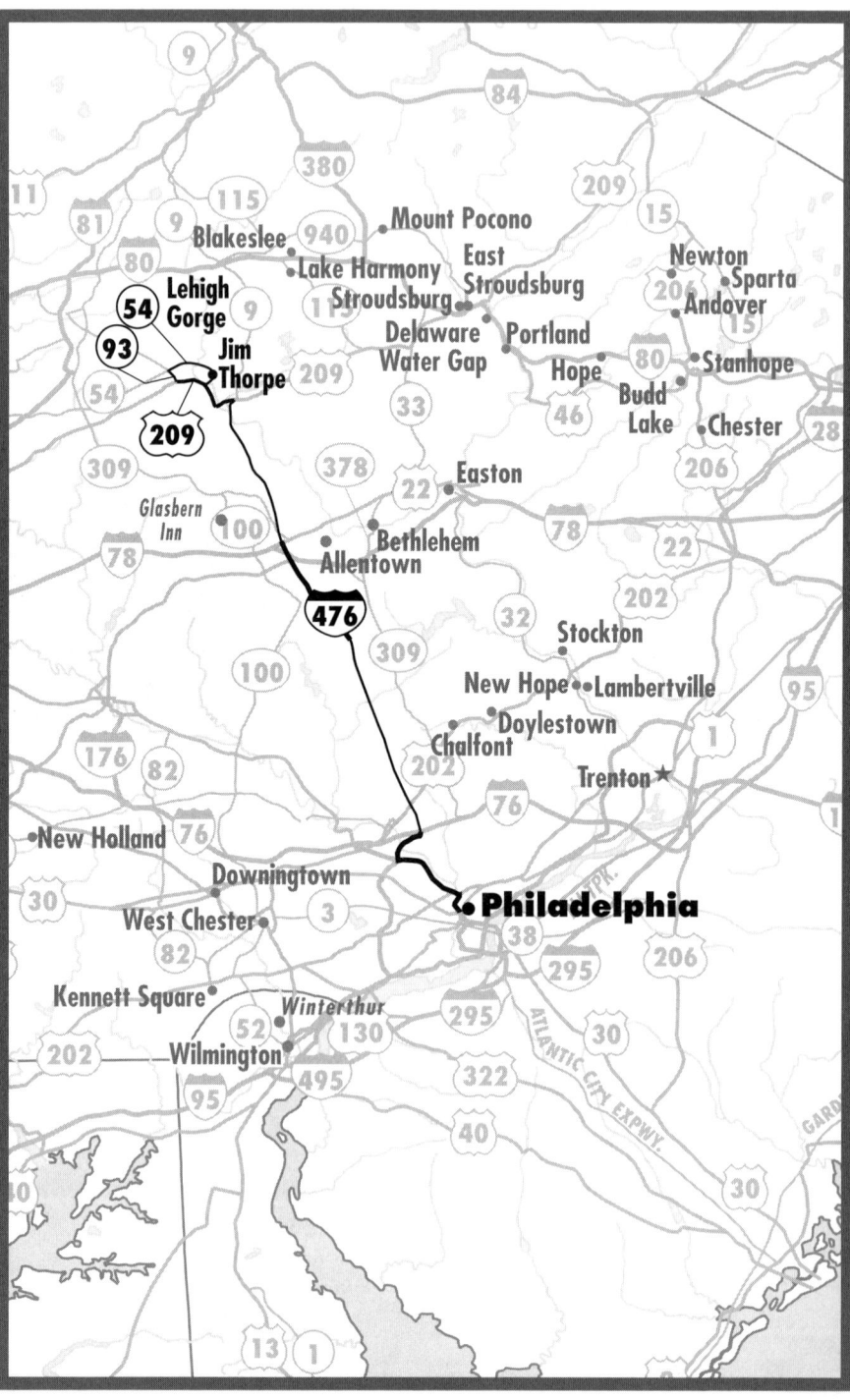

in the world" deserved more. She proposed that the struggling little town in the Pennsylvania mountains build a monument to Jim Thorpe, take his name, and make his memory the focus of a concerted effort to restore his name—and the town—to their former glory.

Day 1 / Morning

Jim Thorpe lies about 90 miles north of Philadelphia, about a 1½-hour drive. Your day is going to be quite full, so be sure to get an early start. To get there, take the Schuylkill Expressway (I–76) to the Northeast Extension of the Pennsylvania Turnpike (I–476) going north for 55 miles; get off at exit 34 and follow Route 209 south 7 miles through Lehighton to Jim Thorpe.

As you enter town on Route 209, you can't miss the centrally located and architecturally distinctive **Jersey Central Railroad Station,** Jim Thorpe, PA 18229 (open daily year-round 9:30 A.M.–5:30 P.M.). Constructed in 1888 as the hub of the town's passenger train activity, it now houses the **Tourist Welcome Center** (888–JIM–THORPE) and a museum filled with artifacts from the town's heyday as an industrial and tourist railroading center. The station still functions as the home base of **Railtours, Inc.** (570–325–4606), an old-fashioned locomotive with vintage coaches that offers thirty-five-minute to 2½-hour themed excursions through this scenic mountain region. Adults $6.00 to $15.00, children $3.00 to $8.00.

The decidedly ecclesiastical architecture and high ornate ceilings of the **Mauch Chunk Museum & Cultural Center** (41 West Broadway, Jim Thorpe, PA 18229; 570–325–9190) are reminders of its origins as a church in 1843. Today it is home to a comprehensive collection of artifacts and photos that trace the history of the area from its geological formation to today and describe the enormous impact the discovery of coal and its subsequent mining and production had on this and other nearby mountain towns. Pay particular attention to the working model of the once world-renowned Switchback Gravity Railway. This extraordinary collaborative effort of man and nature will play a key role in your activities later on in the day. The museum is open Tuesday through Sunday, 10:00 A.M.–4:00 P.M. Admission is $4.00 adults, $1.00 children under eight.

LUNCH: Sunrise Diner, 3 Hazard Square, Jim Thorpe, PA 18229; (570) 325–4093. Normally, it might be a bit early to think about lunch. But you're going to be a long way from town when those midday hunger pangs start to make themselves known. So before you head for the hills, take a short walk down to the diner and grab something hearty to go . . . perhaps a triple-decker club or other big, freshly made sandwich. Inexpensive. Breakfast, lunch, and dinner daily; Friday and Saturday, twenty-four hours.

Afternoon

Head past the railroad station and turn right onto the bridge on North Street (Route 903). About 2 miles down the road, just at the edge of town on your left-hand side, you'll see the **Jim Thorpe Mausoleum,** a twenty-ton granite monument to the athlete. Continue on Route 903 about 5 more miles and you'll come to the **Pocono Whitewater Adventure Center** (570–325–8430), where you'll begin your afternoon's explorations on the back of a mountain bike.

Jim Thorpe has been rated as one of the top three mountain-biking destinations in the United States by *Cycling* magazine. One popular ride is along a downhill 9-mile trail that was once the site of the **Switchback Gravity Railroad.** The first railroad in Pennsylvania, and the second in the United States, the Switchback was originally built in 1827 to transport coal down the mountain from nearby mines to Mauch Chunk for shipment to Philadelphia. In addition to being a railroad industry pioneer, it was unique in that it made its downhill runs powered solely by gravity. In the 1870s, after the major railroad lines had begun servicing the mines, the Switchback continued to make its 65-mile-per-hour downhill runs, this time carrying thrill-seeking visitors who came from far and wide just to take this hair-raising plunge. In fact, it became one of the top tourist attractions in the United States, second only to Niagara Falls. One of the passengers loved the railway so much he made it the prototype for a new kind of amusement park ride—the roller coaster.

Although the Switchback ceased operation in 1933 and the tracks are long gone, the route still provides a breathtaking ride for bikers who take the descent down the mountain, past a lake, and along a creek through a forest dense with hemlock and rhododendron. For your efforts, you will be rewarded with awe-inspiring scenery as you ride and some of the most beautiful backdrops you'll find anywhere for enjoying your picnic lunch. Pocono Whitewater Adventure Center offers bike rentals and shuttle service to the Lehigh Gorge and Switchback Railway Trails ($25 full-day rental, $15 half day, $35 shuttle with rental, and $10 Switchback shuttle).

A visit to Jim Thorpe is like a journey back to yesteryear.

Maps, parking, and child seats are free with rental. Open seven days year-round.

If, upon your return to downtown Jim Thorpe, you find yourself in need of a little refreshment, go right over to **Rainbows End** (46 Broadway, Jim Thorpe, PA 18229; 570–325–9150) for a big, thick, old-fashioned malted, ice-cream float, or sundae. Open year-round.

For another glimpse into Jim Thorpe's history, take a late-afternoon stroll up and down the town's historic district right across from the Jersey Central Railroad Station. Once known as **Millionaire's Row,** the ornately designed Victorian-era town houses that line both sides of Broadway were home to families made wealthy by the coal, lumber, and transportation industries. In reality, few of those who resided in these royal row houses were actually millionaires, but their working-class neighbors viewed them as if they were. Today many of these lovingly maintained houses are living second lives as enticing—and sometimes curious—little shops and art galleries.

At **Marianne Monteleone Design** (97 Broadway, Jim Thorpe, PA 18229; 570–325–3540), the art, which highlights the best of local and national talent, is of the wearable variety. Open Saturday and Sunday noon–5:00 P.M., Thursday and Friday noon–4:00 P.M. And for some dramatic handcrafted jewelry to go with your unique new wardrobe, **Chatelaine** is just a few doors away at 81 Broadway, Jim Thorpe, PA 18229 (570–325–2224).

If you happen to be in the market for a new crystal ball, there's the **Emporium of Curious Goods** (15 Broadway, Jim Thorpe, PA 18229; 570–325–4038), which is presided over by Barrett Ravenhurst, Ph.D., and a Red Lored Amazon parrot named Chester. And if you think twenty-four-hour automatic-teller machines were a great invention, stop by **Four Seasons Sporting Goods** (29 Broadway, Jim Thorpe, PA 18229; 570–325–4364) and see how far modern technology has really come. Right outside the door is a twenty-four-hour bait vending machine that dispenses six different kinds of worms for those day- or night-fishing emergencies.

Evening

DINNER: Emerald Restaurant & Molly Maguire's Pub. 24 Broadway at the Inn at Jim Thorpe, Jim Thorpe, PA 18229; (570) 325–8995. During its days as a bustling coal transportation center, Mauch Chunk attracted many immigrants from Ireland. So it should be no surprise to find a bona fide Irish pub serving shepherd's pie (piped with homemade mashed potatoes), bubble and squeak (a casserole of smoked ham, grilled chicken, onions, carrots, and mashed potatoes baked with brown gravy), and "Dublin-style" fish-and-chips. The rest of the world is well represented as well with such selections as the "Indonesian seafood festival," chicken prosciutto, and Southwestern pork. Prices are moderate.

If you're visiting during the months of December, March, or May, be sure to catch one of the four seasonal performances by the **Bach and Handel Chorale** (570–325–9440), an exquisite collection of local voices. The concerts are held at various locations throughout the town. A donation ranging from $10.00 to $15.00 for adults and $5.00 to $7.50 for students is requested.

LODGING: Harry Packer Mansion, Packer Hill, Jim Thorpe, PA 18229; (570) 325–8566. This eighteen-room Victorian creation of the most elaborate sort has watched over the town from high atop its perch on Packer Hill since 1874. The home was a wedding gift from Harry's father, the illustrious and exceedingly wealthy Asa Packer, and mother. Its distinctive design and otherworldly quality have long fascinated visitors— including the designers of the Haunted Mansion attraction at Walt Disney World, who used the house as their model. Completely restored, the mansion retains many of its original features and appointments, including the 400-pound front doors with cut-glass windows, hand-painted ceilings, carved mantels, and even the detailed English Minton fireplace accent tiles depicting Shakespearean scenes. This place is definitely worth seeing, even if you're not staying overnight. Tours of the first floor are available for a moderate fee for nonguests. Weekday room rates range from $150 to $250 for the mansion, $135 to $175 for the carriage house. The Harry Packer Mansion also hosts Murder Mystery Weekends, with package prices ranging from $495 to $650 per couple.

Day 2 / Morning

BREAKFAST: Harry Packer Mansion. A full breakfast is included in the room rate. Innkeeper Pat Handwerk is justifiably proud of the feasts she lays out each morning for guests, including such house specialties as French toast stuffed with strawberries and cream cheese in a strawberry glaze, croissants l'orange, and a savory crustless quiche.

Before you descend Packer Hill, stop by the mansion next door. You can't sleep at the **Asa Packer Mansion Museum** (570–325–3229), but you can take a fascinating tour of this nineteenth-century home owned by one of the town's only true millionaires and the man responsible for the building of the Lehigh Valley Railroad and Lehigh University in Bethlehem. The inside of the mansion is much the same as it was in 1878 when Packer and his wife moved in on their golden wedding anniversary. Among the many treasures on display is a crystal chandelier, a copy of which was used in the movie *Gone With the Wind*. Tours are offered weekends in April, May, and November; daily June through October, 11:00 A.M.–4:15 P.M. Admission is $7.00 for adults, $6.00 senior citizens, $5.00 students (thirteen to eighteen), and $3.00 for children twelve and under.

At the bottom of Packer Hill and a few blocks straight up on Broadway is the **Old Jail Museum** (128 West Broadway, Jim Thorpe, PA 18229; 570–325–5259), formerly the Carbon County Jail. It was here that, in the late 1800s, seven Irish immigrant coal miners were hanged for being members of the Molly Maguires, an organization formed to fight the dangerous and deplorable working and living conditions imposed on the immigrants by the mine owners. Legend has it that before the hanging, one of the men placed his hand on the wall of his cell and declared that if he was innocent, the print would stay on the wall forever. It's still there. Tours are offered Memorial Day through October, every day except Wednesday, noon–4:30 P.M. $4.00 for adults, $3.50 for seniors and students, and $2.50 for children six to twelve.

Around the corner from Broadway and running parallel to it is Race Street, a charming part of town best known for its group of sixteen houses called **Stone Row.** Said to have been copied from Elfreth's Alley in Philadelphia, these houses are basically identical in design, yet each is individualized by some distinctive decorative feature. Once the homes of railroad engineers and foremen, some of these buildings remain private residences while others provide studio and shop space for local artisans and merchants.

Afternoon

LUNCH: Black Bread Cafe, 45–47 Race Street, Jim Thorpe, PA 18229; (570) 325–8957. This terrific lunch and dinner spot on the ground floor of a 150-year-old Stone Row town house has a moderately priced menu that spotlights Italian cuisine. Favorite lunch selections include chicken panini, Insalada Melissa (spinach with Gorgonzola cheese and mushrooms), and homemade gnocchi quattro formaggi. Closed Monday and Tuesday. Inexpensive to moderate.

Before you leave town, treat your inner child to a visit to the **Old Mauch Chunk H.O. Scale Model Train Display,** right across the street from the railroad station on the second floor of the Hooven Mercantile Company Building (41 West Susquehanna, Jim Thorpe, PA 18229; 570–325–4371). Aspiring engineers of all ages will marvel at the extensive collection of working trains and automobiles. Open year-round; call for seasonal hours). Admission is $3.00 for adults, $2.00 for seniors, $1.00 for children five and older.

On the lower level of the Hooven Building are some interesting stores, including the **Virginia Smith Shops** (570–325–2248; open daily 10:00 A.M.–5:00 P.M.). Be sure to ask about the unique collectibles and jewelry made by local artisans out of coal mined from the nearby mountains. They are really quite beautiful and make highly appropriate souvenirs of your trip to Jim Thorpe.

To return to Philadelphia, simply retrace the route you took to get here. The trip home should take about 1½ hours.

There's More

Lehigh Gorge State Park, Jim Thorpe, PA 18229. A 25-mile, gentle downhill, packed-dirt bike trail between 800- to 1,000-foot-high mountains. One of the highlights is a stop at Glen Onoko Falls. Pocono Whitewater Adventure Center (570–325–8430) offers bike rentals; guided mountain, wetland, and waterfall hikes; and whitewater rafting trips through the Gorge year-round, weather permitting.

Mauch Chunk Opera House, Opera House Square, Jim Thorpe, PA 18229; (570) 325–4439. Throughout the year this rustic 1882 entertainment center hosts concerts, children's theater, workshops, art and fashion shows, and sidewalk festivals.

No. 9 Mine "Wash Shanty" Anthracite Coal Mine and Museum, Dock Street, Lansford, PA 18232; (570) 645–7074. Ride a railcar deep into the mine, back to the time when coal was king. Opened in 1855, this was the world's oldest operating deep anthracite mine until it closed in 1972. Located only 10 miles south of Jim Thorpe on Route 209, the museum is open year-round Wednesday and Thursday noon–4:00 P.M. Mine tours are available May through November, Friday and Saturday 10:00 A.M.–4:00 P.M. Admission for mine tour and museum $7.00; museum only, $3.00.

Camping. Jim Thorpe Camping Resort, Lentz Trail, Jim Thorpe, PA 18229; (570) 325–2644. Features include level wooded sites, 60-foot swimming pool and 15-foot wading pool, playground, camping cabins, free hot showers, laundry facilities, grocery and camping supply store, games and planned activities. Fees for two people are $20 per site, $35 per day for camping cabins. Water, electrical, and sewer hookups; air-conditioning or electric heaters; and cable TV hookups are available at additional cost. Closed in winter.

Special Events

October. Fall Foliage Festival; (888) JIM–THORPE. Local crafters, music, ethnic foods, train rides, tours of museums, historic mansions, and other sites.

December. Old Time Christmas; (888) JIM–THORPE. Weekends in December leading up to Christmas. Horse-drawn trolley rides with Santa, concerts, Victorian carolers, talking snowman.

Other Recommended Restaurants and Lodgings

Jim Thorpe

Inn at Jim Thorpe, 24 Broadway, Jim Thorpe, PA 18229; (800) 329–2599. Located right in the heart of the town's historic district, this restored hotel has been charming guests including General Ulysses S. Grant, President William Taft, Buffalo Bill, Thomas Edison, and John D. Rockefeller for over a century. Rates range from $79 to $139 for a standard room to $149 to $289 for a suite. Continental breakfast buffet is included.

J. T.'s Steak & Ale House, 5 Hazard Square at the Hotel Switzerland, Jim Thorpe, PA 18229; (570) 325–4563. The J. T. stands for—who else?—Jim Thorpe. And the hearty fare is, indeed, suited to the most athletic of appetites. A specialty of the house is the twenty-four-ounce sirloin rib steak. Moderate.

The Manor Bed and Breakfast at Opera House Square, 54 West Broadway, Jim Thorpe, PA 18229; (570) 325–8777 or toll-free (877) 7–TIMEOUT (784–6368). Ask for "The Suite" at this wonderfully private B&B alternative and you'll feel like Victorian royalty. You can even breakfast in your own cozy turret overlooking the town and mountains. Your refrigerator/pantry will be kept filled with all the makings for a lovely continental repast, with fresh-baked goods added each morning. $145 per night. A smaller "Blue Room" with a king-size bed is available for $120 per night. Ten percent midweek discounts.

Victoria Ann's Bed and Breakfast, 68 Broadway, Jim Thorpe, PA 18229; (570) 325–8107. A true nineteenth-century getaway with period furnishings, welcoming atmosphere, and a lovely Victorian garden. Rates range from $85 to $95 for a standard room to $125 to $135 for a suite. Rates include a full breakfast.

For More Information

Jim Thorpe Chamber of Commerce; (888) Jim–Thorpe.
Pocono Mountains Vacation Bureau; (800) 762–6667 or (570) 325–3673; www.800poconos.com.

The Western Poconos, Pennsylvania

Blakeslee and Lake Harmony

2 Nights

In a dictionary of purely Philadelphia terminology, this is the area that would define "up the Poconos" best. Between the generosity of Mother Nature and man's own contribution, the snowmaking machine, these mountains are ready to give you the ultimate experience no matter what time of winter the skiing (or other winter sport) bug bites.

☐ Downhill Skiing

☐ Sporty Days

☐ Romantic Nights

☐ Spectacular Views

Actually, the Poconos are wonderful for a getaway any time of year. In summer there are shimmering lakes for swimming, boating, waterskiing, and fishing; championship golf courses; breathtaking mountains for hiking, biking, and horseback riding; even NASCAR racing. With its slopes covered in the sparkling snow of winter, the lush greens of summer, or the flaming foliage of fall, it's hard to believe that the hustle and hassles of home are only 1¾ hours away.

This itinerary describes a winter escape to the western Poconos. For a summer-oriented Poconos getaway, see the itinerary for Escape Four, Delaware Water Gap.

Day 1 / Evening

Leave right after work so that you can enjoy a nice dinner and some evening entertainment in the mountains. To get to this area of the Poconos, take the Schuylkill Expressway (I–76) to the Northeast Extension of the Pennsylvania Turnpike (I–476)—about 74 miles. Get off at I–80 and continue west about 5 miles to White Haven; get off at exit 273 and you will see the sign for your dinner destination on your right-hand side.

DINNER: Power House Eatery, I–80, exit 273, White Haven; (570) 443–4480. In this converted early coal-to-electricity power plant, you'll dine amid original construction and hardware, surrounded by valves, boilers, and fire doors. Surprisingly, all of this makes for a pretty dramatic setting for a contemporary menu featuring some very innovative dishes such as shrimp and crab française and pork a la Power House stuffed with crabmeat and topped with dill sauce. Moderate to expensive.

If you want to sample a bit of the area nightlife, two of the mountain's hot spots are at **The Resort at Split Rock** (Lake Drive, Lake Harmony, PA 18624; 570–722–9111) on beautiful Lake Harmony. From the Power House Eatery, take I–80 east until you come to Route 940, then continue east on 940 about 10 miles. If you like to keep ahead of musical trends, you can see who's up and coming at the **Rock Bar** at Split Rock Lounge. (The lakeside view is worth the trip by itself.) Or check out the wide variety of live entertainment from comedy to music at Split Rock's Galleria nightclub. Call (570) 722–9111, ext. 522, for a recorded schedule.

Time for a good night's rest before your day on the slopes tomorrow. From the resort take Route 940 east until you come to Route 115 in Blakeslee.

LODGING: Blue Berry Mountain Inn, Thomas Road, Blakeslee, PA 18610, just off Route 115; (570) 646–7144. Although it is located off the beaten path (in this case Route 115) on a dirt road that winds through a beautiful wooded area, don't expect your typical rustic mountain hideaway. When owner Grace Hydrusko decorated her home in 1994, she was inspired by the sunshiny colors of Bermuda . . . which means you can't miss the salmon-colored stucco structure with its white wide-board shutters, unique architecture, and graceful verandas. Just as you think you have Blue Berry Mountain pegged as a totally modern inn, Grace surprises you again with a warm and cozy interior filled with books, antiques, and country charm. Another surprise . . . the inn doesn't have one massive stone heart- and soul-warming fireplace such as you'd expect in the heart of ski country—it has *two!* The five guest rooms and one suite are spacious and individually decorated. Other amenities include a complimentary full country breakfast, indoor swimming pool, and year-round outdoor spa. Weekend rates are $90 to $120 for a room, $135 for the three-room suite. A 10 percent discount is offered for midweek stays.

Day 2 / *Morning*

BREAKFAST: Blue Berry Mountain Inn. Every day Grace offers juices, a huge fresh-fruit salad, a bread basket teeming with a variety of breads and home-baked muffins, and an egg or other entree served with breakfast meats. Saturday morning she really goes all out with semolina French toast, pancakes or waffles, and perhaps some oven-fresh strudel or apricot-cheese pastries. And Sunday brunch is a buffet featuring Grace's famous crustless, creamless quiche; crepes (or blintzes) with hot strawberry sauce; oven-roasted red potatoes; lemon–poppy seed cornbread; and a homey dessert. Lots of guests also make special requests for her old-fashioned oat-meal. Ask in advance and she'll be happy to whip some up for you.

Whether or not a single snowflake has fallen from the sky today, you can be assured of a great time on the slopes at **Big Boulder** and **Jack Frost Mountain** in Blakeslee (800–468–2442), two major ski areas with one ticket price. To get to Big Boulder, take Route 115 south to Route 903 south; turn right and follow the signs.

For novices, families, and anyone who prefers an easygoing downhill run, Big Boulder is the place to go. Opened in 1946, it was the first com-mercial ski area in Pennsylvania and the first to perfect snowmaking. The terrain here is beginner-friendly with vertical drops of 475 feet for runs that are thrilling without being heart-stopping. First-timers from ages nine and up who have never put on a pair of skis before (and the more expe-rienced skiers around them) will appreciate the resort's "Discover Beginner Package," which includes equipment and lift ticket and is $60 for ages nine and over. Private and group lessons are also available.

If you prefer a more challenging run, the Free Domain area at Jack Frost Mountain (Route 940 east just a few minutes away from Big Boulder) has all the trees, glades, bumps, and cliffs your adventurous heart desires—as well as vertical drops of 600 feet.

For a single ticket price, you can move back and forth between the ski areas at will. For adults, a day/night (open to close) ticket is $38 midweek, $45 weekends and holidays; night prices (4:00 P.M. to close) are $25 mid-week, $25 weekends and holidays; and multiday/night $40 per day any-time. Together these two neighboring resorts also offer other popular winter sports, including cross-country skiing, snowboarding, snowmobil-ing, and tubing (more about that this afternoon). Babysitting is available at both locations.

Horseback riding in the Poconos.

Afternoon

LUNCH: The **cafeteria** at Big Boulder or Jack Frost Mountain Lodge. The decor isn't fancy, and neither is the food; but it's good, plentiful, inexpensive, and, best of all, nearby. Try to plan an early (11:00 A.M. or so) or late (after 2:00 P.M.) lunch to miss the noontime rush. Then relax over your choice of mealtime options ranging from pizza, nachos, burgers, and hot dogs to soups, chili, topped baked potatoes, or other homemade hot entrees.

Trade in your skis for a tube and spend the afternoon gliding down hills as much as twelve stories high and more than 1,000 feet long. ($23 for adults, $18 for those twenty-one and under.) As with skiing, Big Boulder tends to be mild, while Jack Frost tends to be wild. After the sun goes down, you can continue tubing (or skiing) "under the lights" at Big Boulder until 10:00 P.M.

DINNER: Villa Virella, Route 115, Blakeslee, PA 18610; (570) 646–3265. "Casual, but nice" attire and a reservation are required at this family-operated restaurant, but you will be rewarded for your efforts with an eight-course Italian feast so exquisite the locals consider this their favorite special-occasion spot. To get there from the Blue Berry Mountain Inn, turn right onto 115 south and follow it for 12 miles; Villa Virella, marked by a little oval sign, will be on your left. The entire meal—from *bagna caoda* (a warm dipping sauce for vegetables and bread sticks) to cappuccino—is traditional northern Italian with an emphasis on homemade freshness and family recipes. How fresh is the food? Well, the Virella family requests that you choose your entree when you call for reservations to ensure that they order everything in just the right amounts. It's hard to believe this elegant old building was once a roadside service station! Fixed-price dinner costs $50 plus tax and gratuity. BYOB.

LODGING: Blue Berry Mountain Inn. After dinner, cozy up to one of the inn's two fireplaces. If you like (and if you have room), your host, Grace, will pop some corn or fix you a nice cup of cocoa or a hot buttered rum (BYOB). You can also play some pool in the game room or settle in with a good book from the inn's library.

Day 3 / Morning

BREAKFAST: Blue Berry Mountain Inn.

Before you set out on your day's adventures, take some time to stroll the inn's 440 acres of nature-decorated walking trails. There's a private lake for admiring, fishing (no license required, but bring your own equipment), or boating in season. Or take a refreshing dip in the indoor pool.

Stay in a leisurely mode for a trip to the **Morgan Gallery of the Arts** (800–621–1654 or 570–646–5333), located on Route 940 about 1 mile east of the inn in Blakeslee. In this 1,500-square-foot gallery, owner and self-proclaimed "chief cook and bottle washer" James Morgan exhibits and sells original paintings, sculptures, and other works by regional artists. Open 11:00 A.M.–4:00 P.M. Tuesday through Saturday.

Alvins Snowmobile Rental, Long Pond, PA 18334; (570) 646–0705. Head east on Route 940 to Long Pond Road on your right, just before Route 380. Turn onto Long Pond Road and drive 4 more miles to Alvins. If there's enough white stuff on the ground, you can go for an hour-long, sixty-acre spin. $60 for single; $80 for double. Call ahead to check conditions.

Afternoon

LUNCH: Piggy's of Lake Harmony, 1 Lake Shore Drive, Lake Harmony, PA 18624; (570) 722–8493. A Pocono tradition famous for its generous portions, inexpensive prices, and fun atmosphere. The specialty of the house is a signature version of French toast called Piggy's Batter Toast. The lunch menu might make you feel nostalgic for home with its Philly cheese steaks, hoagies, and other locally adored delicacies.

From the restaurant, it's about a fifteen-minute drive to **Hickory Run State Park,** White Haven, PA (570–443–0400). Take 940 east to I–80 west, get off at the Hickory Run exit 274 and follow the signs to the park. Year-round this 15,500-acre park offers a veritable smorgasbord of recreational facilities, activities, and options. Bring your own gear, and in winter you can choose from cross-country skiing (16 miles of designated trail), ice-skating, sledding, or tobogganing. If hiking is more your sport, there is a 37-mile trail system in the park. Make sure you pick one ending at Hawk Falls, a natural 25-foot waterfall, or at Boulder Field, where the dramatic 400-by-1,800-foot landscape with its absence of vegetation and its boulders up to 26 feet long has remained relatively unchanged for the past 20,000 years. There's also a large, guarded (Memorial Day through Labor Day) sandy beach for swimming, a family campground (open April through December), picnicking, hunting, and fishing.

DINNER: Britannia Country Inn, Swiftwater, PA 18370; (570) 839–7243. Take Route 940 east to the junction of Route 611. Turn right onto Route 611 south and follow it through the town of Mt. Pocono. The road will become a divided highway. Turn left at the second traffic light (there is a gas station on the left and the Swiftwater Inn on the right). Go approximately $^2/_{10}$ mile and the road makes a Y, bear to the left. The inn is 1½ miles on the right. Owners Joan and Steven Matthews have truly brought a taste of British style, hospitality, and, of course, dining to the Poconos with this charming, moderately priced restaurant. The menu is fun and hearty, and emphasizes such traditional British favorites as roast beef and Yorkshire "pud," "ye olde" steak and kidney pie, bangers and mash (pork sausages and potatoes), and Lancashire hindle wakes, a chicken dish created by Oliver Cromwell. For dessert try King Henry's Olde English trifle, Queen Victoria's fruit jubilee (flambéed with cherry brandy), or the signature Royale chocolate cake. Open year-round Thursday through Saturday; Sunday Memorial Day to Labor Day.

To return to Philadelphia, start at the intersection of Routes 611 and

314 in Swiftwater. Take Route 314 west for about 3 miles until you reach Route 940; go west for 1 mile on 940 to I–380. Go south for 3 miles to reach the entrance ramp of I–80. Take I–80 west for 17 miles to the Pocono Interchange of Northeast Extension of the Pennsylvania Turnpike (I–476). Go east on I–476 for 74 miles until you come to Schuylkill Expressway; go east for 15 miles. The trip home should take you about two hours.

There's More

Whitewater Challengers, White Haven, PA 18661; (800) 443–8554 or (570) 443–9532. Take Route 940 west to Route 80 west. Get off at exit 273 and make a left onto 940 west and continue approximately 2 miles. Challengers will be on the left. Rafting, biking, kayaking, overnight camping, and outdoor adventure weekend packages. Breakfast, lunch ($4.50 in advance, $5.30 otherwise), and dinner ($6.50 in advance, $7.65 otherwise) are available.

A. A. Outfitters, Blakeslee Corners, PA 18610; (570) 643–8000. Guided fishing tours and private instruction available year-round, seven days a week. $150 per person for a full day ($125 per person for two people) and $85 for a half day; rates include equipment rental.

Peterson Ski & Cycle, Route 115, Blakeslee, PA 18610; (570) 646–9223. This convenient shop will rent you all the equipment and accessories you'll need for mountain biking, skiing, and snowboarding. Open year-round.

Memorytown, Grange Road, Mt. Pocono, PA 18344; (570) 839–1680. Open year-round, seven days a week. In operation for more than half a decade, this fun-filled attraction is a complex of museums, dining spots, old-time country shops, and a lake for fishing and boating.

Stock Car Racing Experience, Long Pond, PA 18334; (877) STOCK–CAR (786–2522). Experience firsthand the thrill of riding in or even racing a 600-horsepower Winston Cup–style stock car on the 2½-mile Super Speedway at Pocono Raceway. Programs start at $109 for a three-lap ride in a car with a top speed of 175 mph. Driving experiences start at $469 midweek, $525 weekends. Minimum age to ride is fourteen; eighteen to drive. Open April to November. Located on Route 115, about 5 miles south of Blakeslee on the left.

Special Events

April. Annual Great Brews from Around the World International Beer Festival, The Resort at Split Rock, Harmony, PA 18624; (570) 722–9111. A day filled with international music, food, beer-related crafts, and more than twenty of the world's best brews.

May. Poconos Greatest Irish Festival, Jack Frost Ski Area, Blakeslee, PA 18610; (800) 468–2442. A Memorial Day Weekend (Saturday and Sunday) extravaganza featuring three stages of Irish performers, specialty vendors, and lots of food.

June. Pocono 500 NASCAR Winston Cup Series Race, Pocono International Raceway, Long Pond, PA 18334; (800) RACEWAY or (570) 646–2300.

June. Annual Great Tastes of Pennsylvania Wine & Food Festival, The Resort at Split Rock, Lake Harmony, PA 18624; (570) 722–9111. Two days, usually the last weekend in June, of more than one hundred of Pennsylvania's finest wines from twenty of the state's premier wineries, three stages of live entertainment, wine and food-related seminars, grape stomping, crafts, food, and children's entertainment. Saturday and Sunday, 11:00 A.M.–6:00 P.M.

July. Pennsylvania 500 NASCAR Winston Cup Series Race, Pocono International Raceway, Long Pond, PA 18334; (800) RACEWAY or (570) 646–2300.

August. Annual Poconos Blues Festival, Big Boulder Ski Area, Blakeslee, PA 18610; (800) 468–2442. Enjoy a weekend (usually the first Saturday and Sunday of August) of performances by and workshops with more than a dozen blues artists.

November. Great Brews of America Classic Beer Festival, The Resort at Split Rock, Lake Harmony, PA 18624; (570) 722–9111. More than 200 beers from classic and micro breweries across the country will be served up along with food, live entertainment, and beer-related crafts and seminars (including one specifically for home brewers) during this two-day festival traditionally held the weekend before Thanksgiving.

Other Recommended Restaurants and Lodgings

Blakeslee Area

Woody's Country House, Route 115, Long Pond, PA 18334, south of Route 903 (near Pocono International Raceway) and 4 miles from Blakeslee Corners; (570) 646–9932. Chilis, soups, sandwiches, and the like to chase away the winter chill. Moderately priced dinner fare includes pastas, fresh seafood, charbroiled steaks, and baby back ribs.

The Blakeslee Inn, Route 290, Blakeslee, PA 18610; (570) 643–6000. French with a Tuscan and American infusion, this fine-dining spot features a signature Pocono Mountains Surf and Turf (wild-mushroom ravioli with rosemary cream sauce, grilled medallions of venison, and a roasted lobster). Expensive.

The Resort at Split Rock, Lake Drive, Lake Harmony, PA 18624, 5 miles east of exits 277 and 284 off I–80; (800) 255–7625 or (570) 722–9100. This 500-acre, four-season resort offers a number of options, from the traditional rustic ski lodge to a contemporary posh hotel. Rates, which vary by season and time of week, range from $159 to $299; all-inclusive packages are available.

Swiftwater

Britannia Country Inn, Swiftwater, PA 18370; (570) 839–7243. Transplanted Brits (as they like to refer to themselves) Joan and Steven Matthews have transformed a historic old inn into one with English countryside personality. The decor in each of the rooms ($47.50 per person double occupancy) and suites ($52.50) is pure Laura Ashley. You can also rent a private cottage ($57.50 per person).

For More Information

Pocono Mountains Vacation Bureau, Inc.; (800) POCONOS (762–6667) or (570) 424–6050; www.800poconos.com.

Seasonal snow conditions and fall foliage reports: (570) 421–5565.

Delaware Water Gap, Pennsylvania

Ply Me a River

2 Nights

It doesn't take much imagination to picture this magnificent area as it was when the ancestors of the Leni-Lenape tribe first discovered it sometime between 12,000 and 10,000 B.C., a place of lush woodlands teeming with wildlife, miles of crystal-clear waters, and awe-inspiring waterfalls. That's because it still looks very much like that today.

Inspired by the more than 1-mile-wide S-shaped cleft the river had carved into the mountain ridge they knew as Kittatinny ("endless mountains") millions of years before, the Native Americans called the area Pohoqualin, or "termination of two mountains with a stream passing through them." Over time that name evolved into "Pocono" and came to represent an entire mountain range. However, back then, "Pohoqualin" referred specifically to one area in the eastern part of the mountains, an area we now call Delaware Water Gap.

- ☐ River and Mountain Sports
- ☐ Breathtaking Overlooks
- ☐ Fun Restaurants
- ☐ All That Jazz

When people talk about Delaware Water Gap, they are usually referring to the 70,000-acre national recreation area in Pennsylvania and New Jersey. And it truly is an idyllic spot for nature lovers of all kinds with its more than sixty hiking trails; 40 miles of Delaware River; wide variety of birds, fish, and other wildlife; and virtually unlimited opportunities to enjoy the great outdoors in whatever way you choose. Although each of the seasons has its own distinctive charm, beauty, and activities in the Poconos, spring and summer are really the best times to fully enjoy this area of the mountains. August is peak tourist time here and the area can get pretty crowded; you may want to plan your escape for earlier in the season or even the first few weeks of September.

These are also the best times to explore the *other* Delaware Water Gap,

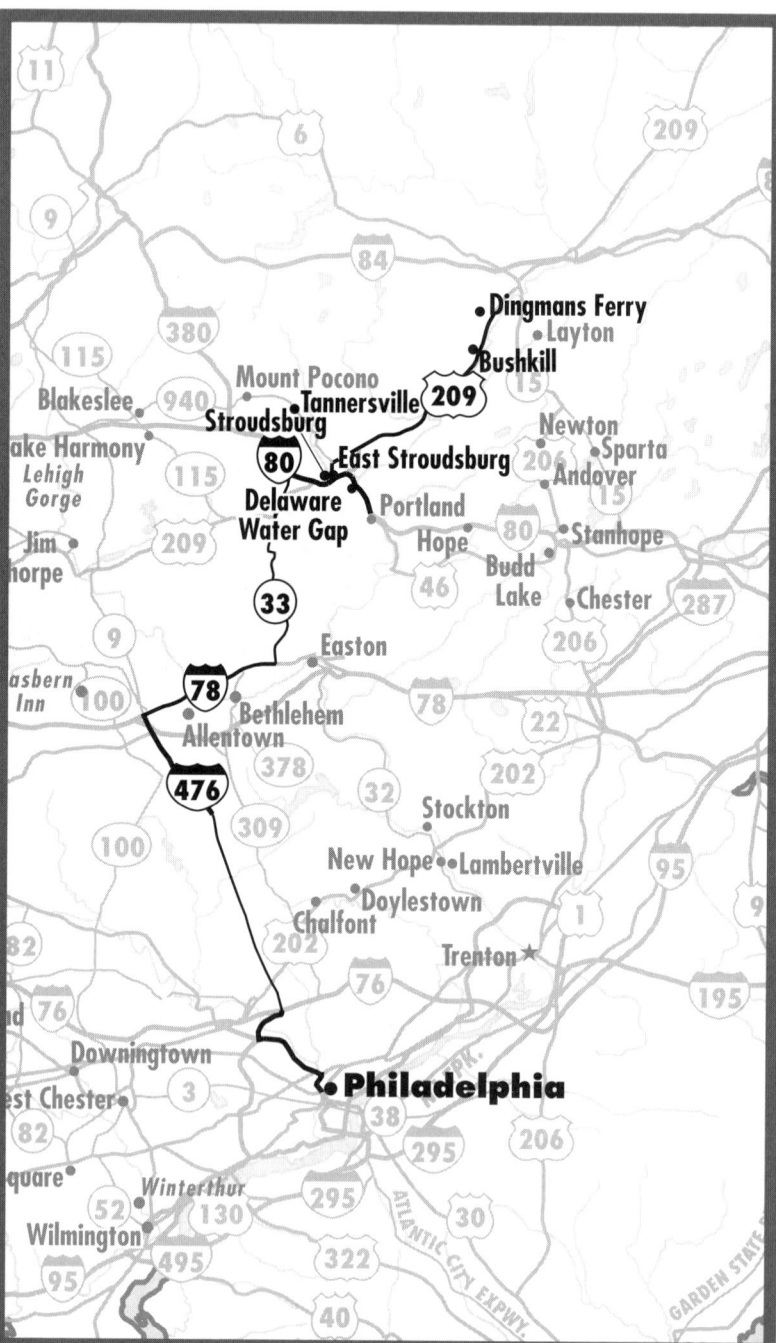

a small nearby town, along with neighboring Stroudsburg, East Stroudsburg, Bushkill, and Portland at your leisure. Their histories and personalities are as varied as the river that flows through the mountains.

Day 1 / Morning

Start out early in the morning for this two-hour drive so that you can do some basic sight-seeing in Delaware Water Gap, the town, before you make your way to Delaware Water Gap, the national recreation area. From Philadelphia, take the Schuylkill Expressway (I–76) to the Northeast Extension of the Pennsylvania Turnpike (I–476); go north to I–78 east. Take I–78 east to Route 33 north then to I–80 east. Get off at exit 310 for Delaware Water Gap and travel Route 611 south, which will take you into the center of town.

As you enter town on Route 611, you'll see the **Water Gap Trolley Depot** (570–476–9766) on your right. Make that your first stop and take the forty-five-minute scenic tour. Of course, you could easily drive the route along 611 yourself, but the history and local lore offered up by your trolley driver/guide make the excursion much more interesting. For example, you might just drive on by and miss **Cold Air Cave**, aka "Mother Nature's Refrigerator," tucked into the mountainside along the road, or the breathtaking Resort Point, Arrow Island, and the Point of Gap overlooks.

Along the route you can also see the remains of the grandest of the nineteenth- and early-twentieth-century grand hotels that catered to well-to-do families from Philadelphia and New York who would summer here. Then there's historic 1752 Shawnee Presbyterian Church, the oldest church in the Poconos, with tombstones from the adjacent cemetery incorporated into its back wall. There's also a natural formation that looks like the profile of an Indian head in the mountain rocks and the place on Main Street where the Appalachian Trail cuts right through the center of town on its 25-mile stretch through the mountains. And if you're of a "certain age," you will probably get a kick out of seeing the home of Captain Kangaroo's longtime sidekick Mr. Greenjeans. Trolley tours are available seven days a week, 10:00 A.M.–4:00 P.M. rain or shine until the weather turns very cold and/or the tourists disappear. Call for current prices.

Right across Main Street from the Trolley Depot is the **Antoine Dutot School and Museum** (570–421–5809). In the 1920s this was the site of a school that was a model for others of its time. Today it is the town's main cultural center and houses an extensive collection of Native American and other historical artifacts, audio and visual exhibits on education in the twenties, and changing displays of works by local artists. Open every Saturday and Sunday from Memorial Day weekend through October. Call for hours and admission prices.

Afternoon

LUNCH: Trails End Cafe, 14 Main Street, Delaware Water Gap, PA 18327; (570) 421–1928. Don't worry, formal dress is not required at this circa 1920 former bus station turned cozy little bistro, even though the doorman—a bigger-than-life wooden raccoon—is wearing coattails. Inside, the sunny country-cabin interior bids you warm welcome with its antiques, pressed-tin ceiling, and colorful array of dried-flower wreaths and swags. The breads are baked on the premises (or "imported" from one of Philadelphia's top artisan bread bakeries on the weekends), and there are more than a few surprises (pierogies Poblano and Thai pie) on the menu. Even such old-fashioned favorite desserts as fruit crisps, bread pudding, and carrot cake are jazzed up with complementary sauces, ice cream, and other delicious additions. Inexpensive to moderate.

Although the restaurant you just dined in is called Trails End, it's actually the beginning of the trail you'll be taking for your afternoon in the sun. Head north on 611 until it intersects Route 402. Follow 402 north about 18 miles to **Pocono Backwater Outfitters** (570–775–7237) at Pecks Pond, Dingmans Ferry, PA 18328. When you see the large wooden fisherman on the right-hand side of the road, you'll know you're there.

There are many places where you can rent canoes, kayaks, tubes, and other watercraft, but Pocono Backwater Outfitters offers a different kind of vehicle . . . and a unique kind of river experience. Upon arrival, you'll be issued a twenty-one-pound "float," which you will carry on your back as you follow your guide on a hike that will take you off the beaten path and onto backwater streams, ponds, and waterways that cannot be accessed by boat. At that time you will don a wet suit and frog fins, place your float in the water, and instantly become one with nature as you glide silently along using only your own kicking power and a small paddle to propel yourself. Because you are creating almost no disturbance or noise, you can enjoy the exquisite beauty of your surroundings and observe the wildlife around you under the most natural of circumstances. A three-hour outback nature trip with equipment costs $59 per person and can be tailored specifically for individuals who want to fish, bird-watch, or take photographs. Six-hour trips are also available at a cost of $110 (includes a hot or cold lunch). Outings may be scheduled during fall, spring, and summer (as long as the water level is high enough for floating).

Evening

DINNER: Everybody's Cafe, Main and Ninth Streets, Stroudsburg, PA 18360; (570) 424–0896. Coming from Delaware Water Gap, head north on Route 611 for about 3 miles until you come to Main Street (Business 209, Stroudsburg). Turn left on Main Street, and the restaurant is just past Ninth Street on the left, in a converted home. This is one of those places that has wonderful architectural and decorative surprises such as ornate doorways with leaded glass, graceful arches, and back-to-back fireplaces just about everywhere you look. The prices are surprisingly modest on the very ambitious, multipage menu. Even more surprising are the huge portions. In light of both these factors, perhaps the biggest surprise of all is that the food is excellent, prepared and seasoned with obvious care to preserve and enhance its fresh flavors. Everybody's is well known for its innovative vegetarian offerings. But as the name suggests, this restaurant isn't just for vegetarians. There are a number of American and internationally inspired meat, seafood, and fowl selections along with infinite pasta combinations. Don't skip dessert—especially the hot fudge pudding cake served warm with ice cream; it's satisfyingly gooey without being overly sweet.

LODGING: Stroudsmoor Country Inn, Stroudsmoor Road, Stroudsburg, PA 18360; (570) 421–6431. Take Route 611 south from downtown Stroudsburg until you come to Route 191 south; turn right and follow 191 to the top of the mountain, where you'll make the first right onto Stroudsmoor Road (the entire trip, including the mountain-climbing expedition, should take five minutes or less). Glowing lanterns line the path leading to the inn, nestled on its 200-acre mountain overlooking the city and surrounded by nature. Gleaming dark woods, colorful flower arrangements, and a big central fireplace greet you at the front door. Owned and operated by the Pirone family, the inn's pretty guest rooms are furnished in Old World style, using as many original pieces and designs as possible. Most guests opt for the bed-and-breakfast plan, which includes a bountiful breakfast each morning. Among the many on-site amenities are the natatorium, with an indoor 40-foot swimming pool and a 10-foot whirlpool spa; the outdoor pool; fitness center; bikes; and scenic trails. The Village Common, right on the property, sells everything from furniture and antiques to clothing (vintage and new), pottery, fine art, and jewelry. Bed-and-breakfast rates start at $109 per couple; suites begin at $250.

Day 2 / Morning

BREAKFAST: Stroudsmoor Country Inn. When staff and guests speak of family matriarch and executive chef Bernadette Pirone's culinary skills—and especially her baking—you can hear the reverence in their voices. The display of some of Bernadette's baked goods (including giant cookies and raisin bread topped with a thick layer of confectioner's sugar icing) in the lobby of the inn hints at her prowess. But breakfast is the real clincher. Aside from a multitude of warm, aromatic muffins, she also whips up some mean pancakes, eggs . . . just about anything you could possibly be craving. Sunday morning's meal is an extravagant buffet, complete with champagne (it's included in your room tab; $17.95 to the general public).

Dress comfortably and pack plenty of suntan lotion. You're going to be spending a good part of the day outdoors exploring the trails, waterfalls, and other natural attractions of the Delaware Water Gap National Recreation Area. Before you head there, however, pick up a single- or triple-decker sandwich-to-go at the **Watergap Diner,** a block off Main Street (Route 611) at 55 Broad Street, Delaware Water Gap, PA 18327 (570–476–0132). To make your sweet tooth happy, make a quick stop at the **Village Farmer and Bakery** (on Main Street, Route 611, across from the Water Gap Trolley Depot in Delaware Water Gap, PA 18327; 570–476–9440), an old-fashioned farm stand that sells oven-fresh cookies, brownies, and other home-baked goods. The Cooper family, who have been operating at this location for over twenty years, also makes thirty varieties of fruit pies (apple is their specialty), crumb cake, apple dumplings, and pot pies.

On your way to the park are two interesting museums situated directly opposite one another on Route 209, but in two different towns. On the left-hand side of the road, off 209 at McCole Road in East Stroudsburg, is the **Mary Stolz Doll Museum** (570–588–7566). Owner Bill Stolz and his wife, Jan, lovingly preserve and display more than 125 dolls from around the world collected by Bill's grandmother, Mary. The collection includes dolls from the 1800s through today, many of which are in original condition, others that were repaired and clothed in authentic period attire handmade by Mary. Also on display are exquisitely detailed miniature rooms. The museum's gift store features—what else?—dolls of all descriptions as well as houses for them to live in, teddy bears, and tin and mechanical toys. Open Monday, Thursday, Friday, and Saturday 11:00 A.M.–5:00 P.M., Sunday 1:00–4:00 P.M. Admission is $2.50, $1.25 children; free on Sunday.

On the left-hand side of the road in Bushkill is the **Pocono Indian Museum** (570–588–9164), dedicated to portraying the history of the Delaware (Leni-Lenape) tribes from prehistoric times (somewhere in the area of 10,500 B.C.) to their first contact with the Europeans prior to the American Revolution. Using the cassette player and thirty-minute tape issued to you with your admission, you can take a narrated self-guided tour through six rooms of artifacts—most of which were discovered within a 20-mile radius of this site—and exhibits showing how these Native Americans lived, worked, and fought for their lives and their land. Highlights include re-creations of a Paleolithic cave and a bark longhouse. The gift shop has an extensive collection of Indian jewelry, crafts, clothing, and other items. Open seven days a week. Call for hours. $5.00 for adults, $3.50 for seniors, $2.50 for children six to sixteen.

Whether you're an experienced hiker at the top of your form or someone who simply appreciates fabulous scenery, the **Delaware Water Gap National Recreation Area** (570–588–2542) has a trail for you. At **Dingmans Falls Trail** (1 mile west of Route 209 at Dingmans Ferry) a ½-mile walk along the forest floor through a hemlock-canopied grove will bring you face to face with Silver Thread Falls, with its graceful 80-foot drop, and Dingmans Falls, with its two-tiered, 130-foot drop. The 1⁸⁄₁₀-mile forested loop at nearby **George W. Child Recreation Site** takes you to three additional waterfalls along Dingmans Creek. Wooden stairs and boardwalks make it easy for you to safely get a close look. About 12 miles north is **Raymondskill Falls,** a seven-tiered 175-foot beauty that drops in seven stages.

Afternoon

LUNCH: George W. Child Recreation Site. A wonderful spot to enjoy your picnic lunch is in the hemlock-shaded glen along Dingmans Creek.

Before you leave the park area, get in your car and take the Dingmans Ferry access road to Route 209; then follow 209 north to the toll bridge to New Jersey. A few hundred yards after you cross the bridge, take the right-hand turn and follow the signs for about 2½ miles to **Peters Valley Crafts Center** (19 Kuhn Road, Layton, NJ 07851; 973–948–5200).

Located in a green, peaceful valley, this center is actually a community of working/teaching studios for resident artists ranging from blacksmiths to photographers to woodworkers. In summer the artists open their studios to the public for two- to twelve-day classes. If you prefer simply to take a self-guided tour, you may also pick up a map at the center's store between 2:00 and 5:00 P.M. on Saturday or Sunday. On-site galleries display and sell current works by the artists-in-residence as well as by craftspeople from around the country. Call for gallery hours.

Evening

DINNER: Deer Head Inn, 5 Main Street, Route 611, Delaware Water Gap, PA 18327; (570) 424–2000. During the town's annual Celebration of the Arts weekend in September, this modest little gathering spot is known as "jazz central" because it's such a popular hangout for the performers and their fans. Actually, that nickname applies all year long—and has for more than forty years. The moderately priced dinner menu is an eclectic mix where the chicken is likely to have a Moroccan or other exotic accent, salmon might come adorned with a cilantro and lime-spiked sauce, and New York strip steak is, well, New York strip steak. For an extra $5.00 to $10.00 (depending on the performers) you can stay for the music. Usually the Deer Head Inn is very easygoing and relaxed . . . except during Celebration of the Arts . . . then it's insane (so make reservations and don't be late)!

LODGING: Stroudsmoor Country Inn.

Day 3 / Morning

BREAKFAST: Stroudsmoor Country Inn.

From Stroudsburg take Route 80 west; get off at exit 304 onto Route 209. Turn right at Shafer's School House Road, then left on Business Route 209. Follow the signs to **Quiet Valley Living Historical Farm** (1000 Turkey Hill Road, Stroudsburg, PA 18360; 570–992–6161), about 1½ miles down the road. In the mid-1700s this sprawling sixty-acre farm was the home of German immigrant Johann Peter Zepper and his family. Today the original house, barn, smokehouse, and tool sheds have been restored, and you can still visit a period-clad farm family, much like the Zeppers, as they go about their spinning, weaving, meat smoking, gardening, fruit and vegetable drying, and cooking. Open mid-June to Labor Day, Tuesday through Saturday 10:00 A.M.–5:30 P.M., Sunday 1:00–5:30 P.M. Admission for adults $7.00, $4.00 for children three to twelve.

Afternoon

Returning to Stroudsburg, don't miss the multitude of antiquing opportunities, starting with the town's two sister co-ops, one housed in a hundred-year-old former machine shop and the other, only blocks away, housed in an equally historic former vinegar distillery. Together the **Olde Engine Works** (62 North Third Street; 570–421–4340) and the **Olde Vinegar Works** (70 Storm Street; 570–421–4441) offer 140 dealers within 35,000 square feet. If books are your passion, head for 740 Main Street, where at **Carroll & Carroll Booksellers** (570–420–1516), owners George and Lisa Carroll specialize in history, philosophy, and fiction—including science fiction—offering thousands of new, used, rare, and out-of-print volumes. For new and old toy soldiers from every era and every part of the world, go to **Stockade Miniatures** at 4 North Sixth Street (570–424–8507).

LUNCH: Smuggler's Cove, Route 611, Tannersville, PA 18372; (570) 629–2277. In this easygoing nautical setting, you can enjoy the catch of the day any way you like it—broiled with tequila lime butter, teriyaki-basted with pineapple mango salsa, blackened with Cajun spices, in Caribbean jerk marinade, or plain broiled or grilled. All kinds of seafood and surf-and-turf combos; special kids' menu, too. From Stroudsburg to Tannersville is about 10 miles, going west on I–80, then south on 611.

From the restaurant, take 611 north and make a left on Route 715 at the traffic light. At the next light, turn right onto Sullivan Trail, then left onto Camelback Road. Follow the signs to **Camelbeach Waterpark** (570–629–1661). Mother Nature didn't create this wild water attraction, but whoever did sure knows kids (and their young-at-heart parents). Fourteen water slides range from relatively tame "kids only" drops to multiperson raft slides to Triple Venom, a trio of scream-producing speed slides. At Kahuna Lagoon, Pennsylvania's largest water-park wave pool, you can play in 1-foot rollers and brave the 4- to 6-foot-high "Big Kahuna." Or catch a tube for an exotic 1,000-foot-long floating journey through waterfalls, past geysers, and across gently bubbling waters. Open weekends in late May, early June, September, and October; daily in July and August. Summer hours are usually 10:00 A.M.–7:00 P.M., but call for early- and late-season variations. Ticket prices for one-day admission are $25.95 for adults, $21.95 for children three to eleven and seniors sixty-five-plus. Camelbeach also offers some pretty good deals such as Bonus Night, which allows you to enjoy the park for free after 4:00 P.M. one day if you purchase a one-day general admission ticket for the next day. Come at 4:00 P.M.

Family fun at Camelbeach Waterpark.

and stay until 7:00 P.M. closing for only $14.95, $12.95 for children under twelve and seniors.

To return to Philadelphia, take I–80 west to the northeast extension of the Pennsylvania Turnpike (I–76) at Lake Harmony; get off at I–76. The trip should take approximately two hours.

There's More

Pecks Pond Rentals, same building as Pocono Backwater Outfitters, Route 402, approximately 18 miles north of Route 611, Dingmans Ferry, PA 18238; (570) 775–7237. Take out a canoe or other small craft for a day of fishing for native bass and trout on one of eight nearby Pocono lakes. They'll take you out in the morning; provide you with a guide, equipment, and supplies; and pick you up at the end of the day. Or you can rent a canoe for $29 for a twelve-hour day. Snowmobile tours may be available in winter. Call for weather conditions and prices.

Pennsylvania Fishing Museum, same as above; (570) 775–7237. Equipment displays and other exhibits follow the history of fishing from the late 1700s to the 1950s. Particularly interesting is the display on ice fishing. Open 9:00 A.M.–6:00 P.M. most times of the year—call for winter hours. $4.00 admission for adults, $2.00 for children six to twelve. There's also a gift shop featuring fishing-related antiques and gifts, handmade wood carvings, tables, and home decor items.

Pennsylvania Craft Gallery, corner of Route 209 and Bushkill Falls Road, Bushkill, PA 18234; (570) 588–9156. This 1746 former house–general store–post office–bar is now the home of the Pennsylvania Guild of Craftsmen, one of the largest craft guilds in the United States, and showcases the traditional and contemporary works of juried members who work in a variety of media from wheat to bronze. Free admission. Call for seasonal hours.

Stroud Mansion, 900 Main Street, Stroudsburg, PA 18390; (570) 421–7703. During the French and Indian War, this was the site of Fort Hamilton, one of a chain of frontier forts extending across Main Street. In 1795 it became the home of Daniel Stroud, the man who planned the town that bears his name, and whose artifacts and personal belongings are on display here today. Open year-round Tuesday through Friday 9:00 A.M.–4:00 P.M., Sunday 1:00–4:00 P.M. (seasonal). Admission is $5.00 for adults, $2.00 for seniors and students.

Shawnee Mountain Ski Area, Shawnee-on-Delaware, PA 18356; (570) 421–7231 or (800) 233–4218. Skiing, snowboarding, and snow tubing on twenty-three slopes and trails, with special instruction for kids as young as three and four years of age, teens, and adults. Late November through late March. Call for hours and rates. There's also a water park geared for young children that's open mid-June through Labor Day 10:00 A.M.–5:00 P.M.

Camping, Delaware Water Gap KOA Campgrounds, Hollow Road, East Stroudsburg, PA 18301; (800) KOA–0375 or (570) 223–8000. Open year-round. Tent sites ($30), RV campsites ($34 with water and electric hookups), and "kamping kabins" ($55) convenient to all local activities and attractions. Special off-season rates are also available.

Special Events

September. Delaware Water Gap Celebration of the Arts, Delaware Water Gap, PA 18327; (570) 421–5791. Held annually the weekend after Labor

Day, this three-day outdoor event attracts thousands of jazz fans from all over for music, arts and crafts, and all kinds of food.

September. Annual Scottish and Irish Festival, Shawnee Mountain Ski Area, exit 309 off I–80, Shawnee-on-Delaware, PA 18356; (570) 421–7231. A weekend of nonstop music and dancing, including bagpipe bands and parade, working sheepdogs, Highland athletics demonstration, pony rides, traditional dancing, gift shops, and lots of food.

October. Annual PMCC/Shawnee Fall Foliage Balloon Festival, Shawnee Inn and Golf Resort, exit 309 off I–80, Shawnee-on-Delaware, PA 18356; (570) 421–7321. Take a ride in one of the bevies of hot-air balloons that ascend to the skies during this three-day event. Also tethered rides, live bands, and children's entertainment and fireworks.

October. Annual Lumberjack Festival, Shawnee Mountain Ski Area, exit 309 off I–80, Shawnee-on-Delaware, PA 18356; (570) 421–7231. Witness amazing feats of strength and skill by world-champion lumberjacks competing in three days of forest-sport events. Also craft exhibits and demonstrations, country line-dancing, jug band and other musical entertainment, food vendors, and the Paul Bunyan Lumberjack Feast.

Other Recommended Restaurants and Lodgings

Delaware Water Gap

Shepard House, 108 Shepard Avenue, Delaware Water Gap, PA 18327; (570) 424–9779. Antique furnishings, a wraparound front porch, and country/Victorian charm make this bed-and-breakfast, located just 1 block from the Appalachian Trail, a delightful place to stay. Rates range from $89 to $120.

Shawnee-on-Delaware

Mimi's Streamside Cafe, River Road, Shawnee-on-Delaware, PA 18356, next to the Shawnee Inn; (570) 424–6455. If you're in the mood for some real native Pocono Mountain brook trout, this moderately priced little restaurant tucked into the mountain is the place to come. Charbroiled steaks are another specialty.

Shawnee Inn and Golf Resort, 1 River Road, East Stroudsburg, PA 18301, exit 319 off I–80; (800) SHAWNEE or (570) 424–4000. This historic hundred-room inn, situated 2½ miles from Shawnee Mountain, features a large indoor pool and Jacuzzi, the area's only full-size indoor ice rink, four dining spots, a large fireplace in the lobby, and a twenty-seven-hole championship golf course.

East Stroudsburg

Dansbury Depot, 50 Crystal Street, East Stroudsburg, PA 18301, exit 308 off I–80; (570) 476–0500. This circa 1864 former railroad station is now a charming restaurant serving moderately priced seafood, chicken, and steak.

For More Information

Pocono Mountains Vacation Bureau, 1004 Main Street, Stroudsburg, PA 18360; (800) POCONOS (762–6667); www.800poconos.com.

Snow and fall foliage reports, in season; (570) 421–5565.

Delaware River Water Gap National Recreation Area; (570) 588–2452.

Berkeley Springs, West Virginia

Eternal Springs

2 Nights

In his famous anthem to West Virginia, John Denver described the Mountaineer State as "almost heaven." Well, after visiting Berkeley Springs, I beg to differ—about the almost part anyway.

☐ Rejuvenating Waters

☐ Heaven-sent Hands

☐ Abundant Art

☐ Country Comforts

Long before the first Europeans set foot in the New World, Native Americans from Canada to the Carolinas were making regular pilgrimages to this lovely Appalachian Mountain valley in West Virginia's Eastern Panhandle to bathe in warm mineral spring waters legendary for their curative powers. Early colonists also believed that "taking the waters" at Medicine Springs or Warm Springs, as it was called back then, could cure their aches and ailments.

In fact, George Washington was so taken with "ye fam'd warm springs" that in 1776 he and a group of his family and friends became landowners in the area and dubbed it "The Town of Bath" after England's premier spa. Bath quickly became a favorite watering hole for the socially prominent—and the site of gambling and parties so wild they prompted a member of the clergy to warn of the "overflowing tide of immorality" that threatened to engulf any who dared to go there.

Today, the only sign of wildlife is the furred and feathered kind you can glimpse from the scenic mountain trails. But the crystal-clear 74.3-degree waters from its springs continue to work their magic on those who come seeking comfort for body and soul.

Five year-round spas offer distinctly different menus of therapeutic and beauty treatments in settings ranging from state-park basic to state-of-the-art luxurious. Berkeley Springs is also a mecca for artists and craftsmen, who provide a feast for the eyes in galleries and shops and on public buildings. Other locals share their talents in the art of hospitality at an abundance of

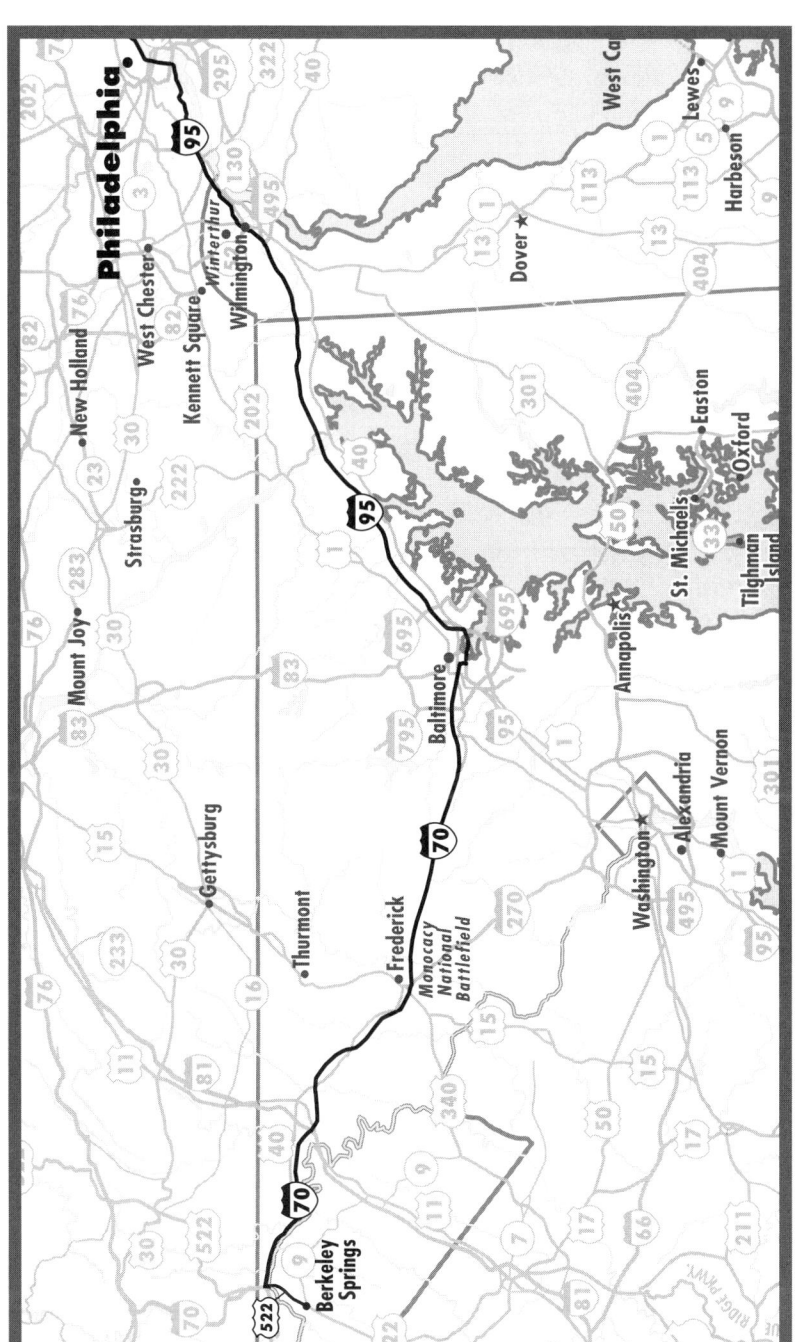

imaginative restaurants and cozy accommodations.

Almost heaven? Decide for yourself, but in my opinion Berkeley Springs is the real thing—no ifs, ands, or almosts about it.

Day 1 / Morning/Afternoon

It's a four-hour (165-mile) drive from Philadelphia to Berkeley Springs, so start early to take full advantage of the smorgasbord of pampering the town has to offer. Take I–95 south to the I–695 west exit (49B), toward I–70/Towson, Maryland. Merge onto I–695 north. Take the I–70 west/I–70 exit (16), toward Frederick. Keep left at the fork in the ramp, then merge onto I–70 west. Stay on I–70 west until you reach the U.S. 522 south exit (18) on the left toward Hancock/Winchester. Merge onto Route 522 south and follow it for 6 miles; it will become Washington Street and take you straight into the heart of Berkeley Springs.

LUNCH: A good place to get your first taste of Berkeley Springs is at **Inspirations Bakery/Cafe** at 312 North Washington Street (corner of North Washington and Union Streets), Berkeley Springs, WV 25411; (304) 258–2292. The eye-catching pink and purple paint job on this restored Victorian home makes it hard to miss. Nor would you want to miss Pam Neiman and Cheryl Tacha's "fresh and funky" menu of seasonal soups and salads, ethnic specialties, and just plain fun stuff. Leave your diet at the door and indulge in a huge, gooey pecan sticky bun, homey cookie, or other oven-fresh sweet. Generous portions, inexpensive prices. Open mid-March through December, 7:30 A.M.–3:30 P.M. Thursday through Monday.

Berkeley Springs State Park may seem like a pretty grandiose name for the five-acre patch of green at the corner of Washington and Fairfax Streets. But considering that the town's lifeblood runs through it, the designation seems much more appropriate.

In the park, be sure to pay homage to **George Washington's Bathtub,** a tongue-in-cheek tribute to—but authentic reproduction of—the hollowed-out crude sand- and rock-lined pools from G.W.'s spa days. In addition to soaking in the waters, our health-seeking ancestors liked to swig it, too. And that hasn't changed. Every day streams of people from all over the county come to fill up their bottles, jugs, and other vessels from the free public tap.

For a truly down-to-earth (and budget-friendly) spa experience, you can't get any more authentic (or inexpensive) than the **Old Roman Bath**

House (800–225–5982 or 304–258–2711). No fancy whirlpools, just totally serene immersion in your own private 750-gallon walk-in tub of mineral spring water heated to 100 to 102 degrees ($10 for a half hour). Open 10:00 A.M. to 6:00 P.M. daily, Friday until 9:00 P.M. April 1 through October 31. (The 1928 Main Bath House across the park also offers Swedish massage, steam, and infrared heat treatments.)

For the main event, simply cross the street to **The Bath House Massage & Health Center** (110–114 Fairfax Street, Berkeley Springs, WV; 800–431–4698 or 304–431–4698). Take your pick from a massage menu that includes deep tissue, pressure point, hot stone, and reflexology ($40 to $100 for thirty to ninety minutes). Also specializing in aromatherapy treatments. Call for hours.

Just a five-minute drive up the mountain is the renowned Robert Trent Jones–designed, eighteen-hole, par 72, championship public course at **Cacapon State Park Resort** (Cacapon State Park, Berkeley Springs, WV 25411; 304–258–1022). From downtown, turn right at the corner of Fairfax and Washington Streets. Washington Street turns into Route 522. Take Route 522 south about 10 miles to the park entrance. Driving range, pro shop, and private lessons ($30) are available. Greens fees vary by season and day of week—for eighteen holes, it ranges from $18 to $30.

Evening

DINNER: Probably the liveliest dining spot in downtown Berkeley Springs is **Tari's Cafe** (123 North Washington Street, Berkeley Springs, WV 25411; 304–258–1196). Owner Tari Hampe-Deneen (she does the cooking) and her "husband, hero and right-hand man," Lovey, serve big portions of "real food" made with homegrown herbs and veggies in season. Specialties include jambalaya, crab cakes, and full-flavored low-fat creations. If peach crisp is on the homemade dessert tray, be sure to order it—the peaches are grown by Tari's dad. On Thursday evening stick around after dinner for some pretty hot jam sessions featuring area talent. Open seven days for lunch and dinner, 11:30 A.M.–9:00 P.M. Moderate to expensive.

If you long for the days when movie theaters had personality (and reasonable prices), take in the 8:00 P.M. show at the **Star Theatre** (Congress and North Washington Streets, Berkeley Springs, WV 25411; 304–258–1404) any Friday through Sunday evening (also Thursday in summer). A true mom-and-pop operation, this vintage Depression-era movie house is as famous as for its popcorn (made in a 1947 popper) as it is for its flicks. $3.50 for adults, $3.25 for seniors, $3.00 for children. For an extra 50 cents, you can cozy up on one of the comfy couches. Take note of the theater's stained-glass windows with the dancing star designs. They were created by a self-taught local artist who calls himself Ragtime, and you can see more of his works displayed at various locations throughout the town along what the town has dubbed the **Ragtime Trail.**

LODGING: To find your bed for the night (and your breakfast tomorrow morning), take Washington Street to Market Street, just south of the park and springs. Turn left onto Market and follow it 2 blocks to the top of the hill to **Highlawn Inn** (on your right at 304 Market Street, Berkeley Springs, WV 25411; 888–290–4163 or 304–258–5700). Originally built for a Victorian bride, this elaborate abode was meticulously restored by innkeeper Sandra Kauffman and her husband, Tim, to regain its aura of romance. Sink-in sofas flank the working fireplace in the antiques-filled parlor area. A wraparound porch takes full advantage of the inn's hilltop perch. Highlawn also includes three adjacent buildings, each distinctive in character. Guest rooms start at $85; with whirlpool tubs, $145. The Carriage House ($190 weekends, $180 Monday through Thursday) is a private hideaway for two.

Day 2 / Morning

BREAKFAST: Highlawn Inn. Sandra is known far and wide for her sumptuous breakfast buffets featuring freshly squeezed juices; homemade breads, pastries, and egg and vegetarian dishes spiked with fresh herbs from her garden; fruited oatmeal; and custom-blended coffee.

Head back up to **Cacapon State Park** for a leisurely stroll or ambitious hike on 20 miles of blazed trails. Park maps and trail guides are available at the front desk of the Cacapon State Park Resort. Throughout much of the year, naturalist-guided walks are also available. At the park's stables you can arrange for a one-hour ($15) or longer trail ride through the forested mountainside.

Need to cool off? There's also an open-to-the-public lake, complete with diving boards, lifeguard, and lovely white, sandy beach. Rowboats and paddleboats are available for rental. Open Memorial Day weekend through Labor Day weekend.

When you're ready to leave the park, take Route 522 north about 9 miles until it intersects with Route 9. Make a left onto Route 9 and go about 4 miles until you come to **Panorama Overlook** (aka Prospect

Peak Scenic Overlook). The breathtaking view from this rugged, rocky peak encompasses the Potomac and Cacapon Rivers nearly 1,000 feet below and three states—Maryland, Pennsylvania, and West Virginia. Although the road is open to hikers year-round, it is accessible by car only from May through October.

Afternoon

A morning of exercise deserves an afternoon of pampering. So turn around on Route 9 and drive back about 2 miles to **Coolfont Resort's Spectrum Spa** (on your right on Cold Run Valley Road in Berkeley Springs, WV 25411; 800–877–8768 or 304–258–4500). Choose from an A to Z of body and beauty treatments available individually or in packages such as "The Ultimate Escape," which includes massage, manicure, pedicure, Black Mud-n-Aloe body treatment, Aveda facial, and lunch in the resort's restaurant ($275). Call for hours.

LUNCH: Coolfont's Treetop House Restaurant offers a lovely view of one of the resort's lakes, woods, and almost constantly occupied bird feeders, along with a menu specializing in creative spa fare that manages to be full of flavor without being heavy on the fattening stuff. Moderately priced for breakfast, lunch, dinner, and Sunday brunch buffet. (The resort also offers a variety of accommodations including a hotel-like lodge and one- and two-bedroom chalets $69 to $259).

To showcase the talents of the many amateur and professional artists and crafters who call Berkeley Springs home, the local Morgan Arts Council (MAC) has opened a gallery (open Saturday and Sunday 11:00 A.M.–5:00 P.M.) on the first floor of a 40,000-square-foot former cold storage building called the **Ice House** (corner of Independence and Mercer Streets, Berkeley Springs, WV 25411; 304–258–2300). On display (and for sale) are works representing a wide range of disciplines, including sculpture, forged iron, abstract mosaics, wearable art, and handcrafted furniture. On selected evenings, the Ice House also hosts lectures, literary discussions, plays and musical performances, and classes on an eclectic variety of topics.

Evening

On Saturday evenings in July and August, MAC sponsors free concerts at Berkeley Springs State Park. Blues, jazz, country, string band, Caribbean, or international music sounds extra good with a magnificent mountain view in the background.

A panoramic overlook in West Virginia.

DINNER: Lot 12 Public House, 302 Warren Street (just 1 block south of Highlawn Inn), Berkeley Springs, WV 25411; 304–258–6264. Owners Damian and Betsy Heath have turned their 1913 "little house on the hill" into a truly classy little restaurant with a sophisticated seasonal menu. Year-round favorites include crisp goat-cheese medallions on baby spinach with mustard vinaigrette and crisp roasted duck with bourbon-flavored pan juices, rosemary potato cake, and pear chutney. Desserts are international in scope and crafted on the premises. Moderate to expensive. Wednesday through Sunday 5:00–9:00 P.M., Saturday until 10:00 P.M.

LODGING: Highlawn Inn.

Day 3 / Morning

BREAKFAST: Highlawn Inn (yay!)

It's time to hit the trail again—this time the antiques trail. For a history lesson, visit J & A Political Collectibles, one of thirty dealers in the **Berkeley Springs Antique Mall** (100 Fairfax Street, Berkeley Springs,

WV 25411; 304–258–5676). **Old Factory Antique Mall** at 262 Williams Street, Berkeley Springs, WV 25411 (304–258–1788), has 20,000 square feet of antiques and crafts plus its signature Almost Heaven Fudge.

LUNCH: Just south of Berkeley Springs State Park is **The Inn and Spa at Berkeley Springs** (1 Market Street, Berkeley Springs, WV 25411; 304–258–2210), resplendent with stately columns, elegant latticework, and English gardens fragrant with mock orange. The inn's dining spot, One Market Street American Grill, gives some familiar American favorites fresh local flavor. Lunch and dinner; moderate prices. (The inn also offers guest rooms and suites for $130 to $175.)

Retrace the route you took to get to Berkeley Springs on day one. The trip home should take about four hours.

There's More

Atasia Spa, 206 Congress Street, Berkeley Springs, WV 25411; (877) 258–7888 or (304) 258–7888. Thai massage a specialty ($55). Open daily 9:00 A.M.–6:00 P.M.

Special Events

Call (800) 447–8797 for more information about the following events:
April. Uniquely West Virginia Wine & Food Festival. A two-day feast of local goodies including smoked trout, shiitake mushrooms, and baked items.
October. Apple Butter Festival. A real hometown harvest celebration with parade, old-time games and contests, street performances, and 225-plus food, craft, and antiques booths.

Other Recommended Restaurants and Lodgings

Lodging at Cacapon Resort State Park, (800) CALL–WV or (304) 258–1022. Cabins range from the rustic ($64 to $88) to the deluxe ($78 to $167); lodge accommodations range from $59 to $78.

Panorama Steak House, Route 9 west across from Panorama Peak, Berkeley Springs, WV 25411; (304) 258–9847 or (304) 258–9370. Great view, prime beef and seafood. Moderate to expensive.

The Troubadour, Highland Ridge, Berkeley Springs, WV 25411; (304) 258–9381. Home of the West Virginia Country Music Hall of Fame and

Museum and inexpensive steak dinners. Tuesday through Thursday 11:00 a.m. to 10:00 p.m., Friday and Saturday noon to midnight.

For More Information

Travel Berkeley Springs Visitor Center; 304 Fairfax Street, Berkeley Springs, WV 25411; (800) 447–8797 or (304) 258–9147; www.berkeleysprings.com. Open Monday through Friday 9:00 A.M.–5:00 P.M., Saturday until 3:00 P.M.

Frederick, Maryland

Eye of the Storm

2 Nights

You won't find the name of this Maryland town written in fire and brimstone in any history book. Nor will you see it on a list of America's most famous battlefields. But through the centuries Frederick has played an important role in many of the major events that have helped to shape our nation.

- ☐ Angels in the Streets
- ☐ Presidential Retreat
- ☐ Unsung Heroes
- ☐ Poetic Heroines

What is it about Frederick that has so often put it in a position of such prominence? One simple explanation is its location. During the French and Indian War, this was the edge of the wild and perilous Western frontier, making it the perfect strategic planning post for then-Colonel George Washington and British General Edward Braddock. During the Civil War it was sandwiched between the Union right above the Mason-Dixon line and the Confederacy across the Potomac, making it a busy crossroads of troop movement and a crucial center of medical care for soldiers from both sides wounded in the nearby battle of Antietam. Today its position halfway between Baltimore and Washington continues to make it a favorite R&R spot for business and leisure travelers.

But Frederick is more than just a town to breeze through on your way to somewhere else. It has a wealth of historical and recreational attractions, absolutely incredible art, fabulous shopping, fine and fun dining, and world-class lodging to share with those who choose to make it the focal point of a quick escape.

Day 1 / Morning

As the crow flies, Frederick, Maryland, is about 128 miles southwest of Philadelphia. But unless you have wings, too, give yourself at least three hours to get there. Take I–95 south toward Baltimore until you come to exit 49 for the Baltimore Beltway (I–695) west toward Towson. Take the Beltway to exit 16 (I–70 west toward Frederick) and stay on I–70 for approximately 35 miles. Take exit 54 to Market Street/Buckeystown. At

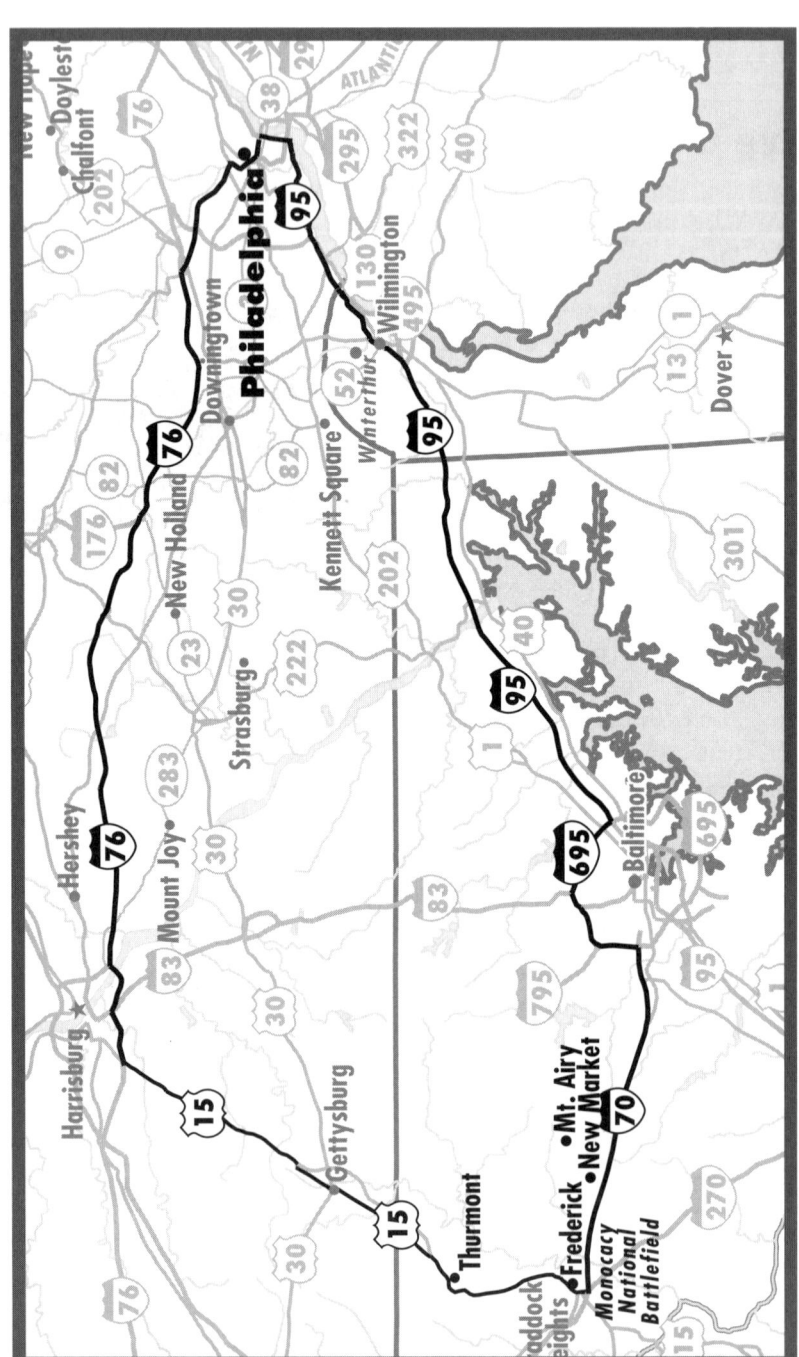

the end of the ramp, turn left onto South Market Street and follow the signs for the **Visitor Center,** 19 East Church Street, Frederick, MD 21701; (301) 644–4047.

Before you embark on the ninety-minute historic-district walking tour offered by the center, get yourself a primo caffeine jolt. You can choose from fifty kinds—all roasted on the premises—and freshly baked pastry at **Frederick Coffee Company & Cafe,** 100 East Street at Everedy Square and Shab Row, Frederick, MD 21701 (301–698–0039). While you're there, order a lunch-to-go to pick up after your tour. The chicken salad is famous, and most of the rest of the inexpensive menu is innovative vegetarian.

During your walking tour of Frederick, along streets lined with beautifully preserved eighteenth- and nineteenth-century homes and churches, the stories your guide shares will be as interesting as the sites. There are stories of Civil War–era families torn apart by divided loyalties. And stories of how the population came together to create makeshift hospitals in their homes, churches, and other public buildings to care for soldiers from both sides wounded on the battlefield at Antietam. Walking tours are offered April through November at 1:30 P.M. on Saturday, Sunday, and most major Monday holidays. Cost is $5.50 for adults, $4.75 for seniors, and free for children under twelve.

The city of Frederick's skyline is famous for the graceful **clustered spires** that rise above its many churches. You can get a breathtaking view of six of these spires (including the tallest at St. John the Evangelist Roman Catholic Church) from the top of the parking deck adjacent to the visitor center. It's the best view in town.

Grab your picnic lunch and head southeast on Route 355 south/Urbana Pike to **Monocacy National Battlefield** (visitor center is at 4801 Urbana Pike, Frederick, MD 21701; 301–662–3515), the site of a strategically important, yet little-known Civil War encounter often referred to as "the battle that saved Washington." It was here that Union troops held off the Confederates who planned to invade Washington, D.C., even though the Southerners outnumbered them by more than three to one. This two-day engagement gave the Union troops time to fortify against and eventually repel the Confederate advance. You can take a ½-mile walking tour of the beautiful farmland and orchards, which look much the same as they did on the day of the battle, and view artifacts, monuments, and an electronic map presentation that offers a detailed account of the action. Open daily.

Afternoon

L U N C H : Have your picnic at one of the designated spots along the now-peaceful river at Monocacy National Battlefield Park.

Back in Frederick's historic district, there are several sites from this morning's tour that you might want to explore in more detail. The first, and most extensive, is the **National Museum of Civil War Medicine,** 48 East Patrick Street, Frederick, MD 21701 (301–695–1864), the only museum in the world dedicated to the practice and development of medicine during the war.

Authentically detailed exhibits and videos trace the medical care soldiers from both sides received, from their initial examination at recruitment stations to the dismal breeding grounds for disease that served as camps to the primitive field facilities and, finally, "fixed bed" hospitals. Particularly fascinating are the exhibits explaining how such important breakthroughs as triage, surgery, sanitation, prosthetics, and veterinary medicine had their origins during this dire period in medical history.

An "immersion exhibit" brings the sights and sounds of the battlefield to life with a reconstructed camp scene—complete with an original Civil War surgeon's tent, murals to replicate the conditions of battle, and mannequins to provide a human face to the tragic tableau.

Open Monday through Saturday 10:00 A.M.–5:00 P.M., Sunday 11:00 A.M. to 4:00 or 5:00 P.M., depending on the season. There is also a museum store filled with medical-related Civil War books and other items. Admission is $6.50 for adults, $6.00 for seniors, $4.50 for children, and free for children under five.

When poet John Greenleaf Whittier wrote the words "Shoot if you must this old gray head, but spare your country's flag," his inspiration was a ninety-year-old Fredericktonian named Barbara Fritchie. The legend has it that Fritchie defiantly waved an American flag at Confederate troops as they marched past her home. Although her original home was ruined by a flood, the **Barbara Fritchie House and Museum** (154 West Patrick Street, Frederick, MD 21701; 301–698–0630), an exact replica complete with salvaged woodwork, hardware, and personal items, was built on the spot in 1926 as a tribute to her patriotic spirit. Open April through September, Monday, Thursday, Friday, and Saturday 10:00 A.M.–4:00 P.M., Sunday from 1:00 P.M.; October through November, Saturday and Sunday only. $2.00 donation.

Barbara Fritchie and Francis Scott Key are among the historically prominent citizens buried a couple of blocks away at **Mt. Olivet**

Cemetery (515 South Market Street, Frederick, MD 21701; 301–662–1164). On the western edge of the cemetery, you can also see the graves of more than 800 Union and Confederate soldiers who died at the battles of Antietam and Monocacy River.

Frederick County is apple country, and since 1938 the name McCutcheon's has been synonymous with fine apple products, not just locally but nationwide. At **McCutcheon's Factory Store** (13 South Wisner Street, Frederick, MD 21701; 301–662–3261), you can get your apples in any form you like—right off the tree or crafted into butter, cider, or syrup. Check out the fruit jellies and preserves, mustards, hot sauces, and other condiments, too.

From May to July one of the most popular destinations in the Frederick area (actually about 8 miles south of Frederick on Route 85) is **Lilypons Water Garden** (6800 Lilypons Road, Buckeystown, MD 21717; 800–999–5459 or 301–874–5133). During the summer blooming season, this sixty-acre aquatic nursery's outdoor displays of water lily–filled ponds, pools, and lush wetlands are breathtaking in color and dimension. Birders also delight in visits by the wide variety of species that are attracted to this natural setting. If you're into aquatic gardening at home, you'll find lots of tips, ideas, plants, statuary, and fountains to create your own paradise. Open year-round Monday through Friday 8:00 A.M.–8:00 P.M., Saturday 9:00 A.M.–8:00 P.M., Sunday until 6:00 P.M.

Evening

DINNER: Hagan's Tavern, 5018 Old National Pike, Braddock Heights, MD 21714; (301) 371–9189. If colonial costumes and menu selections with names like "Jefferson's Fancy" and "Ben Franklin's Favorite" set off your "tourist trap detector," turn it off. This circa 1785 tavern about fifteen minutes west of Frederick, with its low-key setting and inspired offerings, is a delicious surprise. Medallions of pork are sautéed with apple and dried cherry conserve; twin duck breasts are marinated in fresh herbs and molasses and topped with a pear and orange confit. And exactly what did Jefferson fancy? According to Hagan's, it was a stew of lobster, shrimp, and scallops in a Mediterranean-style saffron broth. Serving lunch (moderate to expensive) and dinner (expensive).

LODGING: Hill House Bed and Breakfast, 12 West Third Street, Frederick, MD 21701; (301) 682–4111. Innkeepers Damian and Taylor Branson have turned their circa 1870 Victorian town house into a cozy downtown getaway. Wonderful furnishings collected from antiques hunts and international travels, heirloom family treasures, and original works of art created by Damian and other Maryland artists give each of the four guest rooms its own distinct personality. The third-floor Steeple Suite ($175 per night) offers a spectacular view of the spires of Frederick. The Mexican Room ($125 per night) is a grand and colorful affair filled with acquisitions from the Bransons' frequent forays south of the border. Even the bathrooms are works of art. Room rates start at $105. A full breakfast is included.

Day 2 / Morning

BREAKFAST: Hill House Bed and Breakfast. This is no ordinary breakfast: This is a Maryland breakfast, says Damian, as she sets out baskets of homemade biscuits and dishes of French toast, country ham, bacon, sausage, home fries, some of the best grits I have ever tasted, and such in-season delicacies as fried apples or green tomatoes. Long live Maryland breakfasts!

For thirty-six specialty shops filled with thoughtfully selected antiques, art, jewelry, imports, and many unique apparel and home furnishing items, take a stroll along **Everedy Square & Shab Row** (301–662–6200), where East Street meets Patrick Street. Adding to the charm is the fact that the shops are housed in restored eighteenth- and nineteenth-century dwellings.

If thousands of people were asked to suggest a symbol that best represents the spirit of community, what would they choose? The answers (actually more than one hundred of them), ranging from the whimsical to the profound, are now part of an amazing piece of art and cultural and sociological revelation known as **Community Bridge** on Carroll Street, 1 block east of South Market in Frederick. This trompe l'oeil masterpiece, actually a 2,500-square-foot mural, created by local artist William Cochran over a five-year period, appears to be an old-fashioned stone bridge covered with carvings of icons and symbols. Other "fool the eye" triumphs on the mural include an intricately sculpted statue in a niche, a bronze gate, and a marble fountain. For information, visit the Web site at www.bridge .skyline.net, or call the Frederick Visitor Center.

Three more of Cochran's trompe l'oeil creations adorn—and seem to leap out from—the walls of buildings along Market Street. Part of a series he calls "Angels in the Architecture," they are *The Edge of Gravity* (at Citizen's Way), *Earthbound* (at Church Street), and *Egress* (at Second Street).

To see one of the most intriguing features of Community Bridge exactly the way the artist intended, you must view it from a certain window inside the adjacent **Delaplaine Visual Arts Center,** 40 South Carroll Street; (301) 696–0656. Housed in a restored old mill, the center also offers exhibitions of local, national, and regional fine arts, crafts, and photography year-round. Open Monday through Saturday 9:30 A.M.–5:30 P.M., Sunday 1:00–4:00 P.M. Admission is free.

Take East Patrick Street out toward Route 144 east. Follow Route 144 for about ten minutes and it will become Main Street in the 200-year-old village of **New Market** (301–864–5651), aka "the Antiques Capital of Maryland." With its restored eighteenth-century buildings, mile-long Main Street has a small-town-of-long-ago feeling. Housed in these former abodes are thirty charming little shops, whose proprietors do everything possible to preserve the history and dignity of the area. No bright lights, no garish signs—just tasteful displays of all types of vintage and collectible items from art to armoires, books to beer steins, and teddy bears to textiles. A number of these shops are open during the week, but for full effect—and the widest selection —try to visit on a weekend.

Afternoon

LUNCH: New Market General Store and Cafe Maryland, 26 West Main Street, Old National Pike (Route 144), New Market, MD 21774; (301) 865–6313.You don't even have to interrupt your shopping when you lunch at this combination nineteenth-century general mercantile/casual dining spot.You can enjoy your soup, chili, sandwich, or other light selection inside the cafe or, on nice days, sit outside and watch the other treasure hunters along Main Street. Inside the shop you'll find all kinds of edible and nonedible delights such as homemade fudge, penny candies, antiques, and collectibles. Inexpensive. Open 9:00 A.M.–5:00 P.M. Monday, Tuesday, Thursday, and Friday, 9:00 A.M.–6:00 P.M. Saturday, and 10:00 A.M.–6:00 P.M. Sunday.

Head east on West Main Street/Route 144 until you come to Route 874.Turn left onto 874, then take Route 75 north about 4½ miles. Make a right just before the concrete bridge onto Glissans Mill Road, turn right, then travel another 3⁷⁄₁₀ miles until you come to **Berrywine Plantations/Linganore Winecellars** (13601 Glissans Mill Road, Mount Airy, MD 21771; 410–795–6432).At this 230-acre winery,Anthony Aellen produces some wonderful classic wines and some intriguing surprises.

For instance, when was the last time you had mead (honey wine)—you know, the stuff they drank in Camelot and other medieval kingdoms? How about real, old-fashioned dandelion wine? And if you never thought of fruit wines as sophisticated, you haven't tried Aellen's signature dry and semi-sweet varieties made with 100 percent berries, peaches, and apples. Open daily for tours and tastings.

Evening

DINNER: Mealey's Restaurant, 8 Main Street, New Market, MD 21774; (301) 865–5488. I'll long remember the salmon and crab Wellington from this spot in the heart of New Market. Housed in an eighteenth-century log building enclosed in a larger nineteenth-century brick former hotel, Mealey's is renowned for steaks and seafood and offers a generous taste of both with such house specialties as prime rib of beef and hickory shrimp, and filet mignon and broiled crab cake. Desserts are well worth the calories, especially the homemade peanut butter and Key lime pies. Or you could innocently order a Girl Scout Cookie coffee and pretend that you didn't know it was laced with white menthe and dark cacao. Entrees range from $11.95 for pasta to $26.95 for a "seafood feast."

LODGING: Hill House Bed and Breakfast.

Day 3 / Morning

BREAKFAST: Hill House Bed and Breakfast.

You're going home to Philadelphia today, but you won't be reversing your original route. Instead, get on to Route 15 in Frederick and follow it about 10 miles north. From Route 15, take Route 77 west for 3 miles and follow the signs to **Catoctin Mountain Park** (visitor center, Thurmont, MD 21788; 301–663–9388) in the town of Thurmont.

Aside from its beauty, scenic mountain overviews, and virtually unlimited recreational opportunities, the park is probably best known as the site of the presidential retreat known as Camp David. Although the chief executive's getaway is closed to the public, you can still share the presidential vacation experience by hiking, snowshoeing, or cross-country skiing some of its more than 45 miles of trails, admiring the wildflowers, and visiting the remains of farms once inhabited by early European settlers. You can also go rock climbing if you obtain a free permit from the visitor center.

One particularly interesting site in the park is the **Blue Blazes Whiskey Still,** originally built by western Maryland farmers during the

Whiskey Rebellion of the 1790s and later enlarged for use by Prohibition-era bootleggers.

Right across Route 77 is **Cunningham Falls State Park** (visitor center 301–271–7574) where you'll find a 78-foot waterfall, more hiking trails, and forty-three-acre **Hunting Creek Lake,** where you can swim, fish, or canoe. Only fifty-some years ago, this beautiful park was a devastated area, depleted by years of logging, mountain farming, and the wanton harvesting of resources to fuel a major iron furnace from Revolutionary War times up until 1903. The remains of the **Catoctin Furnace** still stand, but the land—10,000 acres of which were purchased by the federal government in 1935—has come a long way toward returning to its natural state.

The parks are open daily year-round from sunrise to sunset. Peak visitor time is in October, when the foliage is in its most magnificent finery.

Afternoon

LUNCH: Cozy Restaurant, 103 Frederick Road, Route 806, Thurmont, MD 21788; (301) 271–7373. Normally I would suggest getting a picnic lunch and enjoying it amid the trees and wildflowers of one of the parks. But just about everyone who visits the Catoctins or Camp David—from high-ranking government officials to foreign dignitaries to members of the news media—makes at least one special pilgrimage to this seventy-some-year-old spot, as the jam-packed celebrity memorabilia cases will attest. "The Cozy" is also famous in its own right for its outstanding, yet outrageously inexpensive, daily lunch and dinner buffets. Call for open hours.

The return home to Philadelphia from Thurmont, Maryland, should take about three hours. Follow Route 15 north 16 miles into Gettysburg, Pennsylvania; then take Route 30 east for 2 miles and get back on Route 15 north for another 29 miles until you reach the Pennsylvania Turnpike (I–76). Take the turnpike east 92 miles until you come to the Schuylkill Expressway (I–76); then take the expressway east for 22 miles into Philadelphia.

There's More

The Children's Museum at Rose Hill Manor Park, 1611 North Market Street, Frederick, MD 21701; (301) 694–1650. Designed to teach elementary school–age children about life in the late eighteenth and early nineteenth centuries, this tour of a 200-year-old Georgian manor house and its outbuildings offers many interactive exhibits and activities. Admission is $5.00 for adults, $4.00 for children. Your ticket also entitles you to take a self-guided tour of the property's **Farm Museum,** where you'll see exhibits depicting nineteenth- and twentieth-century agricultural tools and techniques. Open April through October, Monday through Saturday; only weekends in November. Hours are 10:00 A.M.–4:00 P.M., Sunday 1:00–4:00 P.M.

Weinberg Center for the Arts, 20 West Patrick Street, Frederick, MD 21701; (301) 228–2828. The setting is a restored 1926 movie palace complete with plush-velvet rocking chair seats, massive crystal chandeliers, satin brocade walls, marble columns, and an old Wurlitzer organ. The fare is everything from silent and classic films to music and dance to community theater. Evening and matinee performances year-round.

Schifferstadt Architectural Museum, 1110 Rosemont Avenue, Frederick, MD 21701; (301) 663–3885. This pre–Revolutionary War farmhouse, the oldest standing structure in Frederick, is considered one of the finest examples of German Colonial architecture in America. Open May through mid-December, Tuesday through Saturday 10:00 A.M.–4:00 P.M., Sunday noon–4:00 P.M. Donations accepted.

Frederick Carriage Company, departure points at 124 Market Street, Baker Park, or Everedy Square, Frederick, MD 21701; (301) 845–7001. Scenic and romantic horse-drawn carriage rides through Frederick's historic district. Price for a half-hour carriage ride for up to four adults is $50; $75 for one hour.

Catoctin Wildlife Preserve & Zoo, 13019 Catoctin Furnace Road, Thurmont, MD 21788; (301) 271–4922. This twenty-six-acre woodland setting is home to more than 300 animals, including many rare and endangered species. Open April through October, seven days a week, 9:00 A.M.–6:00 P.M. Admission for ages thirteen and over $11.95, seniors sixty and over $8.95, children two to twelve $7.95, under two free.

Camping, Catoctin Mountain Park in Thurmont, MD, has two public campgrounds:

- Owens Creek Campground; (301) 663–9330. Sixteen dollars per night per site for five people, available on a first-come, first-served basis. Open April 15 to third week in November.

- Camp Misty Mount; (301) 271–3140. Individual cabin rentals begin at $35 per night. Open mid-April to end of October.

National Shrine of St. Elizabeth Ann Seton, 333 South Seton Avenue, Emmitsburg (north of Thurmont on Route 15), MD 21727; (301) 447–6606 (Monday through Friday), (301) 447–3121 (Saturday and Sunday). Home and shrine of the first American saint to be canonized by the Catholic Church. Open daily 10:00 A.M.–4:30 P.M., except Monday from November 1 to April 1, selected major holidays, and the last two weeks in January.

Special Events

June/July/August. Summer Concert Series, Baker Park Bandshell, Second Street and Carroll Parkway, Frederick, MD 21701; (301) 663–8687. Outdoor musical performances every Sunday evening at 7:00. Free.

September. The Great Frederick Fair, Frederick Fairgrounds, 797 East Patrick Street, Frederick MD 21705; (301) 663–5895. This eight-day event is one of the oldest agricultural fairs in the country. Features include animal exhibitions, food, carnival rides and games, harness racing, and national headliner musical entertainment.

October. Oktoberfest at Schifferstadt, Schifferstadt Architectural Museum, Frederick, MD 21701; (301) 663–3885. Taste Frederick's rich German heritage at this festival of food, oompah bands, and crafts.

Other Recommended Restaurants and Lodgings

Frederick

Brewer's Alley, 124 North Market Street, Frederick, MD 21701; (301) 631–0089. If you've never tried Louisiana alligator, you can get a side of sausage or an entree of medallions. Other Big Easy fare includes a footlong muffuletta, smoked sausage po' boy, gumbo du jour, and boudin (Cajun pork-and-rice sausage). Inexpensive to moderate.

Tyler Spite House, 112 West Church Street, Frederick, MD 21701; (301) 831–4455. A faithfully restored pre–Civil War home with a unique history in the heart of downtown Frederick. Rooms range from $200 to $250 double occupancy on weekends, $125 to $175 weekdays.

Morningside Inn, 7477 McKaig Road, Frederick, MD 21701; (301) 898–3920. Set on 300 acres of fields and forest, this renovated early-1900s Amish-style barn has cozy country-style furnishings and on-site activities that range from an exercise room to playing fetch with Sydney, the resident golden retriever. Rates, which include a full breakfast, range from $95 to $105 Sunday through Thursday, $125 to $250 Friday, and $250 to $300 Saturday.

Buckeystown

Inn at Buckeystown, 3521 Buckeystown Pike, Frederick, MD 21717; (301) 874–5755. This elegant inn, housed in a nineteenth-century former mansion and church, offers five guest rooms and two cottages furnished with period pieces and filled with amenities. You can choose from the traditional bed-and-breakfast plan ($110 to $240 per night) or a plan that includes breakfast and a gourmet dinner ($275 to $300).

Thurmont

Cozy Country Inn, ½ mile off Route 15 on Route 806, Thurmont, MD 21788; (301) 271–4301. The Cozy offers executive rooms, suites, and cottages ranging from $44.50 to $150.00 per night (depending on type of accommodation and time of year), all individually decorated to commemorate the presidents, foreign leaders, and news organizations who have visited the inn or nearby Camp David. Deluxe continental breakfast is included on weekdays.

For More Information

Maryland Office of Tourism Development; (410) 767–3400; (800) 634–7386 or (800) MD–IS–FUN; www.mdwelcome.org.

Tourism Council of Frederick County; (301) 644–4047 or (800) 999–3613; www.fredericktourism.org.

DOWN THE SHORE
ESCAPES

Cape May, New Jersey

Beyond the Gingerbread

1 Night

Cape May—the name undoubtedly sets visions of cozy gingerbread cottages and Victorian painted ladies dancing in your head. And they are well worth seeing, these survivors of history, reminders of an era so prim and proper that men and women were assigned separate hours to bathe in the sea.

- ☐ Brilliant Monarchs
- ☐ Water Safaris
- ☐ Whales
- ☐ Diamond-studded Beaches

But it was the wild side of this beautiful peninsula bounded by the Atlantic Ocean to the east and the Delaware Bay to the west that attracted the first seasonal visitors here almost four centuries ago. In the 1600s the Leni-Lenape tribe used it as their summer home, returning year after year to feast on the bounty offered by its waters, lands, and skies. Later in the century the abundance of whales off the coast brought the Dutch, as well as William Penn's Quakers and migrating colonists from New York and New England, including a few original *Mayflower* families from Plymouth, Massachusetts. Even birds have long recognized this southernmost tip of New Jersey as a hospitable feeding and resting place along their annual migration routes.

Today that wild side of Cape May, the oldest and still one of the most popular of the nation's seashore resorts, remains a major draw for visitors, not just in summer but throughout the year. Like the Indians, they still come to fish the ocean and bay. Like the English colonists, they continue to hunt the whales—only now with cameras instead of harpoons. And nature lovers from all over the world follow the hundreds of thousands of birds and more than one hundred species of butterflies as they converge here each year on their way to warmer climates.

As with most seaside resorts, summer is peak time for tourists. That's when the population swells from its year-round figure of about 5,000 to about 80,000 on any given weekend. If you must come in summer, try to make it during the week rather than on the weekend. Better yet, come in

the fall when there are fewer visitors (unless you count the thousands of migrating raptors and other birds) with whom you will have to share the beaches, trails, cruises, wonderful restaurants, intriguing shops, and awe-inspiring sunrises over the ocean and sunsets over the bay.

Day 1 / Morning

The wildlife gets up early in Cape May, so try to hit the road right after breakfast. To get there, take the Walt Whitman Bridge to New Jersey Route 42 south. Take 42 south to the Atlantic City Expressway east until you come to the Garden State Parkway. Take the Parkway south to Route 109 and follow 109 into Cape May. The total distance from Philadelphia is 97 miles, which translates to two days by stagecoach (the way vacationers came in the 1800s) or about 2½ hours (depending on seasonal traffic) by car.

In 1976 Cape May became one of the only entire cities in America to be designated a National Historic Landmark. Along its lovely tree-lined, gas lamp–lit streets stand more than 600 preserved and restored build-ings—among them the famous gingerbread houses and painted ladies—representing all of the Victorian era's most popular architectural styles. One of the best ways to get an overview of these beauties and learn some inter-esting tidbits about the city's history is to take one of the variety of regu-larly scheduled trolley tours offered by the Mid-Atlantic Center for the Arts. You can purchase tickets at the Washington Street Mall Information Booth, where all the center's tours begin and end. If you have the time, take one of the ninety-minute **Combination Trolley/Physick Estate Tours** ($12.00 adults, $6.00 children three to twelve). This guided excur-sion takes you through Cape May's historic district and includes a tour of the **Emlen Physick House & Estate** (1048 Washington Street, Cape May, NJ 08204), the city's only Victorian-home museum. Open daily in spring, summer, and fall; weekends in winter. Also included with your tour of the estate is a stop to see the current exhibition at the **Carriage House Gallery,** home of the oldest county art league in America. For additional information about arts center–sponsored tours and the Emlen Physick House & Estate, call (609) 884–5404.

If a visit to the shore means stocking up on your favorite seaside sweets, you're in luck. The Washington Street Mall in Cape May is home to **Morrow's Nut House** (321 Washington Street; 609–884–3300), **Fralingers** (324 Washington Street; 609–884–3300), and **Fudge Kitchen** (513 Washington Street; 800–23–FUDGE).

Afternoon

L U N C H : Pick up a lunch-to-go at **Cape May Coffee, Tea and Gifts,** 106 Sunset Boulevard, West Cape May, NJ 08204; (609) 884–7041. Box lunches ($6.25) include a freshly made sandwich on a pita, croissant, or wrap, a helping of savory health salad, and a crunchy pickle. Be sure to add a couple of homemade cookies, fragrant cinnamon buns, or other sweet treat to complete your picnic. Order in advance or just stop in. Open year-round. Hours vary according to season.

Cape May Point State Park, off Sunset Boulevard at the southern tip of New Jersey, about 2 miles west of the city of Cape May (609–884–2159), is a beautiful spot to relax over your picnic lunch. Near the entrance to the park, there's a still-working 157-foot-tall 1895 light-house (609–884–5404)—one of the nation's oldest in continual operation—that you can climb day or evening for a panoramic view. Admission for climbing the tower is $4.00 for adults (one child age three to twelve free per adult) and $1.00 for additional children. Right offshore you can spot a World War II bunker, once 900 feet inland, now slowly eroding away in the sea.

In the skies and on the beach, you can watch the year-round residents and migratory visitors that come for rest and food to the nearby National Audubon Society's **Cape May Bird Observatory.** In mid-September thousands of monarch butterflies add their brilliant colors to the view as they wing their way to Mexico. The park is open daily from dawn to dusk from April to mid-October and weekends from mid-February to March and mid-October to January 1. Closed January to mid-February.

Evening

D I N N E R : **Louisa's,** 104 Jackson Street, Cape May, NJ 08204; (609) 884–5882. At this tiny family-owned dining spot (across from Washington Street Mall), the hand-painted door, walls, and tables are only a preview of the real artistry, which comes from the kitchen. Fresh fish gilded with tomatilla and red pepper salsa or papaya mustard sauce. Chicken breast made sassy with Jamaican jerk seasoning. Savory vegetable cakes made from the season's harvest. For dessert, there are oven-fresh fruit cobblers and irresistible bread puddings. The blackboard menu changes daily. Prices are moderate to expensive. Open Tuesday through Saturday from 5:00 P.M. Reservations are accepted one week in advance starting Tuesday at 4:00 P.M. for Tuesday through Saturday.

Welcome to Louisa's in Cape May.

After dinner, walk back to the parking lot of the Washington Street Mall to see if you're in the right place at the right time to catch one of the free open-air concerts at the **Victorian Bandshell** (Wednesday and Saturday at 8:00 P.M. July through Labor Day). Or you could take a moonlight stroll on Cape May's answer to the boardwalk, an oceanside path stretching from Madison Street to just beyond Broadway called the **Promenade.** If you're looking for a noisy, razzle-dazzle, circus midway, you'll have to go to Wildwood. Although Cape May's version does have a smattering of arcades, cafes, fudge, and T-shirt shops, it is a relatively peaceful place, perfect for some romantic star and surf gazing.

LODGING: **Albert Stevens Inn,** 127 Myrtle Avenue, West Cape May, NJ 08204; (800) 890–2287 or (609) 884–4717. West Cape May is only a ten-minute walk from the beach and the Washington Street Mall, but for some reason it is considered by many tourists to be off the beaten path. Built in 1898 by Dr. Albert Stevens as a wedding gift for his bride, Bessie, this Victorian Queen-Anne classic is furnished with period antiques and historically authentic wall coverings from Burbury & Burbury. A unique floating staircase is suspended from the third-floor turret, which owners Jimmy and Lenanne Labrusciano have turned into the very private Tower Suite. The inn also has nine other rooms and suites, each with its own distinctive personality. If it's some waves you're after, the Labruscianos will supply you with beach chairs and towels for the beach. Or you can just step outside for a soak in the hot tub. Rates, which include full breakfast, range from $90 to $135 for a weekday winter night; summer rates start at $135 and go to $220. (The Tower Suite ranges from $125 to $195, depending on the season.)

Day 2 / *Morning*

BREAKFAST: Albert Stevens Inn. Lenanne loves to bake, so it's likely that you'll find fresh-from-the-oven muffins, bread, or, perhaps, her famous lemon blueberry cake on the breakfast table. But be sure to leave room for the entree, which might be apple French toast, sherried eggs, or a lighter-than-air soufflé.

Head for the beach or, for a truly unique perspective on the Cape May seascape, head north on Ocean Drive over the Cape May inlet bridge into Wildwood Crest and travel about ¼ mile until you see Two Mile Landing Restaurant and Marina on your left. This is the home base of **Atlantic Parasail** (609–522–1869), which offers adventures ($55 per person) 500 feet above the ocean for courageous souls of all ages. The entire experience lasts about 1½ hours, and for ten of those minutes (twelve to fifteen if you sail in tandem), you'll be soaring way above the waves. Open Memorial Day through end of September. During peak season boats depart hourly 8:00 A.M.–sunset; call for off-peak hours.

Afternoon

LUNCH: Zoe's Beachfront Eatery, Beach and Stockton Place, Cape May, NJ 08204; (609) 884–1233. Here you can get another view of Cape May over lunch on the white picket-fenced, flower-box, and planter-adorned patio. Lunch favorites include big-chunk fruit salads, a truly delicious signature veggie hoagie, and fresh-roasted turkey sandwiches. Prices are inexpensive; inside seating is available.

One of West Cape May's best-kept secrets is its abundance of wonderful antiques shops, a number of which are within blocks of the Albert Stevens Inn and are open year-round. **Tabby House Antiques** at 479 West Perry (609–898–0908) features eighteenth- and nineteenth-century

American antiques in room settings. On North Broadway, there's **Bogwater Jim** (201 Broadway, Cape May, NJ 08204; (609–884–4448) for nautical items, vintage jewelry, and "worthy old wearables"; at 523, **Bridgetown Antiques,** (609) 884–8107, displays old architecture, iron items, and other antiques in house and garden settings. The **Antique Doorknob,** located at 600 Park Boulevard (609–884–6282), is a treasure trove of original restored building artifacts, including Victorian lighting, building hardware dating from 1840 to 1910, stained glass, iron, wicker, fireplace mantels, and other architectural antiques.

By now it's late afternoon, time to follow the sun and Sunset Boulevard to the southernmost tip of the peninsula and the state. This lovely spot is called **Sunset Beach**—for good reason. Out in the water you can see the weathered hull of the *Atlantus,* a World War I–era concrete ship that went aground here more than fifty years ago and has been slowly sinking deeper into the sands with each passing year. And while you won't find a lot of seashells on this beach, you will find Indian arrowheads and a wealth of Cape May diamonds—pure quartz crystals of various shapes, sizes, and colors believed by the early Native Americans to possess supernatural powers and bring good luck. While that might be merely wishful thinking, these "diamonds" are still treasured for their beauty; when polished and cut into facets, they closely resemble the real thing. Even if you don't have much luck on the beach, you don't have to go away empty-handed. The adjacent **Sunset Beach Gift Shops** (609–884–7079) carries a large selection of sterling and gold-filled Cape May diamond jewelry ranging in price from just over $20 to more than $100. You can also purchase small uncut polished stones for 94 cents.

Evening

DINNER: Black Duck on Sunset, 1 Sunset Boulevard, West Cape May, NJ 08204; (609) 898–0100. The sunsets here are so spectacular, it's no wonder the beach is named in their honor. Quite frankly, with its unparalleled view of the sunset, a beachfront restaurant here could probably get away with serving a pretty ordinary menu. But it isn't likely that anyone would call Pacific Coast wild-mushroom crepe with truffle salad and red-wine syrup, saffron-braised halibut over Alsatian creamed spinach, or orange almond salad tossed with wild-honey lavender vinaigrette and topped with locatelli cheese ordinary. Expensive.

To return to Philadelphia, retrace your route from day one. The return trip should take about 2 to 2½ hours.

There's More

Cape May Stage, Welcome Center, Lafayette and Bank Streets, Cape May, NJ 08204; (609) 884–1341. The town's resident Actors Equity theater company performs contemporary and regional historical plays from spring through December. Also on the schedule are a children's theater series and poetry readings. Tickets are $22 for adults, $18 for seniors and students.

Haunted Cape May Tour, tickets available at Hotel Macomber, 727 Beach Avenue, Cape May, NJ 08204; (609) 463–8984. Your guide will regale you with tales of buried pirate treasure and other scary stuff on this ninety-minute ghost tour along Jackson and Washington Streets. Available May through November, 7:00 and 9:00 P.M.; call for specific days. Tickets are $10.00 for adults, $5.00 for children ten and under.

Shields' Bike Rentals, 11 Gurney Street, Cape May, NJ 08204; (609) 898–1818. Hourly and daily rentals for the family plus tandems and beach cruisers. Call for hours and rates.

The Colonial House, 635½ Washington Street, behind City Hall, Cape May, NJ 08204; (609) 884–9100. Built before the Revolutionary War, this museum hosts changing exhibits of art and artifacts from Cape May's (or as it was called then, Cape Island) colonial past. Open daily June 15 through September 15, 10:00 A.M.–2:00 P.M. $1.00 donation. Call about off-season special exhibits.

Cape May National Golf Club, Route 9, exit 4A Garden State Parkway, Cape May, NJ 08204; (609) 884–1563. A uniquely beautiful and environmentally sensitive course set amid wetlands, ponds, flower beds, and a private nature preserve and sanctuary. Open year-round. Prices, including cart, range from $35 to $40 in winter and, in summer $85 until 11:00 A.M., $65 from 11:00 A.M.–2:30 P.M., $50 "twilight" (after 2:30 P.M.). Parent/child special—$35 for both, including cart—is offered daily after 4:30 P.M.

Cape May–Lewes Ferry, Route 9 south to Ferry Road, terminal is between Bay Shore Road and Beach Drive, Cape May, NJ 08204; (800) 64–FERRY or (609) 886–1725. Take a relaxing 17-mile (seventy minutes one-way) ride across the Delaware Bay aboard the MV *Twin Peaks* or MV *Cape May,* state-of-the-art vessels, each with expansive passenger deck, cushy lounge, and fine restaurant. Fare: $20 to $25 for passenger car and driver (additional passengers cost extra); $10 to $15 for foot passengers six and over. Operates 365 days a year.

Nature Center of Cape May, 1600 Delaware Avenue, Cape May, NJ 08204; (609) 898–8848. Take a Harbor Safari, a fascinating ninety-minute exploration of this fertile habitat led by a marine biologist, to get up close and personal with the native fish, other vertebrates, and plants. Offered April through November; call for days, hours, and prices.

Camping, Cape Island Campground, 709 Route 9, directly across from Cold Spring Village, Cape May, NJ 08204; (800) 437–7443 or (609) 884–5777. Spacious campsites with accommodations for everything from tents to RVs set on 175 acres of forests and fields. Amenities include two large swimming pools, tennis courts, all hookups, modern bathhouses, and convenience store. Call for rates.

Special Events

April. Spring Festival; (800) 275–4278 or (609) 884–5404. Ten days of seasonal celebration including the new Spring Victorian Weekend (a three-day version of October's Victorian Week) and Tulip and Garden Weekend with secret garden tours, concerts, trolley rides, and golf and tennis tournaments.

May. Cape May Music Festival; (800) 275–4278 or (609) 884–5404. Convention Hall and other venues. This six-week, twenty-concert series features the forty-piece Cape May Festival Orchestra and classical and classic music from the Renaissance to the jazz era, and from Bach to the Beatles.

October. Victorian Week; (800) 275–4278 or (609) 884–5404. Throughout the city. A ten-day extravaganza of historic city and house tours, Victorian fashion shows, vaudeville, brass bands, craft and antiques shows, lectures, and workshops.

October. Lima Bean Festival, Wilbraham Park, West Cape May, NJ 08204; (609) 884–1005 (West Cape May City Hall). Country-western music, games, crafts, food (lots of limas, of course), and the crowning of Miss Lima Bean. The locals absolutely love this one!

Late November–New Year. Christmas in Cape May, throughout the city; (800) 275–4278 or (609) 884–5404. Celebrate an old-fashioned Victorian Christmas in beautiful Cape May with candlelight tours, a wassail party, caroling, arts and crafts, parade, band concerts, food and wine tastings, and other holiday festivities.

Other Recommended Restaurants and Lodgings

Cape May

The Abbey, 34 Gurney Street at Columbia Avenue, Cape May, NJ 08204; (609) 884–4506. Once two summer retreats owned by a wealthy Pennsylvania coal baron and his son, the striking gothic villa with its 60-foot tower, stenciled and ruby glass arched windows, and shaded verandas has been combined with the cottage next door to create one fabulous bed-and-breakfast. Rates range from $100 to $275 per night double occupancy. Open April through December.

Virginia Hotel, 25 Jackson Street, Cape May, NJ 08204; (800) 732–4236 or (609) 884–5700. Established in 1879 as a small, elegant inn, the Virginia Hotel continues its tradition of excellence in this restored gingerbread building with its graceful two-story veranda and impeccably appointed rooms. Open year-round, rates range from $85 to $295 midweek, $145 to $425 weekends. Special rates and packages may be available. The hotel's Ebbitt Room restaurant is renowned for its fresh seafood and New American cuisine specialties.

Union Park Dining Room, Hotel Macomber, 727 Beach Drive, Cape May, NJ 08204; (609) 884–8811. Innovative twists on American and seafood dishes include fennel-roasted lamb loin and lobster and shiitake dumplings. Expensive.

Waters Edge, Beach and Pittsburgh Avenues, Cape May, NJ 08204; (609) 884–1717. The internationally and seasonally inspired menu changes daily. Expensive.

La Patisserie, 524 Washington Mall, Cape May, NJ 08204; (609) 884–7107. Exquisite cookies, cakes, and pastries—especially the jewel-like fruit tarts and the melt-in-your mouth almond, cheese, or chocolate croissants. Give twenty-four hours notice and you can adopt one of the fantasy breads made in the shapes of giant crabs, turtles, alligators, birds, and other local marine inhabitants.

Mad Batter Restaurant, Carroll Villa Hotel, 19 Jackson Street, Cape May, NJ 08204; (609) 884–9619. This charming restaurant has long been famous for its fabulous moderately priced breakfast/brunch batter selections, including specialty pancakes, waffles, blintzes, and orange and almond French toast. Lunch and dinner, too.

West Cape May

Daniel's on Broadway, 416 South Broadway, Cape May, NJ 08204; (609) 898–8770. Currently one of the hottest spots at the Jersey Shore, this handsome restaurant housed in a restored 1870s mansion takes classic American regional cuisine to new heights of elegance. Moderate to expensive. Open year-round.

Mangia Mangia, 110 North Broadway, Cape May, NJ 08204; (609) 884–2429. Moderately priced Italian pasta, seafood, and other specialties. Children's menu.

For More Information

Greater Cape May Chamber; (609) 884–5508; www.capemaycounty chamber.com.

Cape May County Chamber of Commerce; (609) 465–7181.

Cape May Region Welcome Center, Ocean View Service Area, Garden State Parkway; (609) 624–0918. Open daily 9:00 A.M.–4:30 P.M. for information and brochures.

Lewes and Cape Henlopen, Delaware

The Other Side of the Ferry

1 Night

Most Philadelphians know Lewes, Delaware, as the town on the other side of the Cape May–Lewes Ferry. You may have spent a few hours there yourself, strolling along the waterfront, visiting some of the charming shops, or enjoying lunch with an unparalleled view of the Delaware Bay. But if you think this kind of brief foray into Lewes means you've "been there, done that," you couldn't be further from the truth.

☐ Night Fishing

☐ Dolphin Watching

☐ Seas of Lavender

☐ Oceans of Orchids

Lewes and nearby Cape Henlopen State Park have shared an exciting, even tumultuous history: as an ill-fated Dutch whaling settlement in 1631, as target for late-seventeenth-century pirate raids and cannon bombardment during the War of 1812, and as a crucial Atlantic coastline defense post during World War II. You can still see the remnants of those past years in the area's carefully restored homes (one with a cannonball still lodged in its wall), museums, and lookout towers—even on the rolling sand dunes of the cape. Fortunately peace now reigns over this lovely little town as well as over the adjacent miles of virtually unspoiled ocean and bay beaches and the protected lands ranging from dunes to freshwater wetlands to pine forests.

Only 85 miles south of Philadelphia in Delaware's Sussex County, Lewes is not exactly an unexplored treasure, but it certainly is an underexplored one. And here's a tip—if you want to endear yourself to the natives, keep in mind that Lewes is pronounced *loo*-iss, not *looz* as in *youse*.

Day 1 / Morning

It takes about 2½ hours to get to Lewes from Philadelphia. Take the Schuylkill Expressway (I–76) east to I–95. Take I–95 south for 28 miles to I–295. Travel north on 295 for 1 mile until you reach Route 13/Route

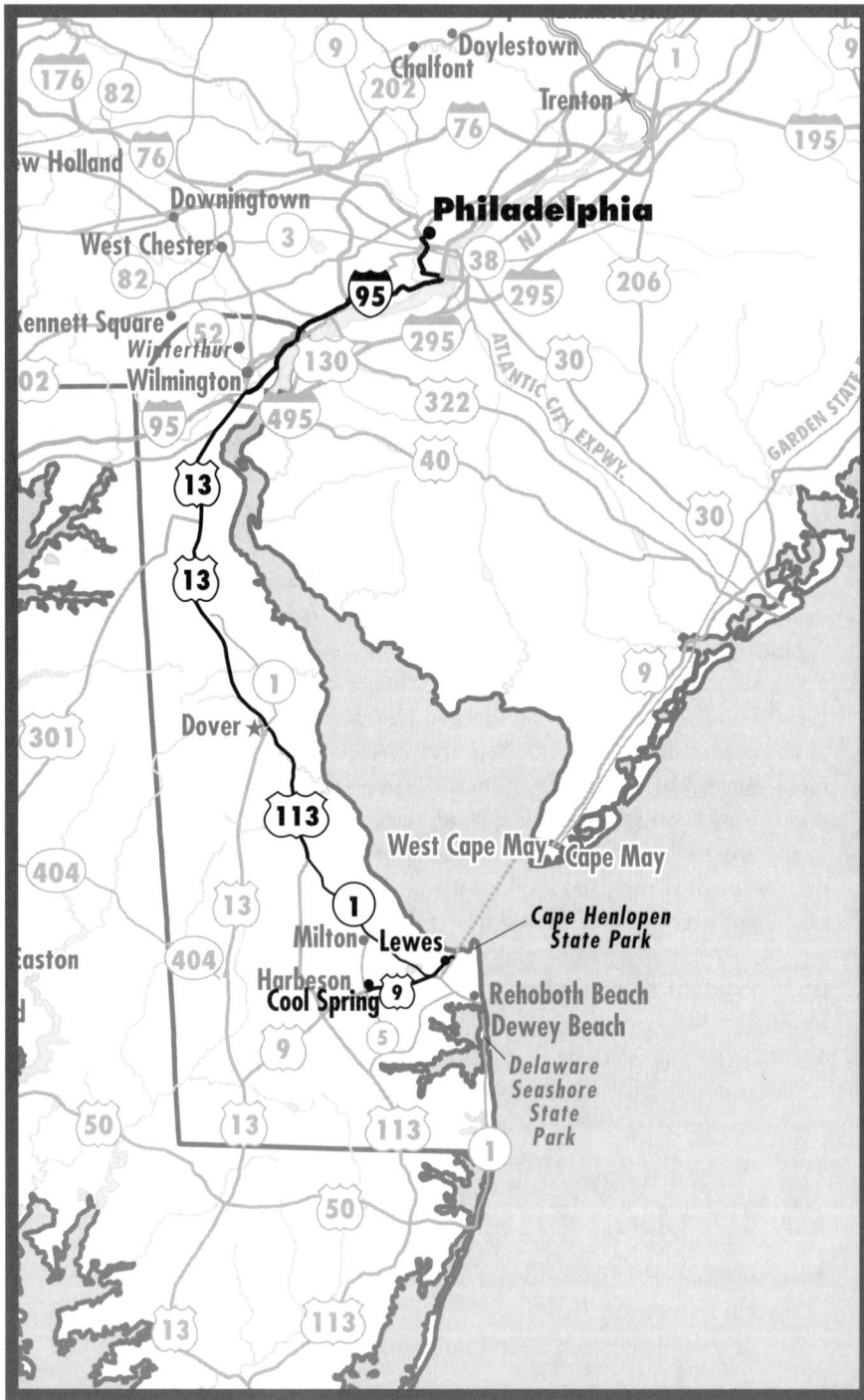

40; then follow Route 13 south for 66 miles to Route 1. Follow Route 1 south 18 miles to Route 9, then Route 9 for 2 miles into Lewes.

To get a hint of Lewes's earliest history, start at the **Zwaanendael Museum** on the corner of Savannah Road and Kings Highway, Lewes, DE 19958; (302) 645–1148. Although its elaborate architecture and stonework facade are decidedly seventeenth-century European, this eye-catching building was actually built in 1931 to commemorate the 300th anniversary of the arrival of the area's—and the state's—first settlers. The original whaling colony quickly came to a tragic end, but this replica of the city hall that stood in their native city of Hoorn, Holland, in 1631 preserves and shares its history and artifacts. Other exhibits and displays tell the stories of the British bombardment of Lewes during the War of 1812, the town's long career as a major port of trade, and the *DeBraak,* a captured Dutch-built ship sailing under the English flag that was sunk by a storm off Cape Henlopen in 1798. Open Tuesday through Saturday 10:00 A.M.–4:30 P.M., Sunday 1:30–4:30 P.M. Free.

A few steps away at 114 West Third Street, Lewes, DE 19958, artist John Austin Ellsworth keeps the craft of blacksmithing alive while producing wonderful items for the home and garden at his **Preservation Forge** (302–645–7987). In this working shop and museum, you can see early blacksmith-made ironwork and watch Ellsworth create new items ranging from fireplace pieces to weather vanes to ornately crafted gates. If you have a particular design in mind, he also takes custom orders. Open summer months 9:00 A.M.–4:00 P.M. every day except Sunday and Wednesday. Hours vary other seasons, so call first.

Afternoon

LUNCH: Second Street Grille, 115 West Second Street, Lewes, DE 19958; (302) 644–4121. CIA graduate Ray Richardson's lovely storefront restaurant offers lunch, light fare, dinner, and Sunday brunch in a relaxed atmosphere filled with art and soft music. Try the spicy Maryland crab soup, a house speciality, and the grilled fresh catch of the day served over Caesar salad. Crispy calamari with chili mayonnaise, the beer-battered flounder sandwich, and the chef's signature Chinese chicken salad are also tasty choices (along with Black Angus burgers for beef eaters). Open year-round, hours vary seasonally. Lunches range from $7.00 to $12.00.

It has long been believed that lavender has the power to heal the spirit and soothe the soul. So to really get yourself into the relaxation mode, travel west on Route 9 and head toward Georgetown. Continue on Route

9 about 4 miles until you come to the railroad tracks. Make a left immediately at the tracks onto Route 290 south (Cool Spring Road); go about ½ mile and straight through the intersection, then an additional ½ mile. On your right you will see a large white farmhouse fronted by a pole light with an orange globe. This is **The Manor at Cool Spring Lavender Farm** (18864 Cool Spring Road, Milton, DE 19968; 302–684–8325). Here Joe Palenik and his wife, Pauline Pettitt-Palenik (known around town as "the Lavender Lady"), grow about thirty varieties of lavender and blend them into a collection of fabulous products, including bath and massage oils, soaps, crafts, jelly, and hard candy. In season they also offer homemade jams, pickles, and fresh vegetables. Call ahead and Joe will take you on a tour of prized fields, where he'll explain the history and uses of lavender and show you his latest experimental plantings. The tours are free.

To sample some bouquets of the liquid kind, head back east on Route 9 until it intersects Route 1; take Route 1 north for about ½ mile. Turn left at the Nassau overpass bridge onto Road 14B; when you reach the farm equipment store, turn left and follow the sign to **Nassau Vineyards** (36 Nassau Commons, Lewes, DE 19958; 302–645–9463). At this truly one-of-a-kind destination in Delaware (it's the only winery in the state), you can take a trip through wine-making history, tour the facility, and savor the fruits of the vines and orchards. Open Tuesday through Saturday 11:00 A.M.–5:00 P.M.; opens at noon on Sunday.

For some prime antiquing, head back to Lewes and take Route 9 east to Route 1. In the 3-mile stretch of Route 1 that extends north and south of Lewes, there are no less than 150 dealers in four warehouse markets offering all manner of antique, vintage, and collectible items. The farthest south is **Heritage Antique Market** at 130 Highway One (302–645–2309) with fifty dealers. The farthest north is the **Antique Village Mall** at 221 Highway One (302–644–0842), with eighty dealers.

Evening

Have an early dinner because you've got an appointment at 6:00 that's going to take up the rest of your evening.

DINNER: Gilligan's Restaurant & Harborside Bar, 134 Market Street, Lewes, DE 19958; (302) 644-7230. If you feared that the fabled SS *Minnow* (the one that took Gilligan and company on their "three-hour tour") was lost at sea forever, you'll be glad to know that it has found a new life and a safe, secure home on the canal in Lewes. In addition to lots

Cape Henlopen State Park.

of atmosphere, this adorable seasonal restaurant also has a terrific menu specializing in American seafood and innovative regional cuisine. Try the jumbo coconut shrimp; Gilligan's crab and sweet corn chowder; and capellini pasta with sautéed shrimp, scallops, and crab tossed in saffron beurre blanc. Moderate to expensive. If the weather permits, ask to sit on the covered deck on top of the *Minnow*, where you can watch the sunset and the boats as they return to the harbor.

Now that you've gotten your sea legs, it's time to take a real boat trip, namely a night fishing expedition offered in season at **Fisherman's Wharf** on Savannah Road by the drawbridge in Lewes; (302) 645–8862. Night fishing trips are available Friday and Saturday late April through mid-July (6:00 P.M.–1:00 A.M.) for $45, half-night Monday through Saturday late May through mid-October (6:00 P.M.–10:30 P.M.) for $25. Daytime trips are also available. Rod and reel rentals are $5.00 extra.

LODGING: Zwaanendael Inn (formerly New Devon Inn), corner of Second and Market Streets, Lewes, DE 19958; (800) 824–8754 or (302) 645–6466. Two huge carved wooden elephant chairs (imported from Thailand and each carved from a single piece of wood, says the concierge) give the lobby of this circa 1926 inn an air of the exotic. While also impressive, the individually furnished, antique-appointed upstairs guest rooms and suites have been decorated with a somewhat lighter touch. Room rates range from $45 weekdays, $70 weekends in winter to $90 weekdays, $135 weekends in summer. Breakfast is included in the room rate.

Day 2 / *Morning*

BREAKFAST: **The Buttery,** 142 Second Street (Second and Savannah Streets), Lewes, DE 19958; (302) 645–7755. Treat yourself to a lavish Sunday brunch here at its lovely restaurant where, for only $17.95 per person, you get a fresh-fruit plate, bakery basket, choice of champagne, mimosa, or bloody Mary, and one of nine entrees, including sirloin steak and eggs or Eggs Savannah topped with spinach, lump crabmeat, and hollandaise.

Lewes may be a small town, but it is an absolute treasure trove of historic sites. For a single $6.00 admission price, you can tour a number of these significant sites, beginning with the **Lewes Historical Society Complex** at Shipcarpenter and West Third Streets, Lewes, DE 19558 (302–645–7670). For this ambitious and highly successful project, the society transported eighteenth- and nineteenth-century buildings, including an early Swedish log house, doctor's office, one-room schoolhouse, country store, and residences, from all over Lewes and its neighboring towns to this beautifully landscaped site. It then restored and accurately furnished them to give us a glimpse of the personal and working lives of their former occupants.

Also included in that $6.00 admission is the historical society–operated **Cannonball House Marine Museum** (118 Front Street, corner of Front and Bank) with its patched-over hole in the wall where a British cannonball from the War of 1812 remains lodged. (Appropriately enough, right across Front Street you'll find the **1812 Memorial Park,** then the site of an important defense battery, now a commemorative park marked by guns from that encounter (as well as one from an abandoned pirate vessel and another used during World War I). You can also visit two other Lewes Historical Society sites, the **Ryves Holt House** (Second and Mulberry Streets), built in 1665, the oldest known house in the state, and the **Lightship Overfalls** (on Pilottown Road on the Lewes & Rehoboth Canal), commemorating the ship that protected the entrance to Delaware

Bay from 1892 to 1961. All of the sites are open Monday through Friday 10:00 A.M.–4:00 P.M., Saturday 10:00 A.M.–1:00 P.M. from mid-June until the Saturday before Labor Day.

Husband-and-wife entrepreneurs Gavin and Louise Braithwaite own two of the most fun shops in Lewes. Their traditional and contemporary handicrafts shop called the **Stepping Stone** (107 Market Street, Lewes, DE 19558; 302–645–1254) offers the works of about 175 artists from all across the United States and includes an international collection of handmade musical instruments, such as a gourd piano and two different types of musical spoons. **Puzzles** (111 Second Street; 302–645–8013), another Braithwaite offspring, has everything from rustic handcrafted wooden designs to the latest Rubik's mind teasers. For jigsaw beginners, there are two- or three-piece models, and ones with 2,000 to 3,000 pieces for the pros. For crossword addicts, there are word games at every level of complexity and in just about every language. Best of all, there's a great babysitting area where impatient young ones (and spouses) can happily occupy themselves testing their puzzle-solving skills.

Afternoon

LUNCH: At **Daily Market** (420 East Savannah Road, Lewes, DE 19558), you can pick up a deli sandwich and your favorite snacks for your picnic at the beach. While you're there, be sure to check your sunscreen supply. Inexpensive. Open 365 days a year.

About 1 mile east of Lewes is **Cape Henlopen State Park** (302–645–8983), a naturalist's paradise with 4,000 acres of every type of terrain, including ocean and bay beaches, rolling dunes (such as the 80-foot-high **Great Dune**), pine forests, salt marshes, and freshwater wetlands. These varied environments make the park the perfect habitat for a wide variety of plants and animals, including a number of rare and endangered species. During migrating seasons, it provides a much-needed resting place and feeding area for many types of birds. And for us it offers a place to swim, sun, fish, and explore the interpreted nature trails for hours without ever getting bored. You'll also find an unparalleled view of the Delaware Bay and Atlantic coastline from the top of the **World War II Observation Tower.** Open to the public; admission is included with your park entrance fee.

Before you begin your explorations, pay a visit to the **Nature Center** (open 9:00 A.M.–4:00 P.M. year-round), which has five 1,100-gallon marine aquariums, a touch tank, and interpretive exhibits. For a few extra dollars, you can participate in guided canoe trips, bird-watching expeditions, wetland explorations, and other educational and recreational programs that are available on a regular basis.

The park is open from 8:00 A.M. to sunset year-round. For lunch, bring your own to the picnic pavilion or visit the concession stand. A $5.00 entrance fee is charged for out-of-state vehicles daily during the summer season and on weekends and holidays in the spring and fall.

Evening

DINNER: La Rosa Negra, 1201 F Savannah Road, Lewes, DE 19958; (302) 645–1980. Homemade pastas, including twenty types of ravioli, and other Italian specialties at moderate prices make this a popular spot year-round. Delectable signature dishes include red salmon with lump crabmeat and seafood lasagna. Also not to be missed are the award-winning ice-cream creations ranging from scoops of simple yet luxuriously rich vanilla to elaborate truffles and pies. Inexpensive to moderate.

To return to Philadelphia, reverse your original route. The trip should take about 2½ hours.

There's More

Dogfish Head Craft Brewery, 22 Nassau Commons (near Nassau Vineyards) Lewes, DE 19958; (302) 644–4660. Take a tour of this popular thirty-barrel microbrewery and check out its flagship Shelter Pale Ale, with its strong malt backbone. You also won't be able to resist such memorably named, handcrafted creative concoctions as oak-aged Immort Ale; deep, mahogany Raison D'Etre; Midas Touch Golden Elixir, an occasional offering made from a recipe based on residue from drinking vessels found in King Midas's tomb; and Punkin' Ale, a September through April specialty brewed from pumpkins and spices. Call for hours.

Beach Plum Island Nature Preserve, just north of Lewes; (302) 739–4702. A satellite of Cape Henlopen State Park, most of this 129-acre barrier island is protected to preserve the habitat for native plants. But you are welcome to stroll the beach, do some surf fishing (required permit is available at the park office), and listen to the sounds of nature. Open 8:00 A.M. to sunset year-round.

Cape May–Lewes Ferry, Cape Henlopen Drive, Lewes, DE 19558; (800) 64–FERRY or (302) 645–6364. Take a relaxing 17-mile (seventy minutes one-way) ride across Delaware Bay aboard the MV *Twin Capes* or MV *Cape May,* state-of-the-art vessels with expansive passenger decks, cushy lounges, and fine restaurants. Fee: $20 to $25 for passenger car and driver (additional passengers cost extra); $10 to $15 for foot passengers six and over. Operates 365 days a year.

Camping, Cape Henlopen State Park, 42 Cape Henlopen Drive, Lewes, DE 19558; (302) 645–2103. From April 1 through October 31, the park offers 139 campsites with water hookups for $28 per night for nonresidents.

The Rookery Golf Course, Route 1 just north of Lewes (mailing address RR 3, Box 183, Milton, DE 19968); (866) 313–GOLF. Built in 2000, this eighteen-hole public course, adjacent to wetlands, features fourteen acres of ponds, including an island green. Pro shop on the premises. Open year-round; peak season fees are $59 for eighteen holes.

Special Events

April. Great Delaware Kite Festival, Cape Henlopen State Park, Lewes, DE 19558; (302) 645–8983. Held annually on Good Friday for more than thirty years, this event features kite-flying competitions, kite vendors, food, and entertainment.

May. British Motorcar Show, Blockhouse Pond Park, Lewes, DE 19558; (877) 465–3937. If your taste in autos runs to Austin Healeys, Jaguars, MGs, Morgans, Triumphs, and their ilk, you'll want to be in the stands as the best of the best of the British vintage and new autos compete for prizes. You can choose your favorite, too, in a special "Best of Show" category, the winner of which is selected by popular vote.

October. Boast the Coast Maritime Festival, town of Lewes. Actually two events in one, this exciting weekend begins on Saturday with the Boast the Coast Festival (877–465–3937) celebrating the area's maritime history with exhibits and programs for the whole family, a craft show and sale, food, schooner tours, and a spectacular lighted boat parade. On Sunday the University of Delaware presents Coast Day (302–832–8083) to showcase educational programs and exhibits at the university's College of Marine Sciences in a festival atmosphere that includes entertainment, boat tours, arts and crafts, and a marine petting zoo.

October. Lewes Historical Society Craft Fair, Historic Complex,

Shipcarpenter Street; (302) 645–7670. Held annually on the second Saturday in July and October.

Other Recommended Restaurants and Lodgings

Lewes

Inn at Canal Square. 122 Front and Market Streets, Lewes, DE 19958; (888) 644–1911 or (302) 644–3377. Besides the spectacular views, Lewes's only waterfront B&B offers generously sized rooms (most with balconies overlooking the harbor) decorated in gracious eighteenth-century English style. Continental breakfast is included, with room rates of $105 to $250 per night depending on day of week and season.

Lighthouse Restaurant, Savannah and Anglers Road by the drawbridge on Lewes Harbor, Lewes, DE 19958; (302) 645–6271. This unmistakably seashore dining spot offers well-prepared seafood specialties and lovely harbor views. Inexpensive to moderate. Open year-round.

King's Homemade Ice Cream Shop, 201 Second Street, Lewes, DE 19958; (302) 645–9425. The best. Seasonal.

For More Information

Lewes Chamber of Commerce and Visitors Bureau, 120 Kings Highway, Lewes, DE 19958; (302) 645–8073.

Southern Delaware Tourism Office, 103 West Pine Street, Georgetown, DE 19947; (800) 357–1818 or (302) 856–1818; www.visitsouthern delaware.com.

Delaware Tourism Office, 99 Kings Highway, Dover, DE 19901; (866) 2–VISIT–DE (284–7483); www.visitdelaware.net.

Beaches of Southern Delaware

Rehoboth and Dewey

2 Nights

Although "down the shore" traditionally refers to the beaches of South Jersey, the Garden State certainly does not have a monopoly on fun by the sea. The southern Delaware side-by-side beach towns of Rehoboth and Dewey have long been favored escape destinations for the people who live and work in Washington, D.C.—and for good reason.

☐ White-Sand Beaches

☐ Natural Hideaways

☐ Family Days

☐ Romantic Nights

Rehoboth is the sister that likes to shine in the spotlight. By day it's an old-fashioned kind of place with lots of town-sponsored activities for the whole family. By night it takes on a more sophisticated personality, its streets sparkling with the lights of myriad eclectic shops, restaurants, and nightspots. Directly to the south of Rehoboth is Dewey, the quiet sister characterized by boundless natural beauty and a tranquillity that can soothe the most stressed-out soul.

Like most East Coast shore points, peak season at the beaches of southern Delaware is from Memorial Day to Labor Day. So if you want to miss the crowds, consider going in the late spring or early fall. The beaches are just as beautiful then, and most of the shops are open.

Day 1 / Morning

Rehoboth Beach is 118 miles (nearly three hours driving time) southeast of Philadelphia. To get there, take the Schuylkill Expressway (I–76) east to I–95. Travel south on I–95 about 28 miles to I–295; going 1 mile north you'll come to Route 13/Route 40. Stay on Route 13 south for about 66 miles until you reach Route 1. Then take Route 1 south for 18 miles to Route 9 north. Take Route 9 north for 1 mile until it intersects with Route 1; then take Route 1 another 4 miles or so into Rehoboth.

Go east on any street and you'll find yourself face to face with the

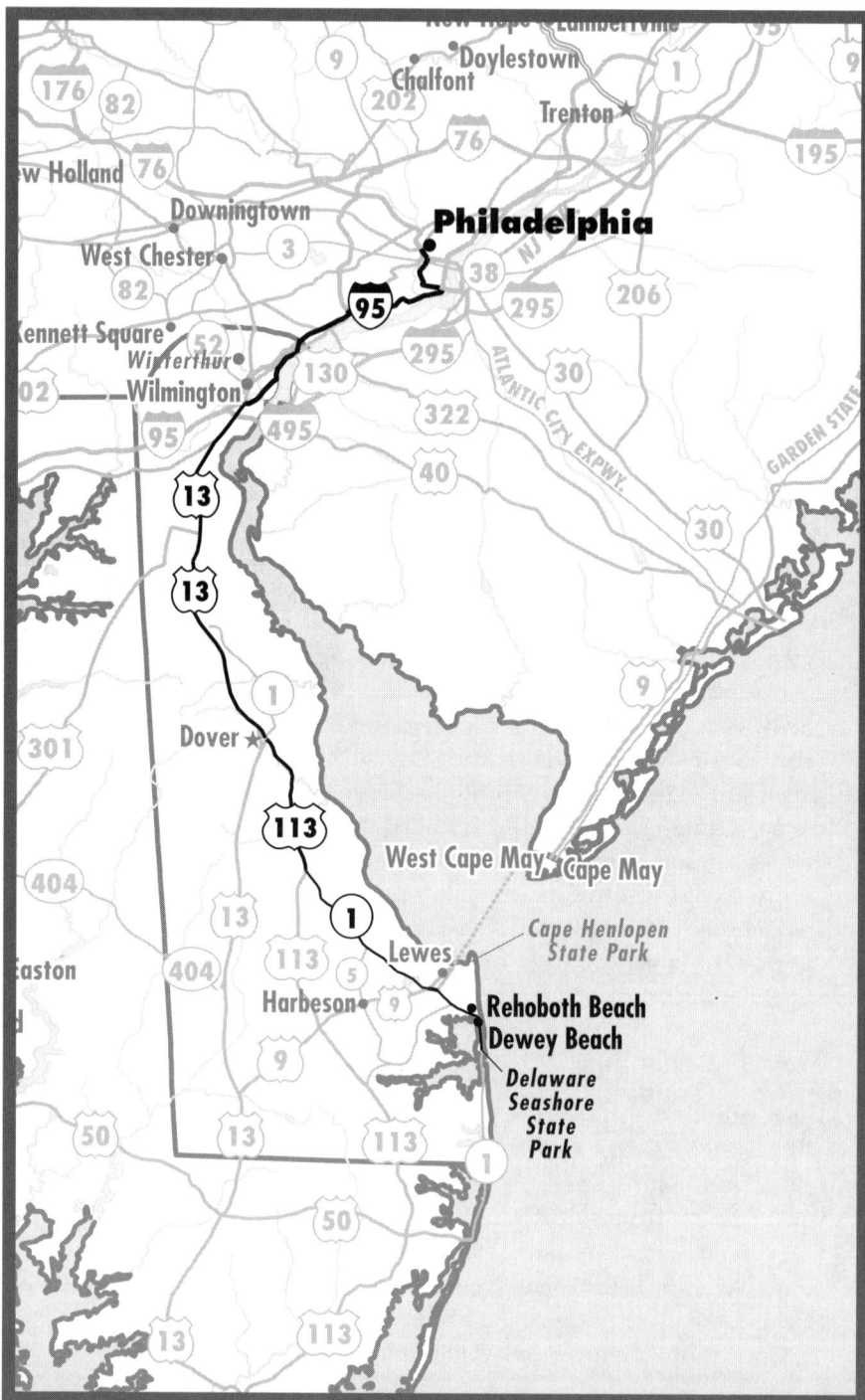

white sands, natural dunes, and foaming surf of **Rehoboth Beach.** Don't fight the urge—kick off your shoes and dig your toes into the wet sand along the water's edge. Then take a leisurely walk and let the sounds of the waves and calls of the shorebirds melt your city stress away. Be sure to keep your eye on the horizon. If you're in the right place at the right time, you might even see dolphins frolicking right off the shoreline.

Afternoon

L U N C H : Nicola Pizza, 8 North First Street, Rehoboth Beach, DE 19971 (right off the boardwalk); (302) 227–6211 or (302) 226–BOLI. This is the home of the Nic-o-boli, a locally beloved creation of ground beef, cheese, and sauce rolled in dough, and its cousins the Nic-spin-oli with spinach and the "Nico e Bolito" with chicken and jalapeño peppers. Open seven days from 11:00 A.M. until the "wee hours of the morning." Inexpensive.

Then break out the heavy-duty sunscreen and head back to the beach for an afternoon of sunbathing, swimming, and sand castles. If the winds cooperate, you might even want to fly a kite. Don't have one? No problem! Just take a short walk over to **Rehoboth Toy & Kite Company** at 67 Rehoboth Avenue or One Virginia Avenue (on the Boardwalk), Rehoboth Beach, DE 19971; (800) 250–KITE or (302) 227–6996. The shapes and colors here will set your imagination soaring no matter what the wind conditions or your personal kite-flying skill level. You'll find the basic single-line Deltas for beginners, a wide array of stunt models, and whimsical shapes, including a parrot in full flight.

Evening

D I N N E R : Back Porch Cafe, 59 Rehoboth Avenue, Rehoboth Beach, DE 19971; (302) 227–3674. This real treasure of a restaurant located in a late 1900s former guest house features a savvy, sassy menu that belies its quaint, understated exterior. Locally grown ingredients give an extra intensity to such creations as pork with ancho-chili crust and Thai green curry duckling. As for dessert, I have only one thing to say—bourbon pecan steamed pudding with bourbon hard sauce accompanied by a cup of coffee en flambé. If the weather is amenable, ask to sit outside on the upper or lower deck.

After dinner check out the sights and sounds on the **boardwalk,** a mile-long fun but not frantic promenade with miniature golf, arcades, and a small amusement park. If you're here at 8:00 P.M. on any summer weekend, you can gather round the **Rehoboth Beach Memorial Bandstand** (302–227–6181), right off the boardwalk at Rehoboth Avenue, for a free old-fashioned band concert.

LODGING: **The Bellmoor,** 6 Christian Street, Rehoboth Beach, DE 19971; (302) 227–5800 or (800) 425–2355. A romantic getaway spot, the Bellmoor is tucked away on a quiet side street, yet only a couple of blocks from the heart of the action. Some of the pretty rooms and suites offer private balconies with garden views, marble baths, fireplaces, hydrotherapy tubs, and/or wet bars. If you're vacationing sans children, there's a separate outdoor swimming pool and indoor-outdoor hot tub designated for adults only. Extra pampering can be arranged at the on-site spa. Breakfast and afternoon tea and cookies are included in room rates, which range from $85 to $485 during "value season" (mid-November through mid-February) and $150 to $575 during peak "summer season" (mid-June through mid-September).

Day 2 / *Morning*

Wake up early so that you can enjoy an early bike ride on the boardwalk (permitted 5:00–10:00 A.M. May 15 through September 15). If you need a rental, **Wheels Bicycle Shop,** (318 Rehoboth Avenue, Rehoboth Beach, DE 19971; 302–227–6807), has all kinds, including cruisers ($4.00 per hour/$13.00 per day), tandems ($12.00/$23.00), tricycles ($9.00/$18.00), road ($8.00/$25.00), and mountain ($6.00/$19.00) bikes.

BREAKFAST: The Bellmoor. Linger over your complimentary country breakfast in the garden.

Pack your bathing suit, sneakers, and more sunscreen for an excursion to Delaware Seashore State Park. But first, stop in at **Arena's Famous Bar & Deli Restaurant** (149 Rehoboth Avenue, Village by the Sea Mall, Rehoboth Beach, DE 19971; 302–227–1272) to pick up your picnic lunch. Arena's offers a wide variety of big sandwiches (including some yummy veggie combos) and fresh salads. Open daily 11:00 A.M.–4:00 P.M. Inexpensive to moderate.

As you continue south, First Street becomes King Charles Street, then, after bearing to the right, Lake Drive, which borders **Silver Lake.** Keep your eye on the sky, or at least on the higher tree branches, near the electrical transformer, and you might be lucky enough to spot one of the wild Monk Parakeets (a type of South American parrot with shocking green plumage) that nest there year-round. How they originally got there is any-

Surf fishing on Rehoboth Beach.

body's guess (many locals believe they are the descendants of a pair of runaway pets), but watching these beautiful birds make themselves at home so
far from their tropical native habitat is a thrilling experience.

When you have finished parrot-seeking, follow Lake Drive to Bayard
Avenue, which will intersect with Route 1; then take Route 1 through
Dewey to **Delaware Seashore State Park** (Rehoboth Beach, DE 19971;
302–227–2800). This 2,000-acre recreational area and nature preserve has
everything. There are two patrolled ocean swimming areas for challenging
the waves and a family-friendly Rehoboth Bay bathing area with calmer
waters for less strenuous dips. Just north of the inlet is one of the few designated surfing areas in the state, and other beaches are set aside for surf
fishing. So that you don't have to go back to town all wet and sandy, the
park has modern bathhouses with showers and changing areas.

Afternoon

LUNCH: **Delaware Seashore State Park** has two very nice pavilions
where you can enjoy your picnic lunch.

After lunch, you can do some more bird watching along the 1½-mile
nature trail on **Burton's Island** in the park. The salt marshes here are a

favorite summer nesting place for gulls and terns. If you would like to do some ocean fishing, the **Indian River Marina** (302–227–3071) offers excursions and a well-stocked bait-and-tackle shop. Delaware Seashore State Park is open seven days a week from 8:00 A.M. to sunset year-round. A daily park fee of $5.00 for out-of-state-registered vehicles is charged Memorial Day weekend through Labor Day, and Saturday, Sunday, and holidays in May, September, and October.

Back in town, in Henlopen Gardens bordering Rehoboth Beach on the north, see what's going on at the **Rehoboth Beach Art League** (302–227–8408). This cluster of four rustic buildings and lovely gardens is the setting for a wide variety of exhibits, programs, and special events all year long. It is also the site of the 1743 **Homestead House,** now a museum featuring restored rooms of period furnishings. Admission is free. Open 10:00 A.M.–4:00 P.M. Monday through Saturday, 1:00–4:00 P.M. Sunday.

Evening

DINNER: Cultured Pearl, 19 Wilmington Avenue, Rehoboth Beach, DE 19971; (302) 227–8493. It's the big picture window filled with lively parakeets and canaries that initially captures your attention, but it's the food that keeps it. For the timid, a section of the menu devoted to "East meets West" compromises pairings of shrimp and vegetable tempura with filet mignon and mashed potatoes. But for an authentic experience, stick to the sushi bar, hosomaki, and other Japanese specialties. Moderate to expensive.

Rehoboth Beach's shopping district, concentrated along Rehoboth Avenue and Wilmington Street, comes alive at night when locals and visitors alike come out to stroll, window-shop, and enjoy the cool ocean breezes. Many of these establishments have an international flavor that makes them fun to visit and their merchandise hard to resist. At the **Tideline Gallery** (146 Rehoboth Avenue; 302–227–4444) riveting Deco blue swirl jazz art sculptures share shelf space with colorfully painted rolling pins (signed by the artists), adorably whimsical animal banks, and decorative yet practical cylindrical stoneware bread bakers.

It's hard to believe that the intricately detailed, ultradelicate hanging sculptures at **Scandinavian Occasions** (125 Rehoboth Avenue; 302–227–3945) are actually paper cuts, a traditional Scandinavian craft. For all things nautical, there's the **Sea Shell Shop** (119 Rehoboth Avenue, Rehoboth Beach, DE 19971; 302–227–6666). Not your typical little souvenir stand, this place is 10,000 square feet filled with unusual home decor items from rugs and afghans to fish netting and pilings. For that hard-to-please person on your gift list, they have a harpoon that just might hit the spot. Also for sale is a collection of authentic shipwreck treasures that may appeal to the history buff (or pirate) in you.

LODGING: The Bellmoor.

Day 3 / Morning

BREAKFAST: Victoria's, Boardwalk Plaza Hotel, Olive Avenue and the Boardwalk, Rehoboth Beach, DE 19971; (302) 227–0615. Don't miss the renowned brunch (in season, $24 per person) or breakfast any time of year. Among the delightfully different selections are lingonberry French toast, Chesapeake omelet (with lump crab imperial), veggie frittata, and Scottish oatmeal brûlée on spiced peach compote. Special children's menu. Expensive, but dining out on the boardwalk patio with its ornate iron furniture and arched trellises is a truly wonderful way to start the day.

If you want to get one more dip in at the beach, the innkeepers at the Gladstone Inn kindly provide an outdoor shower so that you won't have to ride home with sand in your pants.

Afternoon

LUNCH: Jake's Seafood House Restaurant, First Street, between Baltimore and Maryland Avenues, Rehoboth Beach, DE 19971; (302) 227–6237. You can't go to the shore without indulging in a traditional seafood feast, and this has been one of the best places to find one since 1929. Open seven days for lunch and dinner 11:30 A.M.–10:00 P.M. Entree prices range from inexpensive for clam strips to expensive for lobster tail stuffed with crab imperial.

To return to Philadelphia, reverse your route from day one. The return trip should take 2¾ to 3 hours.

There's More

Rehoboth Outlets, 1600 Ocean Outlets, Route 1, Rehoboth Beach, DE 19971; (888) SHOP–333 or (302) 226–9223. Save 20 to 60 percent off original retail prices at more than 150 name-brand outlets along this 2-mile stretch of Route 1. (Remember, shopping in Delaware is tax free!)

Rehoboth Bay Marina, Collins Street, Dewey Beach, DE 19971; (302) 226–2012. Half- and full-day rentals of pontoon boats ($200 and $300, respectively); skiffs ($75 and $105); and runabouts ($115 and $205). Half day can be 8:00 A.M.–noon or 1:00–5:00 P.M. Full day is 8:00 A.M.–5:00 P.M. Marina is open Memorial Day through Labor Day, seven days a week, 7:00 A.M.–6:00 P.M.; call for hours during April, September, and October.

Camping, Delaware Seashore State Park, Route 1 (south of Dewey Beach), Rehoboth Beach, DE 19971; (302) 539–7202. A variety of accommodations for everything from tents to large recreational vehicles. Three-point hookups for electricity, water, and sewer service are available on some sites. Campsites are available on a first-come, first-served basis. $26 to $34 for nonresidents. Cabins from $54 to $74.

Special Events

Easter. Easter Promenade, Rehoboth Beach Convention Center, 229 Rehoboth Avenue, Rehoboth Beach, DE 19971; (800) 441–1329 or (302) 227–2233. Parades and other seasonal family activities. Free.

August. Annual Delaware State News Sand Castle Contest, Fisherman's Beach, north end of Rehoboth Beach boardwalk; (302) 741–8204 or (302) 741–8210. Amateur sculptors compete for cash prizes. Free.

October. Rehoboth Beach Autumn Jazz Festival, over thirty venues throughout Rehoboth and Dewey Beach areas; (800) 29–MUSIC. Three days filled with seventy-five events including a free midday concert, seminars, jazz brunches, club shows, and art exhibits. Call for ticket prices.

October. Annual Sea Witch Halloween & Fiddler's Festival, throughout Rehoboth Beach; (800) 441–1329 or (302) 227–2233. Costume contests, parades, hayrides, craft shows, entertainment, and shop-to-shop trick or treating for the kids. At the Fiddler's Festival, musicians compete for $1,500 in cash prizes.

November. Rehoboth Beach Independent Film Festival, Midway Shopping Center, Route 1, Rehoboth Beach, DE 19971; (302) 645–9095. Three days of critically acclaimed national and international films. Workshops and guest speakers.

Other Recommended Restaurants and Lodgings

Rehoboth Beach

Blue Moon Restaurant, 35 Baltimore Avenue, Rehoboth Beach, DE 19971; (302) 227–6515. The look and personality of this fabulously renovated old beachhouse-turned-restaurant is constantly changing along with the menu, which features modern American cuisine using the freshest locally grown produce. Expensive. Open seven days year-round.

LaLa Land, 22 Wilmington Avenue, Rehoboth Beach, DE 19971; (302) 227–3887. There's nothing modest about this place, with its almost psychedelic hand-painted blue, purple, and pink dining room. There's nothing shy about its menu either—the gnocchi is served with truffle oil and asparagus tips, the mahimahi with corn bacon salsa and guacamole, and the grilled pork chop with a cumin-chili rub. Expensive. Seasonal.

Sydney's, 24 Christian Street, Rehoboth Beach, DE 19971; (800) 808–1924 or (302) 227–1339. Located in one of the first schoolhouses in Rehoboth Beach, this sophisticated spot specializes in hot New Orleans–style cuisine and cool blues and jazz. Open year-round.

Crystal Restaurant and Lounge, 620 Rehoboth Avenue, Rehoboth Beach, DE 19971; (302) 227–1088. It doesn't look like much from the outside, but this unassuming little restaurant has endeared itself to the locals with breakfasts starting at $2.50, lunches from $3.95, and dinners from $7.95. Open year-round.

Eden, 122 Rehoboth Avenue, Rehoboth Beach, DE 19971; (302) 227–3330. Try the signature Going Nuts pasta with a pesto made from pine nuts, pecans, and walnuts! Moderate.

Boardwalk Plaza Hotel, Olive at the Boardwalk, Rehoboth Beach, DE 19971; (800) 33–BEACH or (302) 227–7169. Family-owned and -operated, this gracious Victorian hotel offers beautiful rooms furnished with antiques and period reproductions. One exquisite amenity is the indoor-outdoor spa pool. Depending on time of month and week, rates range from $59 to $274 for a standard double. Ask about money-saving off-season package plans.

Sea Witch Manor, 71 Lake Avenue, Rehoboth Beach, DE 19971; (302) 226–WITCH. It's hard to believe that this dramatic bed-and-breakfast was built in 1994. For a romantic getaway, you won't find better. Memorial Day through Labor Day rates range from $140 to $195; off-season rates from $99 to $135.

For More Information

Rehoboth Beach/Dewey Beach Chamber of Commerce, 501 Rehoboth Avenue, Rehoboth Beach, DE 19971; (800) 441–1329 or (302) 227–2233; www.beach-fun.com.

Southern Delaware Tourism Office, 103 West Pine Street, Georgetown, DE 19947; (800) 357–1818 or (302) 227–1818; www.visitsouthern delaware.com.

Delaware Tourism Office, 99 Kings Highway, Dover, DE 19901; (866) 2–VISIT–DE (284–7483); www.visitdelaware.com.

Annapolis, Maryland

Maritime Masterpiece

2 Nights

For more than three centuries, the Chesapeake Bay has been a primary source of commerce, culture, and cuisine for the people in Annapolis. Known as "America's Sailing Capital," it remains a city of sailors from the midshipmen of the U.S. Naval Academy to the after-work yacht racers.

Annapolis is also a great walking city, with streets that fan out from its centerpiece state capitol. It's a good thing, too, because there's plenty to see here, including the nation's largest collection of surviving seventeenth- to nineteenth-century buildings, ranging from humble, early wood-frame abodes to lavish English-style mansions.

☐ Three Centuries of History

☐ Harborside Feasts

☐ Evening Races

☐ Artistic Pursuits

And history is still being made—or at least being uncovered—at an archaeological dig only fifteen minutes south of the city. There are even public dig days when you can try your hand at unearthing a few buried treasures yourself.

Day 1 / Morning

Annapolis is only about a 130-mile, 2½-hour drive from Philadelphia. To get there, take the Schuylkill Expressway (I–76) to I–95 and drive south on I–95 past Baltimore, about 120 miles to Route I–97. Travel south on I–97 for 21 miles and you will come to Routes 301/50. Take Route 50 east to exit 29A (St. Margarets Road). Turn right at the light and go straight 2³⁄₁₀ miles. Make a left U-turn onto Brownswood Road; then take the first right onto Forest Beach Drive for a delicious introduction to Maryland's famous crabs.

Afternoon

LUNCH: Cantler's Riverside Inn, 458 Forest Beach Drive, Annapolis, MD 21401; (410) 757–1311. At this restaurant, about 1½ miles down at

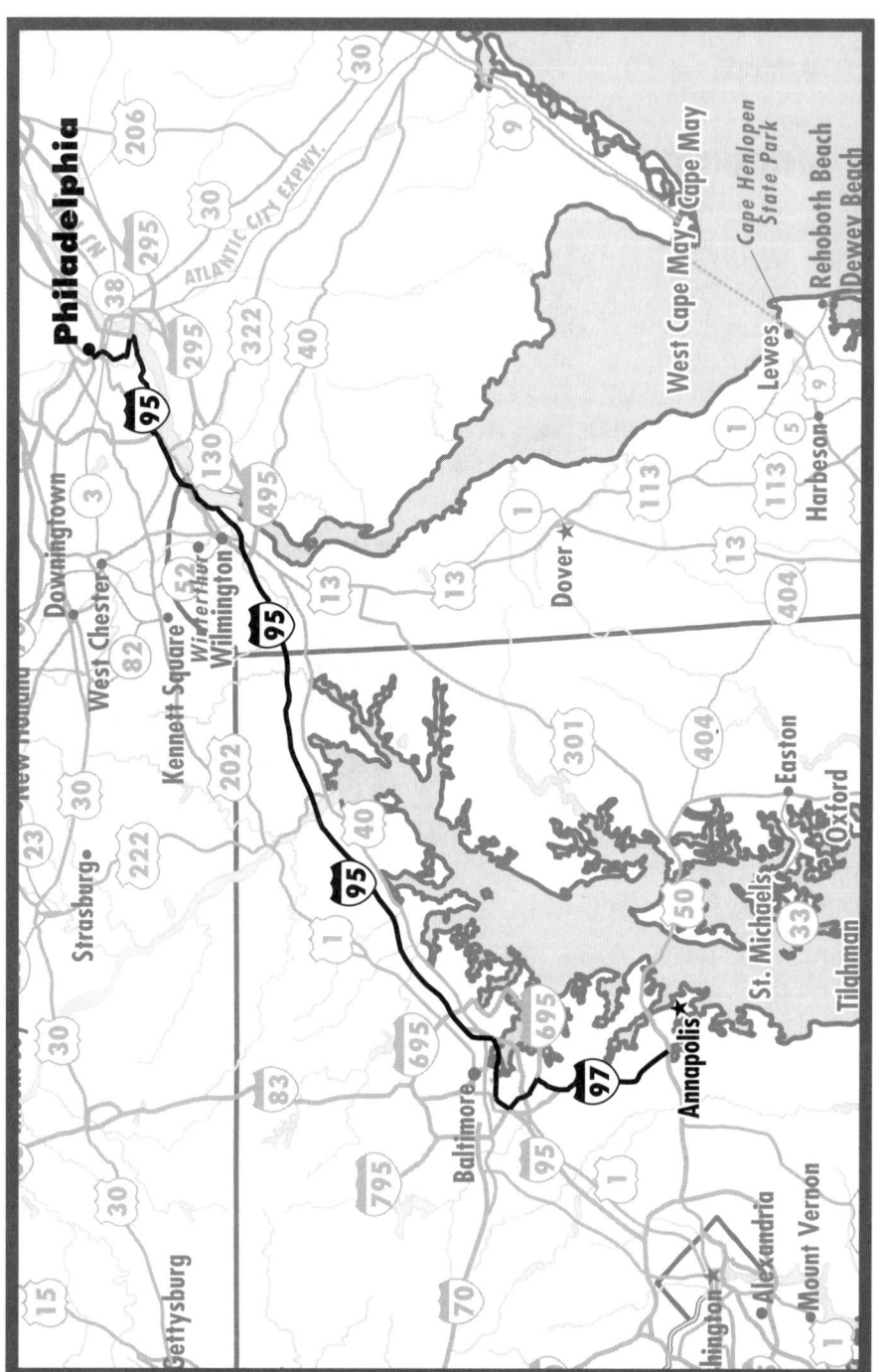

the end of the road, you can feast on award-winning seafood specialties, including just about every preparation of crab from dip to soup to steamed (year-round) to cakes. You can even have your rockfish (striped bass) or New York strip stuffed with Maryland's treasure from the bay. Oysters served in a variety of ways are also available in season.

Reverse your tracks back to Route 50 west, which will take you across the Severn River Bridge. Take exit 24A Rowe Boulevard/Route 70. Follow Rowe Boulevard to State Circle, crowned by the Maryland State House. Bear right on Rowe Boulevard to Northwest Street, then left. Turn right into **Gotts Court Garage,** which is located next to the **Visitor Center,** 26 West Street, Annapolis, MD 21401 (410–280–0445). At Gotts, your first hour is free; then it's $1.00 per hour, maximum $8.00.

The **Maryland State House** (91 State Circle, Annapolis, MD 21401; 410–974–3400) sits on a hill at the hub of the city. The state capitol—and, for nine months in 1783–84, the nation's capitol as well—this impressive structure has a remarkable history and split personality . . . literally. A broad black line on the floor divides the original 1770s wood and plaster section from the early 1900s marble addition.

One of the many highlights of your tour is the room where, in 1783, George Washington resigned his commission as commander in chief of the Continental Army and where, less than a month later, the Treaty of Paris officially ending the Revolutionary War was ratified. Open Monday through Friday 9:00 A.M.–5:00 P.M., Saturday and Sunday 10:00 A.M.–4:00 P.M. Tours are given at 11:00 A.M. and 3:00 P.M.

In the eighteenth century Maryland Avenue was the most fashionable residential street in the city. Stretching from State Circle to the gate of the U.S. Naval Academy, it is still the epitome of style with its diverse collection of exclusive galleries and shops. At **Annapolis Pottery** (40 State Circle, Annapolis, MD 21401; 410–268–6153) you'll never find anyone asleep at the wheel, especially Monday through Thursday, when you can watch the artisans handcraft original stoneware vases, pots, and other decorative items. You'll find more local arts and crafts at the **Maryland Federation of Art—Gallery on the Circle** (18 State Circle, Annapolis, MD 21401; 410–268–4566) and the **League of Maryland Craftsmen** (216 Main Street, Annapolis, MD 21401; 410–626–1277).

From Maryland Avenue, turn right onto Prince George Street. At No. 186 is the **William Paca House & Garden** (410–263–5553), the private residence of one of the four Marylanders who signed the Declaration of Independence. The five-part restored structure is a splendid example of eighteenth-century architecture. Particularly beautiful is the two-acre terraced Eden out back, where you can admire the brilliant colors of the flowers, the clever fish-shaped pool, and the air of absolute serenity. Open Monday through Saturday 10:00 A.M.–5:00 P.M., Sunday noon–5:00 P.M. March 18 to December 31; Saturday 10:00 A.M.–4:00 P.M., Sunday noon–4:00 P.M. January 1 to March 17. Admission for combined house and garden tour is $8.00, $7.00 seniors, and $5.00 for children under seventeen.

Evening

DINNER: Carrol's Creek, at 410 Severn Avenue, Eastport, Annapolis, MD 21403; (410) 263–8102.

Continue south on Prince George Street until you come to Randall Street; turn right. Straight ahead is **City Dock.** At the head of the dock on the sidewalk is the **Kunta Kinte–Alex Haley Memorial** commemorating the arrival in 1767 of the African slave who was immortalized in his descendant Haley's book *Roots,* as well as all of the others who were brought here in bondage. The dock is also one of the stopping points for **Jiffy Water Taxi** (410–263–0033), which you'll be taking for the five-minute ride ($2.00 to $4.50) across Spa Creek to Eastport for dinner.

In addition to its spectacular bayfront view, Carrol's Creek is renowned for its Maryland-accented American cuisine. There are crab cakes, and raw and fried oysters, as well as a killer pecan-and-coconut–crusted mahimahi. But spring for the Carrol's Creek Chef's Dinner, which allows you to add cream of crab soup, salad, and dessert to any entree for an extra $12.

After dinner in season you can sit out on the restaurant's deck/lounge and watch the yachts returning to the neighboring Annapolis Marina from the Wednesday evening races. Better yet, the Kaye family will take you for a two-hour sunset sail aboard their 74-foot *Schooner Woodwind* (410–263–7837), a replica of the luxury "yachts" of the early twentieth century. *Woodwind* departs from Pusser's landing at the Annapolis Marriott Waterfront Hotel next to City Dock seven days a week at 6:30 P.M. mid-May to Labor Day, 5:30 P.M. in early May and September. Sunset cruises are $29 per person for adults, $27 for seniors, $15 for children. (Daytime cruises are $25, $23, and $15, respectively.) From May to the end of September, the Kayes also offer Friday and Saturday overnight boat-and-breakfast packages for two ($235 plus 10 percent tax) that include a double stateroom, two-hour sail, and breakfast.

LODGING: Historic Inns of Annapolis, 58 State Circle, Annapolis, MD 21403; (410) 263–2641. This is really three eighteenth-century inns— **Governor Calvert House, Robert Johnson House,** and **Maryland Inn**—all centrally located across from State Circle and adjacent to Church Circle. Each of the three is distinctive in personality, and all are delightfully furnished with period antiques and reproductions. If you have a favorite among the inns, you can make a request to stay there when you make your reservation. Innkeeper Peg Bednarsky, who happens to be the very soul of hospitality, will try to accommodate your request, subject to room availability. Double occupancy rates range from $155 to $245, suites from $180 to $285.

Day 2 / Morning

BREAKFAST: Treaty of Paris Restaurant, 16 Church Circle at the Maryland Inn, Annapolis, MD 21403; (410) 263–2641. Here you can enjoy a real Maryland-style breakfast in an authentic eighteenth-century setting. The moderately priced breakfast menu includes the traditional morning fare, but for some genuine local flavor, try a smoked salmon or lump crab omelet, or the eggs Maryland—poached eggs and sliced fresh tomatoes with backfin crabmeat and Old Bay hollandaise.

Head east on Maryland Avenue until it dead-ends at King George Street; turn right on King George, keep going straight, and you will find yourself at Gate 1, the main visitors entrance of the **United States Naval Academy.** One of Annapolis's best-known landmarks for the past 150 years, this 338-acre campus—officially known as the "Yard"—is home to a brigade of 4,000 and a faculty of 580. Right inside the gate is the **Armel-Leftwich Visitor Center** (410–263–6933), where you can arrange for a guided tour of the Yard's many attractions. Guided tours are offered year-round, seven days a week. Fees are $7.00 for adults, $6.00 for seniors, $5.00 for students (first through twelfth grades).

At precisely 12:05 P.M. weekdays, the entire brigade assembles for noon meal formation, an impressive event complete with ceremonial swords and drums and bugles that takes place in front of **Bancroft Hall,** the largest dormitory in the western hemisphere and home to the entire brigade. Close by is a statue of the famous Indian warrior **Tecumseh,** to whom the midshipmen send their pleas for benevolence prior to important football games and important tests.

One of the most prominent features of the Yard—and of the Annapolis skyline—is the **Chapel,** with its magnificent Tiffany Studios–designed stained-glass windows. Beneath the Chapel is the elaborate and eerily beautiful "undersea" **Crypt of John Paul Jones** with its black-and-white marble sarcophagus supported by carved porpoises, covered with sculpted seaweed, and surrounded by models, photos, and mementos tracing the career of this famed Revolutionary War hero.

Preble Hall houses the **U.S. Naval Academy Museum** (410–267–2108), with four galleries showcasing a collection of more than 35,000 artifacts and artworks spanning centuries of naval history. Among the exhibitions are 1,210 medals from thirty countries dating from 254 B.C. to A.D. 1936, and 600 historic American and captured flags, including some that have been to the moon. One of the most riveting exhibits is the **Class of 1951 Gallery of Ships** with its awe-inspiring selection of precision-carved ship models crafted from wood, gold, and bone by artisans from the sixteenth to the nineteenth centuries. By the way, the last mentioned were carved from leftover beef bones by French prisoners of war being held in England during the Napoleonic conflicts. The museum is open Monday through Saturday 9:00 A.M.–5:00 P.M., Sunday 11:00 A.M.–5:00 P.M. Admission is free.

Afternoon

LUNCH: Harry Browne's, 66 State Circle, Annapolis, MD 21403; (410) 263–4332. This longtime lunch and dinner tradition for Annapolitans and visitors has a moderately priced menu full of delicious surprises. It offers homemade soups, pastas, and quiche that regularly change with the availability of fresh ingredients and the imagination of the chef. Always available are the excellent cream of crab soup, chili served in a sourdough boule, and, of course, signature crab cakes.

During the warm weather, one Saturday a month is public dig day at **Historic London Town House and Gardens** (839 Londontown Road, Edgewater, MD 21037; 410–222–1919), Maryland's largest archaeological dig. Take Route 50 west to Route 665/Aris T. Allen Boulevard. Get off at the second exit and make a right-hand turn onto Route 2. You'll go over the South River Bridge. The third traffic light is Mayo Road; turn left onto Mayo, then left again onto Londontown Road and continue to the end of the road. On those special Saturdays, you can get some very old dirt under your fingernails as you work alongside the pros who are searching for the lost forty dwellings, shops, and taverns that once comprised the bustling seventeenth-century tobacco port called London. On other days this site is still worth visiting for a tour of the one building that remains, an eighteenth-century mansion where you can learn about life in old-time London, and eight acres of gorgeous gardens. Open Tuesday through Saturday 10:00 A.M.–3:00 P.M., Sunday noon–3:00 P.M. April through December; gardens only Tuesday through Saturday 10:00 A.M.–3:00 P.M. January through March. Guided house and Acoustiguide site tour $7.00, $5.00 seniors, $3.00 children seven to twelve.

DINNER: Rams Head Tavern, 33 West Street, Annapolis, MD 21403; (410) 268–4545. Adjacent to State Circle is the second major focal point of the city, Church Circle. Go halfway around Church Circle to West Street to reach your destination for dinner. This lively tavern is conveniently located right next to (and, is in fact kin to) **Fordham Brewing Company,** Annapolis's first brewery, established in 1703. So it's no surprise that the moderately priced menu is quite beer-friendly and that more than a few of its signature recipes include different incarnations of the brew. Nonspiked specialties include innovations like Jump Back Jambalaya and, of course, a signature version of the Maryland crab cake (market price). The Ram's Head offers diners free parking at Gotts Garage, so if you're driving, be sure to get your ticket validated.

Follow up your dinner with an evening of music from performers such as Livingston Taylor, Leon Russell, Jose Feliciano, and Arlo Guthrie at the **Rams Head On Stage** (410–268–5111), an on-premise 215-seat theater. Ticket prices vary per performer, but they tend to be in the mid-teens to mid-twenties range. The tavern offers a great dinner and show combo that gives you 10 percent off your entire meal check and a free beer nightcap (with ticket stub) after the show.

LODGING: Historic Inns of Annapolis.

Day 3 / Morning

BREAKFAST: Cafe Normandie, 185 Main Street, Annapolis, MD 21403; (410) 263–3382. There's nothing quite as romantic as savoring cups of cinnamon-laced coffee at a cozy table in a rustic French country bistro. Have a fresh croissant with your seafood or apple and cheddar omelet. Or try something a bit more exotic, perhaps eggs Basque with ratatouille or eggs Florentine with spinach and cheese. Moderate. This is also a great dessert stop either during the day or after dinner. The crepes are heavenly and the tarte tatin divine.

If you want to take home a piece of Maryland history, head for the City Dock area for a stop at the **Historic Annapolis Museum Store and Welcome Center,** 77 Main Street, Annapolis, MD 21403; (410) 268–5576. This extensive collection reflects the architectural, social, cultural, and maritime history of the city through eighteenth-century reproductions, handblown glassware, books, and other decorative and educational items. Open Monday through Saturday 10:00 A.M.–5:00 P.M., Sunday noon–5:00 P.M. For the best selection of U.S. Naval Academy and Annapolis clothing and accessories, go to **Peppers,** 133 Main Street, Annapolis, MD 21403; (410) 267–8722. They even have Navy-style gear for newborns!

To pick up the fixings for a fabulous picnic lunch, head to the **Market House** (410–269–0941) at City Dock. In operation since 1690, this market features nine merchants selling fresh seafood (there's even a raw bar), fried chicken, deli sandwiches, all kinds of cheeses, and heavenly breads and pastries. Open 365 days a year.

You can say a fond farewell to the waters of Annapolis at **Sandy Point State Park,** 786 beautiful acres along the Chesapeake Bay that you'll find

Annapolis Harbor.

at 1100 East College Parkway (off Route 50/301 at the Bay Bridge western terminus); (410) 974–2149. The park has lovely beaches for swimming and boating (boat rentals are available), a pier for fishing, and hiking and biking trails for exploring. Home to a wide variety of woodland and marsh birds and located on the migratory route of waterfowl, it is one of the premier bird-watching spots on Maryland's western shore. Bathhouse facilities are available at the park so that you can refresh before you hit the road for home. The park is open daily year-round, 6:00 A.M.–9:00 P.M. from Memorial Day to Labor Day and only for daytime use in other months. Admission is $3.00 per person on weekdays, $4.00 on weekends; seniors (sixty-two and over) and children under four in car seats are free.

Afternoon

LUNCH: Picnic tables under covered pavilions are available on a first-come, first-served basis at Sandy Point State Park.

To return home, get on Route 50 heading west and retrace your route from day one. It should take about 2½ hours to get back into Center City Philadelphia.

There's More

Hammond Harwood House, 19 Maryland Avenue, Annapolis, MD 21403; (410) 263–4683. This restored pre–Revolutionary War residence provides a look at Annapolis history from the perspective of a family who lived here. Open April through October, Wednesday through Sunday noon –5:00 P.M. Admission is $6.00 for adults, $5.50 for students, $3.00 for children under six.

Three Centuries Tours of Annapolis, 48 Maryland Avenue, Annapolis, MD 21403; (410) 263–5401. A colonial-garbed guide will take you on a walking tour along the city's architecturally diverse and historically significant streets. Call for seasonal hours. $11.00 adults, $6.00 students.

Annapolis Summer Garden Theatre, 143 Compromise Street, Annapolis, MD 21403; (410) 268–9212. This outdoor community theater performs Shakespeare and Broadway musicals under the stars from Memorial Day to Labor Day. Performances Thursday through Saturday evenings.

Maryland Hall for the Creative Arts, 801 Chase Street, Annapolis, MD 21403; (401) 263–5544. The city's primary community arts center is home to the Annapolis Symphony Orchestra, Chorale, Opera, and Ballet Theater.

Banneker-Douglass Museum, 84 Franklin Street, Annapolis, MD 21403; (410) 216–6180. Open Tuesday through Friday 10:00 A.M.–3:00 P.M., Saturday noon–4:00 P.M. This museum of African-American arts and culture features changing exhibits, lectures, films, and publications. Free.

Horizon Organic Farm & Educational Center, 100 Dairy Lane, Grambrills, MD 21054; (410) 923–7600. From Annapolis take Route 97 north to Route 3 south. Turn right at first light onto Route 175 west; after about 1 mile, turn left onto Dairy Lane. Dozens of interactive exhibits on this 875-acre demonstration farm (complete with cows) provide kids and adults with a dynamic lesson on agriculture and the environment. Open fields of grass for romping, a pavilion for picnicking, organic milk for tasting. Guided tours $5.00, children under two free. Call for hours.

Special Events

May. Chesapeake Bay Bridge Walk; (800) 541–9595. Lots of locals and visitors gather every year to take this 4%₁₀-mile stroll. Why? Because it's there!

June. Annapolis JazzFest, St. John's College Campus; College Avenue, Annapolis, MD 21403; (410) 349–1111. Three days of nonstop music. Bring a chair and blanket.

August. Kunta Kinte Heritage Festival; St. John's College Campus, College Avenue, Annapolis, MD 21403; (410) 349–0338. This two-day event celebrates the heritage, culture, history, music, and cuisine of Africans, African-Americans, and African-Caribbeans. Mask making, storytelling, crafters, artists, two stages of entertainment, educational workshops, health screenings, and African displays. Lots of traditional and ethnic foods. Admission charge.

End of August through late October. Maryland Renaissance Festival, Crownsville Road (between Routes 450 and 178), Annapolis, MD 21302; (800) 296–7304. Held Saturday, Sunday, and Labor Day Monday, this bawdy, brawling, and absolutely brilliant re-creation of a sixteenth-century English village features 250 performers, Shakespearean and other productions, and combat jousting. More than 130 shops with crafts by artisans from all over North America, and lots of food (including those giant turkey legs said to be favored by King Henry VIII).

September. Maryland Seafood Festival, Sandy Point State Park, Annapolis, MD 21403; (410) 268–7682. A three-day seafood extravaganza starring crabs, shrimp, oysters, and clams in just about every possible form. Also Maryland crab soup cook-off, live entertainment, and crafts.

September. Anne Arundel County Fair, Route 178 (General's Highway), Crownsville, MD 21032; (410) 923–3400. The real old-fashioned kind with four days of carnival midway rides, agricultural and craft demonstrations, outdoor skills contests, livestock sale, live bands, tractor pulls, skunk races—even a watermelon-eating contest.

Other Recommended Restaurants and Lodgings

Annapolis

Charles Inn Bed-and-Breakfast, 74 Charles Street, Annapolis, MD 21403; (410) 268–1451. With its period art and furnishings, fresh flowers, and cozy feather-topped beds, this restored Civil War–era home combines comfort and history. A luxurious full breakfast is included. Rates range from $125 to $225.

McGarvey's Saloon and Oyster Bar, 8 Market Space, City Dock, Annapolis, MD 21403; (410) 263–5700. There's a twenty-some-year-old ficus growing through the middle of the floor and real Blue Angels helmets above the long wooden bar at this jovial spot known for its award-winning burgers, uniquely flavored chili, steaks, and seafood. Moderate.

Middleton Tavern, 2 Market Space, City Dock, Annapolis, MD 21403; (410) 263–3323. Home of the oyster shooter (a gulp of raw oyster followed by a short beer) and other bivalve delights. Prices on the primarily seafood and steak menu generally hover around the mid-twenties. Also open for lunch and weekend "champagne and strawberry" brunch.

For More Information

Annapolis & Anne Arundel County Conference and Visitors Bureau; (410) 280–0445; www.visit-annapolis.org.

Anne Arundel County Economic Development Corporation; (410) 222–7410.

Maryland Office of Tourism Development; (800) 634–7386 or (800) MD–IS–FUN; www.choosemaryland.org.

Maryland's Eastern Shore

Follow the Dotted Coastline

2 Nights

"The mildness of the aire, the fertilitie of the soile, and the situation of the rivers are so propitious to the nature and use of man as no place is more convenient for pleasure, profit and mans sustenance."
—Captain John Smith, 1612

☐ Skipjacks and Yachts

☐ Secret Seasonings

☐ Street Music

It isn't only the Chesapeake Bay Bridge that separates Maryland's Eastern Shore from the rest of the world. It is an entire way of life.

Here, the last of the once extensive fleet of oyster-dredging skipjacks—and their rugged crews—still ply the bay and deliver their catch of the day directly to the kitchens of waterfront restaurants. And boat-builders still practice their centuries-old craft to construct and restore majestic wooden sailing ships for work, display, and pleasure.

As you travel south, then east along the coast, you'll pass through little dots of towns only about fifteen to twenty minutes apart, some with names you know (such as St. Michaels and Tilghman Island), and others, such as Grasonville, Oxford, and Easton, that may not be quite as familiar. Along the way you'll become acquainted with beautiful rivers named Choptank, Tuckahoe, Wye, Miles, and Tred Avon.

Peak visitor time along the Eastern Shore is during the summer. But the early fall brings a back-to-normal tranquillity as well as awe-inspiring arrays of fall foliage for those who like to avoid the crowds.

Day 1 / Morning

Although there are shorter, more-direct routes to St. Michaels from Philadelphia, this one allows you to have a taste of some of the Eastern Shore's best seafood and visit one of the area's most beautiful wetlands sanctuaries along the way. The trip will take about three hours and twenty

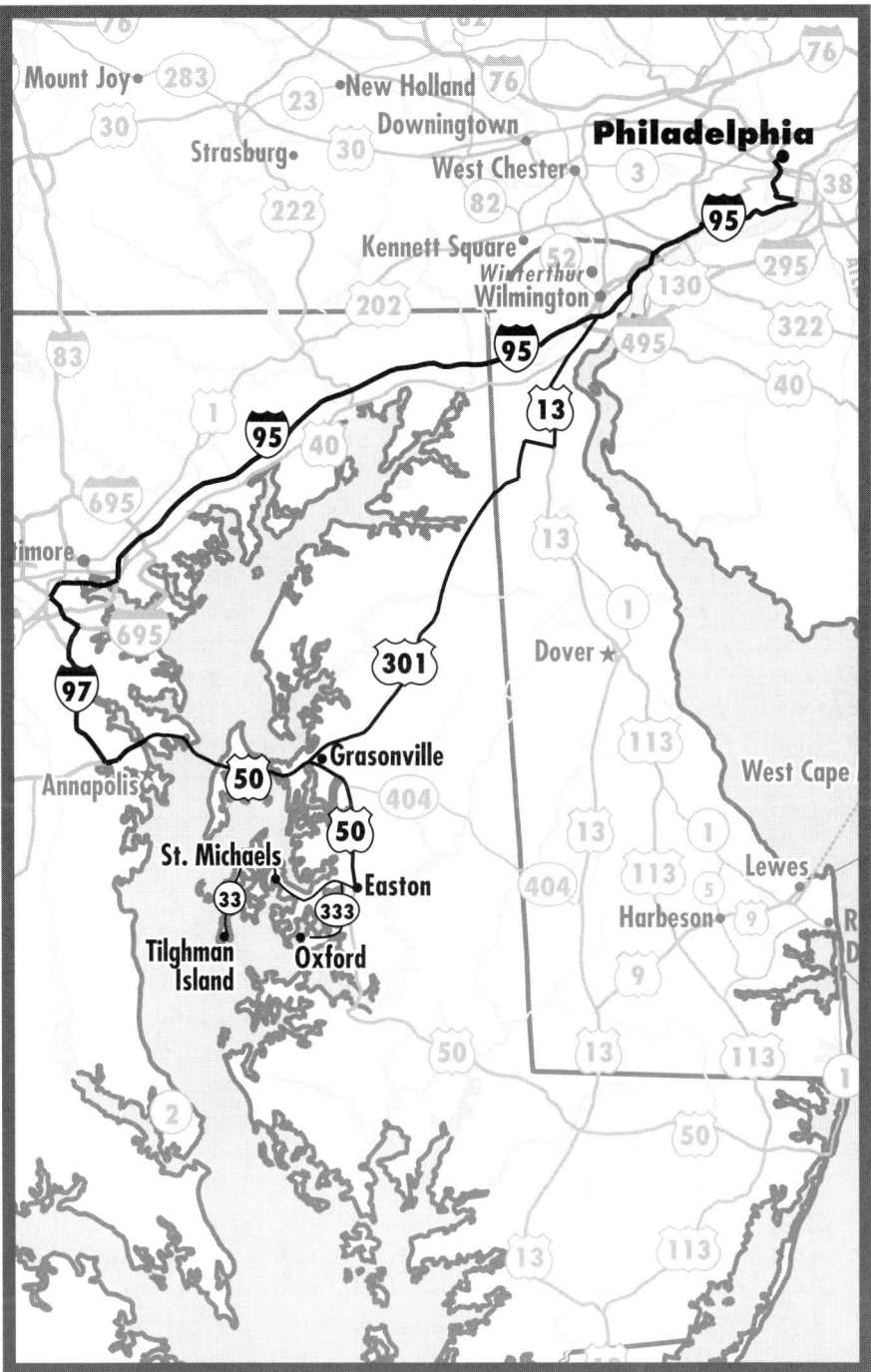

minutes (about ½ hour longer than usual). Take I–76 (Schuylkill Expressway) to I–95 south past Baltimore. Just beyond the city, follow signs for I–695 east toward Glen Burnie. This is a left-hand exit. Follow I–695 until it merges with I–97 south (also a left-hand exit). Take I–97 south until it merges with Route 50 east. Follow Route 50 past Annapolis and across the Bay Bridge to exit 42, Kent Narrows. Follow the blue directional signs to Harris Crab House in Grasonville.

Afternoon

LUNCH: Harris Crab House at the Kent Narrows, 433 North Kent Narrows Way, Grasonville, MD 21638; (410) 827–9500. You know the seafood is fresh because while you eat you can watch the local watermen deliver their day's catch of clams, crabs, and oysters right to the dock of the Harris family's processing plant next door. The Maryland vegetable crab and cream of crab soups are to die for. And the local catch combination platters; "lobster bucket" (comes with shrimp, softshells, mussels, and sides); and, of course, the steamed crabs are exquisite. Harris offspring Karen Oertel explains that the reason Maryland crabs are better than you can find anywhere else is the way they're cooked and the special secret seasonings that are used. If she has any of the Harris special blend available for sale, buy it. It spices up everything from chicken to vegetables. Open for lunch and dinner 11:00 A.M.–10:00 P.M. 365 days a year. Prices are moderate.

Go back toward Route 50, but instead of getting back onto the highway, turn left onto Route 18 and follow it for about 2 miles. Turn right at Perry Corner Road and go ½ mile to the entrance of the wetlands center, which is on the right.

Horsehead Wetlands Center (Wild Fowl Trust of North America) in Grasonville, MD 21638 (800–CANVASBACK, 410–827–6694), is 500 acres of protected land, mostly salt marshes, where you can see Mother Nature at her wildest. Stop at the **Visitor Center** for a brief acquaintance with some of the types of butterflies, insects, and other forms of life that call this environment home. Outside the picture window is one of six ponds where you can watch the resident and visiting waterfowl in their natural habitat. For a panoramic view of the sanctuary and its inhabitants, take the Boardwalk ⅔ mile across the salt meadow and climb to the top of the 15-foot tower. Explore the beautiful trails that wind past the butterfly-and-hummingbird garden, wildflowers, and habitat ponds. You may even spot a bald eagle soaring overhead. Canoes are also available for self-guided water tours of the center. Open 9:00 A.M.–5:00 P.M. daily year-round.

Admission is $5.00 for adults, $4.00 for seniors, and $2.00 for youths (five to eighteen).

Retrace your steps from Horsehead to get back onto Route 50 east. When the road divides into Route 301 and Route 50, keep following Route 50 east toward Ocean City. As you approach Easton, watch for signs for St. Michaels. Turn off Route 50 onto Route 322; you'll pass the Black and Decker plant on your right. At the light near the shopping centers, turn right onto Route 33 toward **St. Michaels.** Route 33 will turn into Talbot Street, the town's main thoroughfare, lined with shops, restaurants, and other enticing places.

Make a right-hand turn from Talbot onto Mill Street at Navy Point and you'll come to the **Chesapeake Bay Maritime Museum** (410–745–2916). Highlights include a floating fleet of restored workboats and the three-story **Hooper Strait Lighthouse,** built in 1879, one of only three of the once typical cottage-style, screwpile lighthouses that formerly lined the bay. And you can pull up a crab or eel pot or tong for oysters at **Waterman's Wharf,** a re-created crabber's shanty. The museum is open seven days a week year-round. Hours are 9:00 A.M.–6:00 P.M. in summer, until 5:00 P.M. in spring and fall, and until 4:00 P.M. in winter. Admission is $8.50 for adults, $7.50 for seniors, $4.00 for youths six to seventeen, and free for children under six. Check out the Museum Store for Bay-inspired books, toys, gourmet foods, and other wonderful items.

Evening

DINNER: Tilghman Island Inn. 21384 Coopertown Road, Tilghman Island, MD 21671; (410) 886–2141 or (800) 866–2141. From St. Michaels, follow Route 33 South for about 12 miles, across the Knapps Narrows Drawbridge onto Tilghman Island. Turn right onto Coopertown Road at the second light after the bridge, and the entrance to the inn will be on your right. Inn co-owner and chef David McCallum creates "trendy American" cuisine featuring fresh ingredients from local growers and watermen. House specialties include Oysters Choptank in a Pernod-scented champagne sauce on puff pastry and Blackeye Pea Cakes with fresh tomato salsa. On Saturday nights five-course prix fixe tasting dinners are available for around $50. Pairing their food and wine savvy, McCallum and partner Jack Redmon also host innovative monthly pairing dinners (including seasonal "Wind and Wine" cruises on the skipjack *Rebecca T. Ruark*).

LODGING: Tilghman Island Inn. Tranquillity is the byword at this intimate spot overlooking the Chesapeake Bay and marshes. Settle back with a glass of wine and watch the yachts and migratory birds sail past your window. Cuddle up in front of an in-room fireplace or sink into the soothing warmth of your own Jacuzzi. Pets are welcome by all, including full-time resident citron-crested cockatoo Blanche Dubois and gentle standard poodle Jasmine. Rooms range between $200 and $300 per night. Continental breakfast is included.

Day 2 / Morning

BREAKFAST: Sherwood Landing. Inn at Perry Cabin, 308 Watkins Lane, St. Michaels, MD 21663; (800) 722–2949 or (410) 745–2200. Luxurious surroundings make this restaurant at the Eastern Shore's most elegant inn a meal to linger over. On warm days, savor the water views from the outdoor patio along with your smoked-salmon omelet or lobster hash, poached egg, and citrus hollandaise. Expensive.

Had you visited the Eastern Shore in the late nineteenth century, you would have seen hundreds of sailing boats called skipjacks dredging for oysters out in the Chesapeake Bay. Today you can still see—and sail on—the real thing, as fifth-generation waterman Captain Wade Murphy Jr. takes you on a two-hour adventure on his skipjack the ***Rebecca T. Ruark*** (410–886–2176). Based in Dogwood Harbor, just across the drawbridge on Tilghman Island, the *Rebecca,* built in 1886 and now the oldest U.S. Coast Guard–certified vessel in the nation, may be retired from dredging, but Captain Wade still offers demonstrations as part of his journey into maritime history. $30 per person, $15 for children under twelve, under five free.

Along the several blocks of Talbot Street that make up the center of town in St. Michaels, a number of unique mom-and-pop shops offer goods that range from fine to fun. Take the **Mind's Eye Craft Collection** (201 South Talbot Street, St. Michaels, MD 21663; 410–745–2023), where you might see a giant totem pole/lighthouse, a bigger-than-life wire dragonfly, and who knows what else might spring from the inspired minds and hands of the more than 250 American artists represented here. At the **Ship Shop** (211 North Talbot Street, St. Michaels, MD 21663; 410–745–6268), you will find handcrafted model ships and other nautical art created by more than twenty artisans and artists, as well as model kits, books, and supplies so that you can make your own.

Belly-up to the tasting bar and sample some of the more than 4,000 salsas, hot sauces, and mustards at **Flamingo Flats** (100 South Talbot

Unspoiled Tilghman Island.

Street, St. Michaels, MD 21663; 410–745–2053). They also have those wonderfully tacky pink flamingos and windup crabs you've been looking for. For crustaceans of the chocolate variety, head to **St. Michaels Candy Company** (216 South Talbot Street, St. Michaels, MD 21663; 410–745–6060).

Afternoon

LUNCH: Bay Hundred Restaurant, Route 33 (right before the drawbridge), Tilghman Island, MD 21671; (410) 886–2126. Exquisite view from the open-air grill and bar of the watermen plying their trade and yacht and sailboat sailors taking their leisure on Knapps Narrows. And you can't get fresher seafood—from Eastern Shore crabs every which way; oysters polenta-fried and in a velvety stew; steamed mussels, clams, and shrimp; sandwiches and salads. All under $10 for lunch. Serving breakfast and dinner, too. Open year-round. Hours vary by season.

From St. Michaels, head east on Route 33 until it intersects with

Route 329. Follow 329 south to the **Oxford-Bellevue Ferry** (410–745–9023). Established in 1683 and believed to be the oldest privately operated ferry in the nation, this charming reminder of the past takes the scenic route over the Tred Avon River to the lovely little town of **Oxford.**

The ferry offers crossings every twenty to twenty-five minutes from June 1 to Labor Day, Monday through Friday 7:00 A.M.–9:00 P.M., Saturday and Sunday 9:00 A.M.–9:00 P.M. From Labor Day through November and March 1 to June 1, the ferry runs until sunset. Car and driver $6.00 one-way, $10.00 round-trip; passenger $1.00 each way.

At the dock you'll see a replica of Oxford's first **Customs House** (410–226–5760), which was built in the late eighteenth century.

Founded in 1683, Oxford is another Eastern Shore town with a long maritime history. You can learn more about it at **The Oxford Museum,** Morris and Market Streets, Oxford, MD 21654; (410) 226–0191. Call for hours and admission.

Another local landmark is the world-renowned **Cutts & Case Shipyard** (306 Tilghman Street, Oxford, MD 21654; 410–226–5416), where state-of-the-art technology and more than 450 years of craftsmanship combine to produce and renovate some of the finest yachts and other private wooden sailing craft afloat today. You can visit the shipyard and wander around at any time, but if you call ahead, you might be lucky enough to get a guided tour from owner Edmund A. Cutts, a man of many talents and fascinating stories.

Right across from the waterfront park in the center of town at 111 South Morris Street is **Americana Antiques** (410–226–5677), a 2,000-square-foot treasure trove of eighteenth- and nineteenth-century furniture, paintings, and period accessories as well as American folk art and antique carved carousel figures. And you never know what you're going to find among the "necessities, gifts, and other non-essentials" at **The Oxford Mews** at 103 South Morris (410–820–8222), but it's fun to poke around.

Evening

DINNER: Robert Morris Inn, 314 North Morris Street, Oxford, MD 21654; (410) 226–5111. Author James Michener must have sampled a lot of seafood during the research for his best-seller *Chesapeake* and, apparently, he was quite vocal about his preferences. The Carpenter Street Saloon in St. Michaels claims to serve his favorite crab soup, and here at the Robert Morris Inn, right by the ferry landing overlooking the beautiful Tred Avon River, you can find the crab cakes that he actually rated best on the Eastern Shore. The inn's tavern has a comfortable, colonial feeling. The mostly moderately priced menu also features such specialties as baked seafood au gratin cake, which you can also order atop a burger for a deliciously different combination. Make sure you order a side of the tavern's signature Chesapeake fries, seasoned and cooked using a five-step process to make them extra tasty and crispy. During strawberry season, the inn also makes a dynamite fresh-fruit pie. Dinner hours are 6:00–9:00 P.M. in season (April to November). The inn also has a formal, white-tablecloth restaurant on the premises.

It's only a 12-mile drive to the next town of **Easton** for an evening's entertainment at the **Avalon Theatre** (40 East Dover Street, Easton, MD 21601; 410–822–0345), a restored 1921 Art Deco movie/vaudeville palace that now features musical concerts, plays, films, and other wonderful stuff year-round. To get there, head away from the water down Morris Street, which will become Route 333. Follow 333 all the way out to Route 322. Cross 322 and get onto Peach Blossom Road. At the light, past the schools and the church, take a hard left onto Washington Street and you will find yourself in the main part of Easton's downtown area. After the theater, head back to Oxford and the Robert Morris Inn for your night's lodging.

LODGING: Robert Morris Inn. The inn was constructed prior to 1710 by ships' carpenters using paneling made with hand-hewn beams, oak pegs, and handmade nails. If you're a history buff, ask for a room in the old part of the house, which features an Elizabethan staircase and white pine floors. The common rooms should also be of interest with their three magnificent murals, 280-year-old handmade wall panels, and a brick fireplace made in England around 1812. Open April through November, some weekends in winter. Rates range from $130 to $350; ask about midweek reductions. Deduct an additional $20 from your room for each night you have dinner in one of the inn's dining rooms.

Day 3 / Morning

BREAKFAST: Start your morning on the banks of the Tred Avon with a picnic breakfast at Oxford's waterfront park. A great place to pick up a quick repast of freshly made breakfast sandwiches, muffins, bagels, and coffee is **Oxford Market** at 203 South Morris Street, Oxford, MD 21654; (410) 226–0015.

Sunday is a relatively sleepy day on this part of the Eastern Shore. So, after breakfast, drive back to Easton, where although many of the shops, restaurants, and other attractions are closed, there are still some wonderful things to see and do.

In recent years, the face, economy, and social dynamics of Talbot County seem to change as swiftly as the tides. To preserve the area's legacy, the **Historical Society Museum** (25 South Washington Street, Easton, MD 21601; 410–822–0073) exhibits furnishings, pictures, paintings, and memorabilia that span pre-Revolutionary to modern times. Open Monday through Saturday, 10:00 A.M.–4:00 P.M.; free. The society also offers guided tours of three historic seventeenth- and eighteenth-century homes, one with the intriguing name Ending of Controversie, Tuesday through Saturday at 11:30 A.M. and 1:30 P.M. for $5.00.

For more history, visit the **Third Haven Friends Meeting House** at 405 South Washington Street, Easton, MD 21601; (410) 822–0293. Erected in 1682, this building has the distinction of being the oldest religious building still in use in the United States, the oldest frame building in continuous use, and the earliest dated building in Maryland. Visitors are welcome any time.

Afternoon

LUNCH: Washington Street Pub, 20 North Washington Street (across from the courthouse), Easton, MD 21601; (410) 822–9011. This year-round local favorite serves hot and cold sandwiches with names like the Barnyard Brawl and the Sly Fox; Sonoma Shrimp Pasta with jumbo shrimp, spinach, black olives, and mushrooms in a light cream sauce; St. Louis BBQ ribs; and "cowboy" steak. Prices are moderate to expensive. Open weekdays and Sunday 11:00 A.M.–9:00 P.M., Friday and Saturday until 10:00 P.M.

At the intersection of Routes 50 and 309, just north of town is the Easton Airport, where pilot Hunter Harris of **Aloft, Inc.** (410–820–5959) keeps his 300-horsepower, 1942 open-cockpit Stearman biplane. For prices ranging from $37 to $135, you can feel the wind in your hair as Harris takes you on a ten-minute "hop around the patch" over Easton or twenty-minute flight over St. Michaels; a thirty-minute tour of St. Michaels, Oxford, and Easton; or a forty-five-minute deluxe aerial tour of these three towns plus the Bay Bridge and Kent Island. Rides are available April through October. Call for hours.

Since you are heading back to Philadelphia from Easton following the most straightforward route, it should only take you a little more than 2½ hours to get home. Go west on Route 50 for about 20 miles until you come to Route 301. Take Route 301 north for 52 miles to I–95. Head north on 95 into Philadelphia.

There's More

Academy Arts Museum, 106 South Street, Easton, MD 21601; (410) 822–ARTS (2787). Exhibits in this renovated schoolhouse include works by such famous nineteenth- and twentieth-century artists as James McNeil Whistler and Grant Wood. Open year-round Monday and Tuesday and Thursday through Saturday 10:00 A.M.–4:00 P.M. Wednesday hours are 10:00 A.M.–9:00 P.M. Call for exhibition schedule and admissions.

Hog Neck Golf Course, Old Cordova Road, Easton, MD 21601; (410) 822–6079. One of the top twenty-five public golf courses in the country according to *Golf Digest,* Hog Neck offers a par 71, eighteen-hole championship course, a par 32 executive nine, a driving range, and a pro shop.

Canton Row Antiques, 216-C South Talbot Street, St. Michaels, MD 21663; (410) 745–2440. This eighteen-dealer antiques mall offers European, country, and Victorian furniture, jewelry, and collectibles. Open year-round, seven days a week, 10:00 A.M.–6:00 P.M.

St. Mary's Museum, off Talbot Street between Chestnut and Mulberry, St. Michaels, MD 21663; (410) 745–9561. Two nineteenth-century structures—a waterman's family home and a former town lockup/mortuary/barbershop—have been joined together and filled with furnishings and personal possessions of local families to offer a glimpse of life in St. Michaels in the 1800s. Open May to October, Saturday and Sunday 10:00 A.M.–4:00 P.M., or by special appointment. A donation is requested.

Tilghman Island Marina, 6140 Mariners Court, Tilghman Island, MD 21671; (410) 886–2979. Watercraft rentals, including fishing and crabbing boats, 15-foot sailboats, Wave Runners, jet boats, kayaks, and canoes.

Lady Patty, Knapps Narrows Marina, Tilghman's Island, MD 21671; (800) 690–5080 or (410) 886–2215. Veteran seaman Captain Mike Richards offers two-hour excursions aboard his 1935 classic bay ketch. The price for a two-hour sail is $30 per person.

Special Events

April. St. Michaels Food & Wine Festival. (410) 745–0411 or (800) 808–7622. An entire weekend of nonstop culinary excitement showcasing local and national talent.

October. Tilghman Island Day, on the harbor; (410) 770–8000 or (410) 886–2677. A celebration of the Eastern Shore's maritime history and world-renowned seafood with a full schedule of waterman's games, workboat races, crab-picking and oyster-shucking contests, cruises, music, and, of course, oceans of clams, crabs, oysters, and other gifts from the sea.

November. Annual Waterfowl Festival, Easton, MD 21601; (410) 822–4567. More than 450 of the nation's premier wildlife artists and exhibitors are invited to participate in the eighteen exhibits spread throughout the town.

Other Recommended Restaurants and Lodgings

St. Michaels

Inn at Perry Cabin, 308 Watkins Lane, St. Michaels, MD 21663; (800) 722–2949 or (410) 745–2200. Built right after the War of 1812, this splendid English-style country house on twenty-five manicured acres overlooking Chesapeake Bay is considered the height of luxury on the Eastern Shore. Rates range from $295 to $745 weekdays, $445 to $795 weekends.

Parsonage Inn, 210 North Talbot Street, St. Michaels, MD 21663; (800) 394–5519 or (410) 745–5519. The architecture of this 1883 brick Victorian is a real attention-grabber. Inside it's genteel in a cozy sort of way with Queen Anne–style furnishings, brass beds, shell pedestal sinks, period light fixtures, and Laura Ashley bed linens. Room rates range from $100 to $195; ask about winter specials. A full gourmet breakfast is included.

Harbour Lights, St. Michaels Harbour Inn, 101 North Harbour Road, St. Michaels, MD 21663; (800) 955–9001 or (410) 745–9001. The food is as delicious as the magnificent view from this beautifully appointed, firelit dining room. Recent selections on the seasonal menu have included onion-encrusted rockfish with sautéed chanterelle mushrooms and leek fondue, roasted Moulard breast with wild-rice mélange, and cane-seared tuna with molasses soy glaze. Open year-round for lunch and dinner. Expensive, but exceptional.

Bistro St. Michaels, 403 South Talbot Street, St. Michaels, MD 21663; (410) 745–9111. This casual Parisian-style restaurant serves a lively marriage of Eastern Shore specialties and classic French bistro fare. Famous for its mussels in white wine and garlic sauce. Open year-round (except February) for dinner Thursday through Monday at 5:30 P.M. Expensive.

Tilghman Island

Lazyjack Inn Bed & Breakfast, 5907 Tilghman Island Road, Tilghman Island, MD 21671, on Dogwood Harbor; (800) 690–5080 or (410) 886–2215. Magnificent harbor views from the sitting room and outside deck, home-cooked breakfasts, and guest rooms filled with unique architectural accents and antique furnishings are among the amenities that make this 160-year-old inn so welcoming. Midweek rates range from $119 to $219; weekends, from $149 to $259.

Easton

Coffee East, 5 Goldsborough Street, Easton, MD 21601; (410) 819–6711. Fresh-brewed coffee drinks and teas, pastries and muffins, soups, quiches, sandwiches, gourmet pizzas, and sushi (on Wednesday). Inexpensive to moderate.

Columbia, 28 South Washington Street, Easton, MD 21601; (410) 770–5172. One of the hottest dining spots on the Eastern Shore, Columbia's "contemporary innovative American menu" is deliciously influenced by the cuisines of France, Portugal, Italy, and other romantic locales. Expensive.

For More Information

Maryland Office of Tourism Development; (800) 634–7386 or (800) MD–IS–FUN; www.mdwelcome.org.

Talbot County Office of Tourism (St. Michaels, Tilghman Island, Oxford, and Easton); (888) BAY STAY or (410) 770–8000; www.tourtalbot.org.

Long Island, New York

North and South Shores

2 Nights

Separated from bustling New York City by only about 15 miles at its closest point and bounded by Long Island Sound on the north and the Atlantic Ocean on the south and east, Long Island has been a favorite getaway for the rich and famous for more than a century. Tycoons with names such as Vanderbilt, Guggenheim, and Roosevelt built their palatial summer mansions on the island's North Shore, which, for obvious reasons became known as the Gold Coast (and, inspired the "East and West Egg" settings in F. Scott Fitzgerald's *The Great Gatsby*).

- ☐ Heritage Trail
- ☐ Gatsby's Eggs
- ☐ Nautical Niches

Traversing the North Shore is a 45-plus-mile west-to-east road known in the early 1700s as "Kings Highway" and after the Revolutionary War until today as the Long Island Heritage Trail. A drive along this scenic route will take you through some beautiful and diverse countryside as well as three centuries of history.

Long Island's South Shore has three barrier beaches, the largest of which is in Jones Beach State Park, a public playground with more than 6 miles of oceanfront and ½ mile of bayfront public beaches, 2 miles of boardwalk, and all types of outdoor recreational facilities. Between the two shores are so many fabulous gardens, charming little towns, and famous landmarks that you'll want to be stopping every few miles to visit them.

Yes, I know that Long Island is notorious for its traffic jams—especially during the summer tourist season. But if you plan your trip for late spring or early fall and do most of your driving on the peaceful and well-marked Heritage Trail (Route 25A), you should miss most of the chaos.

Day 1 / Morning

Time your trip to miss New York's frantic morning rush hour and you'll find the drive to Long Island's South Shore a lot more pleasant. Take I–95 north to the New Jersey Turnpike. Turn off at exit 13/278B (Verrazano Narrows Bridge), go over the Goethals Bridge and continue on Route

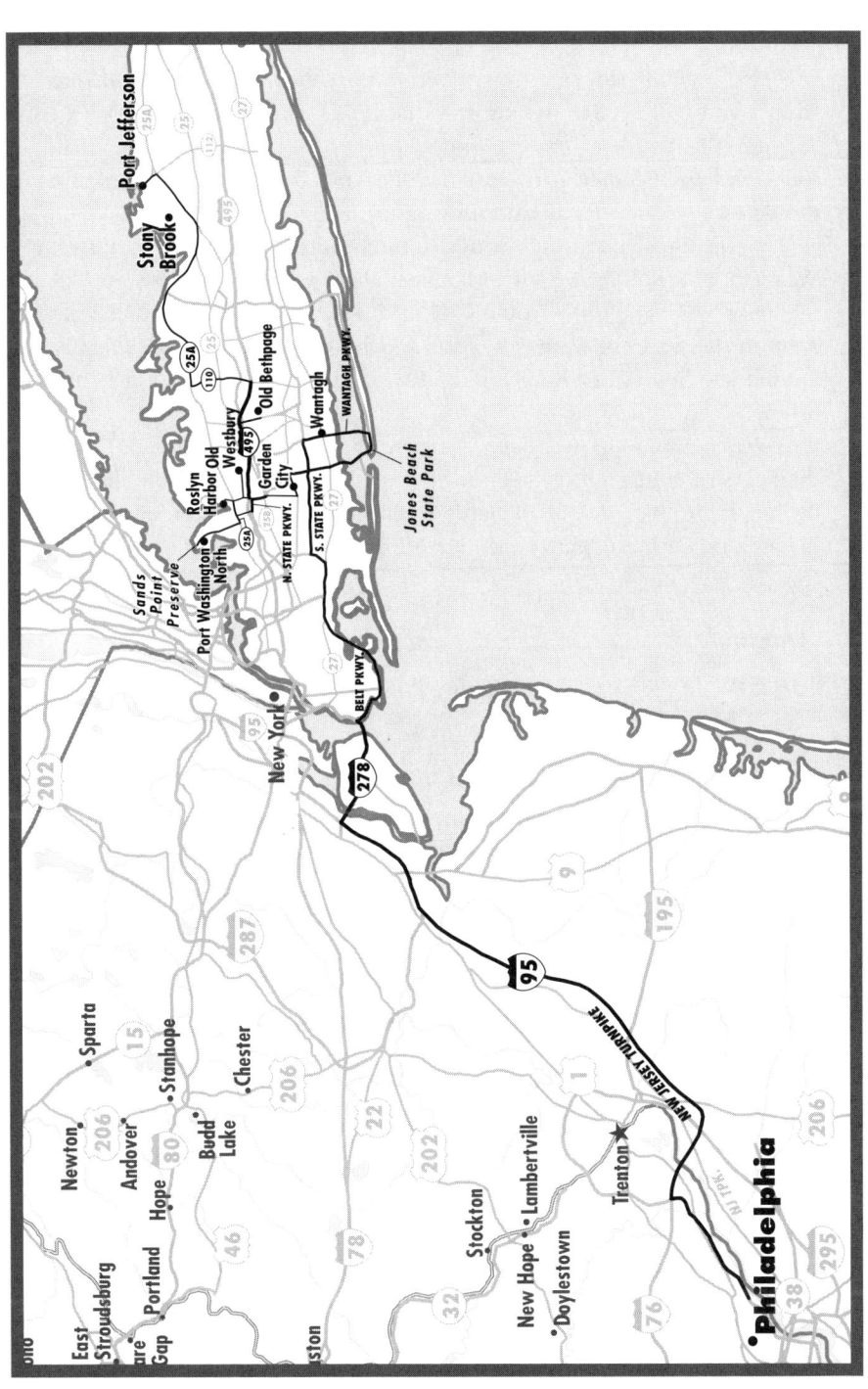

278 east, watching for signs to the Verrazano. Get into the left-hand lane so that you will be able to exit onto the Belt Parkway, and look for exit 25A for the Southern State Parkway. Follow to the Wantagh Parkway south and to the state park entrance. The trip is about 145 miles and should take somewhere around three hours.

By the time you get to **Jones Beach State Park** (Ocean Drive, Wantagh, NY 11793; 516–785–1600), you'll be ready to stretch your legs with a brisk seaside stroll on the sand or the 2-mile-long boardwalk. Take a dip in the waves or in the bay's still waters (there are two conveniently located bathhouses), or head for the west end of the park for some surf fishing.

For maximum fun in the sun, there are also basketball, deck tennis, and shuffleboard courts; an eighteen-hole pitch-and-putt golf course; fishing docks; playgrounds; and other outdoor recreational facilities. Admission to the park is free, but there is a fee for parking from Memorial Day to Labor Day.

Afternoon

LUNCH: At the hub of the boardwalk is the **Central Mall,** one of Long Island's best known landmarks, a 231-foot-high brick-and-stone water tower modeled after the Campanile of St. Mark's Cathedral in Venice, Italy. Here you will find concession stands (some remain open all year) offering a wide variety of sandwiches and other luncheon fare that you can take to one of the park's picnic areas. Or, if you simply can't tear yourself away from the beach, mobile "dune diners" will come to you with cold drinks, snacks, and ice cream.

In 1999 part of the west end of Jones Beach State Park that had been abandoned and run-down for a number of years was brought back to life as the **Theodore Roosevelt Nature Center** (516–679–7254). Now it is a vibrant, fun-filled place for families to learn about the environment through educational exhibits, a butterfly garden, a live animal touch tank, a boardwalk for viewing the natural habitat, and interactive activities for children. Open Memorial Day through Labor Day Wednesday through Sunday 10:00 A.M.–4:00 P.M., until 8:00 P.M. Thursday and Friday; open weekends only in the off-season.

DINNER: **Boardwalk Restaurant** (516–785–2420). This pretty dining spot is a great place to enjoy some of the ocean's bounty, whether it's oysters or shrimp fresh from the seafood bar, clams in a creamy New

Prepare for beautiful sunlit days at Jones Beach on Long Island.

England–style chowder, or pan-seared salmon filet with mango-kiwi salsa. Open for lunch and Sunday brunch, too. Mostly moderate prices.

Your bed for the evening is about twenty minutes away. To get there, go north on the Wantagh State Parkway until you come to the Southern State Parkway west; then take Meadowbrook Parkway north. Get off at exit M–3, West Stewart Avenue; turn right on Stewart and continue 3 miles to the end. Turn left on Hilton Avenue and right on Seventh Street. Look for the Garden City Hotel on the right.

Evening

LODGING: The Garden City Hotel, 45 Seventh Street, Garden City, NY 11530; (800) 547–0400 or (516) 747–3000. You may not own a Long Island mansion, but you can live like those who do when you stay at this historic and luxurious boutique hotel. Deluxe rooms run about $269 per night, but definitely check out the hotel's special packages.

Day 2 / Morning

BREAKFAST: The Garden City Hotel. Select from the buffet in the Atrium Café, laze over breakfast in bed with a special delivery from room service, or feast on Sunday brunch at the Polo Restaurant. Expensive.

For your introduction to the Gold Coast at its most opulent, begin the half-hour drive to Port Washington by going back to Stewart Avenue and taking a slight left onto Clinton Road. Clinton Road becomes Glen Cove Road; turn left when you get to Jericho Turnpike (Route 25). Get on the Northern Parkway west toward New York, and take the Willis Avenue exit (exit 28), toward Roslyn/Mineola. Turn left onto Willis, which will become Mineola Avenue and eventually Center Drive. Turn left onto Northern Boulevard/Route 25A (the Heritage Trail), then right onto Port Washington Boulevard and continue until it becomes Middle Neck Road. Continue until you come to the entrance of **Sands Point Preserve** (95 Middle Neck Road, Port Washington, NY 11050; 516–571–7900).

Be prepared to spend the rest of the afternoon here, because there is quite a lot to see on this 216-acre nature preserve, where two generations of the superwealthy Guggenheim family lived in two magnificent castles overlooking the Long Island Sound. One now houses a changing array of impressive interactive natural science exhibits; the other remains a "living museum" reflecting its owners' interests in medieval, Renaissance, and modern art; horse racing; and aviation. There is also an extensive exhibit of more than 2,000 pieces of Wedgwood ceramics dating from 1759 to the 1970s. Open Tuesday through Sunday 10:00 A.M.–5:00 P.M. Admission prices vary.

To continue your Long Island art feast (and have an outstanding lunch), get back onto Route 25A (Northern Boulevard) and drive east for 6 or so miles until you see the sign for the **Nassau County Museum of Art** (1 Museum Drive, Roslyn Harbor, NY 11576; 516–484–9338). Once the Gold Coast estate of the son of U.S. Steel founder Henry Frick, this elegant neo-Georgian mansion and its 145 acres of beautifully landscaped grounds now showcase ten galleries exhibiting changing world-class art exhibitions, a miniatures museum, and one of the East Coast's largest publicly accessible sculpture gardens. Open year-round, Tuesday through Sunday 11:00 A.M.–5:00 P.M. Adults $6.00, students and seniors $5.00.

Afternoon

LUNCH: Cafe Musee at the Nassau County Museum of Art. Imaginative little touches such as lingonberry mayonnaise on the smoked turkey sandwich and roasted garlic knots with fresh mozzarella, tomato, and basil salad elevate simple foods to elegance. Everything's homemade, from the soups to the dreamy desserts. Moderate prices.

For a very different perspective on Long Island's past, take Route 25A to Glen Cove Road; then head south on Glen Cove Road until you come to the Long Island Expressway east. Get off at exit 48 south and follow the signs to **Old Bethpage Village Restoration** (Round Swamp Road, Old Bethpage, NY 11804; 516–572–8400).

Historic eighteenth- and nineteenth-century structures from all over the island have been moved to this hundred-acre site and painstakingly restored to re-create a typical mid-nineteenth-century rural village, complete with costumed interpreters, working crafters, animals on the working farm, and even, on spring and summer weekends, period-style "base ball" games. Open Wednesday through Sunday from March through December 10:00 A.M. (noon on Sunday)–5:00 P.M. Adults $7.00; children over five $5.00, under four free.

Although you could take a quicker route to your final destination of the day, **The Village of Stony Brook,** you won't find any more scenic and pleasant than the Heritage Trail. Take the Long Island Expressway to exit 49 (Route 110 South); then continue until it intersects Route 25A. Drive east into the village of Stony Brook.

You can still see the waterwheel release its powerful cascades as millers grind wheat and corn at the **Stony Brook Gristmill** (Harbor Road off Main Street, Stony Brook, NY 11790; 631–516–2244) as they did in the 1600s when the first mill (which was washed away by a flood and replaced in 1751) was built here. Open April to September; days and hours vary. Adults $2.00, children $1.00.

Evening

DINNER: Three Village Inn, on the harbor at 150 Main Street, Stony Brook, NY 11790; (631) 751–0555. Dining in a place built by a mid-eighteenth-century farmer and, later, the home of Captain Jonas Smith, Long Island's first millionaire, is right in keeping with the spirit of the rest of your Long Island adventure. Specialties include Long Island duckling and New England seafood pie with lobster, shrimp, and scallops. Expensive.

LODGING: Three Village Inn. Four old working fireplaces create an inviting glow in the winter, but you get an equally warm welcome any time of year at this charming inn. Ask to stay in the original 1751 wing and you can imagine the time when it was home to "Rich Jonas," as the locals called him. Or you can stay in one of the adjacent country cottages that overlook Stony Brook Harbor. Double occupancy $179, $225 for a room with a fireplace.

Day 3 / Morning

It's only about a ten-minute drive east on Route 25A to the end of the Heritage Trail, the town of **Port Jefferson,** which from the early-eighteenth to mid-nineteenth centuries was a major shipbuilding and port center.

BREAKFAST: 25 East American Bistro at Danfords on the Sound, 25 East Broadway, Port Jefferson, NY 11777; (631) 928–5200. Sunday's champagne brunch (around $27.95 for adults, $12.95 for children four and over) is an extravaganza that includes omelet and shrimp bars, carving station, and oven-fresh breads and pastries.

Port Jefferson is a village filled with unique little shops, galleries, and other arts-oriented establishments, including **Prism Gallery** (503 Main Street); **Studio 703** (703 Main Street); **Jezebel's Workshop** (206 East Main Street), a crafter of mosaic painted furnishings; and **Theatre Three** (412 Main Street), a professional theater that offers live productions throughout the year.

From May to October, historic tall ships often dock at **Danfords Inn Marina** and offer tours as well as daytime or sunset sails (631–474–4725).

On your way back toward Philadelphia, stop at Stony Brook Village once again for a 1½-hour, naturalist-led wetlands preserve cruise aboard the *Discovery* (631–751–2244), a 32-foot-long covered pontoon boat. May to October; adults $18, children under twelve $10.00. Before you leave town, go to **The Golden Pear Cafe** in the Stony Brook Village Center (97 Main Street, Stony Brook, NY 11790; 631–751–7695) to get a picnic lunch (the sandwiches and pastries are some of the best I've had anywhere). Inexpensive.

Take the scenic route (25A, of course) east all the way back to Glen Cove Road, where you'll make a left-hand turn, then a right onto Willets Road, then another left onto the service road. Go 1⅗ miles onto the first road on the right, which is Old Westbury Road.

Afternoon

LUNCH: Old Westbury Gardens, 71 Old Westbury Road, Old Westbury, NY 11568; (516) 333–0048. How many times do you get to picnic in a 150-acre Garden of Eden that has also starred in such classic movies as *Love Story* and *Age of Innocence*? After you've eaten, take a walk around and admire nature's and man's cooperative handiwork. You can also take a tour of the eighteenth-century art-and-furnishings–filled three-story mansion that was once home to early-nineteenth-century financier John Phipps. Open late April through Christmas, Wednesday through Monday. Adults $10.00, seniors $8.00, $5.00 for children six to twelve.

To return to Philadelphia, take Glen Cove Road to the Long Island Expressway (I–495 west), heading toward New York City. Continue for 20 miles. Take the Thirty-fifth Street exit on the left toward Thirty-fourth Street/Downtown; turn slightly left onto Tunnel Exit Street, right onto East Thirty-fourth Street, and right onto Dyer Avenue, which becomes the ramp for I–495 west. Take the New Jersey Turnpike South exit on the left toward Trenton/Newark Airport; merge onto I–95 south, which becomes the New Jersey Turnpike. Take exit 4 (Route 73) toward Philadelphia/Camden. It should take you about 2½ hours to get home.

There's More

Vanderbilt Museum, 180 Little Neck Road (off Route 25A), Centerport, NY 11731; (631) 854–5555. Gold Coast mansion on forty-three-acre estate contains mind-boggling collections of fine and decorative arts, historic memorabilia, and marine and wildlife specimens assembled during the 1920s and 1930s; adjacent planetarium. Open year-round. Various admissions.

Sagamore Hill National Historic Site, Cove Neck Road (off Route 25A), Oyster Bay, NY 11771; (516) 922–4447. Theodore Roosevelt's "Summer White House" has been restored to its early-twentieth-century splendor. Guided tours daily 9:30 A.M.–4:00 P.M.; closed Monday and Tuesday in fall and winter. Adults $5.00.

Special Events

September. Medieval Festival at Sands Point Preserve, 95 Middle Neck Road, Port Washington, NY 11050; (516) 517–7900. Jousting tournament, castle siege, street performers, medieval games. Admission.

October. Long Island Fair, Old Bethpage Village Restoration, Round Swamp Road, Old Bethpage, NY 11804; (516) 572–8401. Prize-winning crafts, animals, flowers, and produce; Old Time Base Ball Championships; contests for all ages. Admission.

Other Recommended Restaurants and Lodgings

Port Jefferson

Holly Berry, 415 West Broadway (Route 25A), Port Jefferson, NY 11777; (631) 331–3123. Candlelight, soft music, fresh flowers, and elegant continental breakfast in a restored 1800s farmhouse. $120 to $160.

Pasta Pasta, 234 East Main Street, Port Jefferson, NY 11777; (631) 331–5335. Innovative pastas, gourmet pizzas, seafood, and homemade desserts. Upscale casual. Moderate to expensive.

The Village Way Restaurant, Chandler Square, 106 Main Street, Port Jefferson, NY 11777; (631) 928–3395. Moderate prices for lunch and dinner; good variety of pasta, chicken, and seafood offerings.

For More Information

Long Island Convention and Visitors Bureau and Sports Commission; (877) FUN–ON–LI or (631) 951–3440; www.licvb.com.

BETWEEN AND BEYOND
ESCAPES

Brandywine Valley, Pennsylvania

Memories of War, Images of Peace

1 Night

In the valley of the tranquil Brandywine River, south of Philadelphia, lies a place where Pennsylvania and Delaware come together, united not by bridges but by miles of rolling green hills, history, and a common spirit. As a result, many people tend to combine the Brandywine Valley into one getaway experience. But there's really too much to see and do to try to cram everything into one trip.

☐ River Walks

☐ Scenic Balloon Rides

☐ Historic Reenactments

For convenience, I have split the region into two parts, using the state borders as my dividing line. In this chapter we'll stay on the Pennsylvania side of the valley; in Escape 2 of "Between and Beyond" escapes, we'll visit the Delaware side. And because both sides of the Brandywine Valley are only about an hour south of Philadelphia on I–95, we have the advantage of being close enough to return again and again to savor the particular delights of each area and each season.

Day 1 / Morning

BREAKFAST: Hank's Place, intersection of Routes 1 and 100, Chadds Ford, PA 19317; (610) 388–7061. This modest-looking roadside luncheonette has a not-so-modest sign: HOME COOKING AT ITS BEST. But the locals—and even *Gourmet* magazine—agree that Hank's Place has every right to make that boast. Grab a table or a stool at the counter, where you might find yourself seated next to the local plumber, stockbroker, or artist-in-residence (native son Andrew Wyeth often stops by for breakfast). The prices are extraordinarily inexpensive. But the real draw is the food, which includes buttermilk pancakes, Belgian waffles, Southern-style biscuits, and one incredible shiitake omelet.

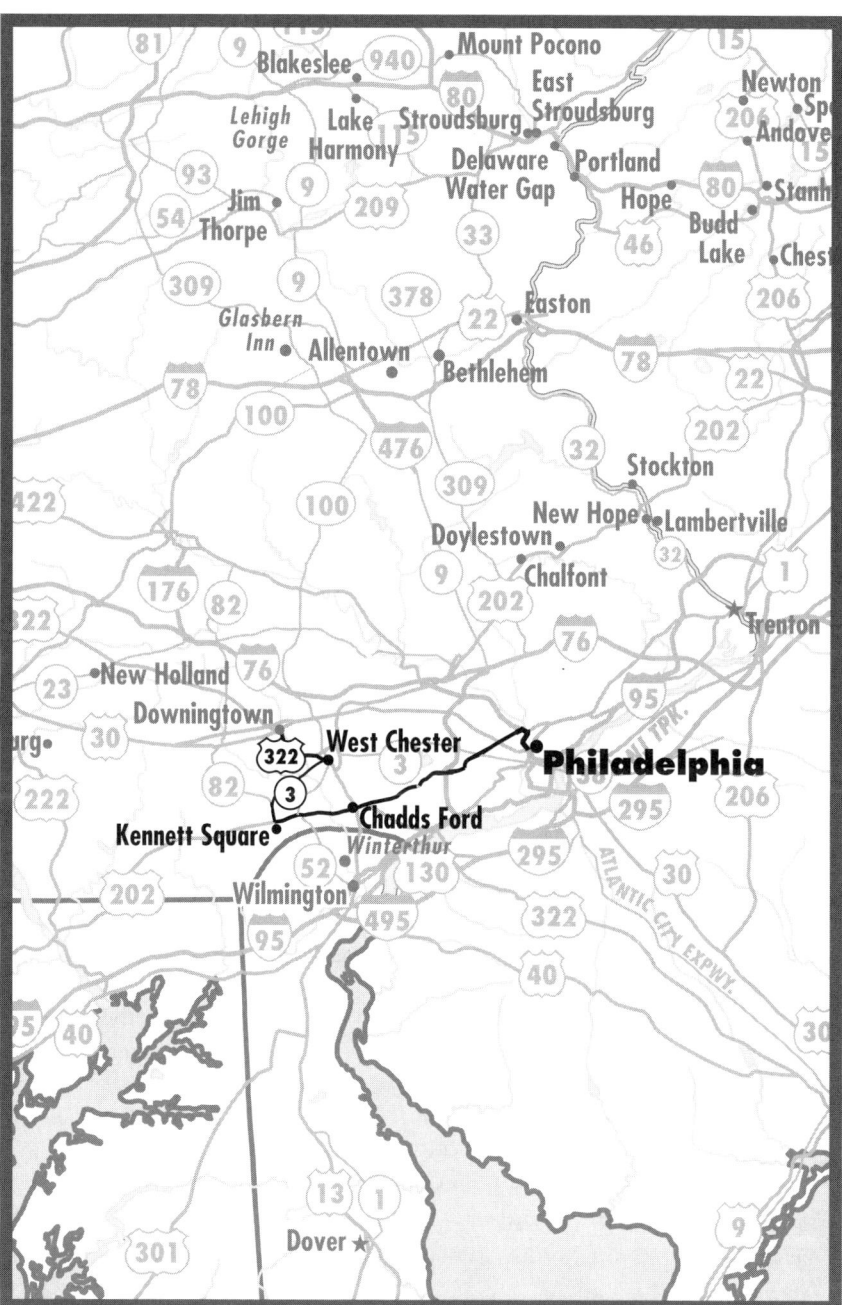

After breakfast, get back on Route 1 and resume your drive south. About 4 miles ahead in Kennett Square, Pennsylvania, you will enter another world, one of gracious living, dazzling colors, and intoxicating perfumes.

For generations, the land that is now known as **Longwood Gardens** was home, hunting, farming, and fishing grounds to the Native Americans who lived in the area. In 1700 a Quaker family named Peirce turned it into a working farm and nationally renowned arboretum. Over the years the property changed hands several times until it was purchased by a company with a sawmill intent on turning the historic trees into just so much timber. However, in 1906 local industrial and financial giant Pierre S. duPont rescued the property, built himself a weekend retreat there, and designed a paradise of plants and flowers inspired by the pleasure gardens of Europe.

Today Longwood Gardens features 1,050 acres of gardens, woodlands, and meadows; 11,000 different types of plants; twenty indoor gardens; and spectacular illuminated fountains.

Make your first stop the **Visitors Center,** where a brief orientation film will help you get your bearings. From there, follow the well-marked paths and trails past the outdoor gardens of roses, topiary, and wildflowers to the conservatories, which boast creative year-round displays. For green thumbers, the Idea Garden offers creative inspirations for home gardens. Climb the Chimes Tower for a bird's-eye view of the gardens and fountains.

Also on the grounds is the **Peirce-duPont House,** originally built by the Peirce family in 1730 and used as a weekend retreat by the duPont family. The house now tells the story of life on the property through artifacts (dating from the Leni-Lenape tribe), photographs, home movies, and personal possessions of the Peirce and duPont families. Many of the original trees are still standing in **Peirce's Arboretum** adjacent to the house. The house is open daily 10:00 A.M.–6:00 P.M. (5:00 P.M. in winter). The outdoor gardens open daily at 9:00 A.M., the conservatory at 10:00 A.M. Closing times are generally between 5:00 and 6:00 P.M. from January to late November, and at 9:00 P.M. from Thanksgiving through December. Admission is $12.00 for adults ($8.00 on Tuesday) mid-January through March, $14.00 ($10.00 Tuesday) April to day before Thanksgiving, $15.00 Thanksgiving through early January, $6.00 for youths ages sixteen to twenty, $2.00 for children ages six to fifteen, free for children under six. Call (610) 388–1000.

Afternoon

LUNCH: **Terrace Restaurant–Cafeteria,** located right on the grounds; (610) 388–6771. If you're hungry yet don't want to tear yourself away from all of these natural wonders, grab yourself an outdoor table or window seat. The atmosphere is quite nice, the food is fresh and kind to the budget, and the view is terrific. After all of today's walking, go ahead and splurge on a big, chewy cookie or warm-from-the-oven cobbler. There is also a full-service white-tablecloth restaurant adjacent to the cafeteria.

Once a hotbed of antislavery activity, the Kennett Square was an important part of the Underground Railroad, with over two dozen documented sites or "stations" within an 8-mile radius (possibly the largest concentration in the nation). Through exhibits and other educational activities, **The Kennett Underground Railroad Center,** (505 South Broad Street, Kennett Square, PA 19348; 610–347–2237) allows you to follow this "trackless trail" and learn the human stories behind the operation of this daring escape system. Exhibit hours are from September through June 1:00–4:00 P.M. each weekend, or call to arrange for individual appointments throughout the year. Free. The museum also offers a narrated one-hour van tour of the "stations" the third Sunday of each month from June through September. $8.00; reservations are necessary.

Evening

DINNER: **Simon Pearce on the Brandywine,** 1333 Lenape Road (junction of Routes 100 and 52), West Chester, PA 19382; (610) 793–0948. If you're a fan of the distinctive pottery and glassware designed by the Irish-born Pearce, you may be familiar with his original glassblowing workshop/restaurant/retail shop in Quechee, Vermont. For his Vermont site, Pearce renovated an old woolen mill; for this one, a Brandywine Valley dining institution, the Lenape Inn. At first the overall industrial look of the restaurant may be a shock to anyone who remembers the old Lenape. But Pearce has made the space distinctly his own with an open, airy feeling and warming maple and cherry-wood accents. And, of course, everything is served on Pearce glass and pottery. The kitchen respectfully acknowledges the Brandywine Valley's status as the "Mushroom Capital of the World" (U.S. cultivation of these fabulous fungi got its start in Kennett Square in 1896) with seasonal selections that have included Marsala-roasted Chester County mushrooms with baby lettuces;

Maine crab and Gulf shrimp cakes; and bay scallop risotto with wild mushrooms, sweet shallots, and truffle essence. Very extensive wine list— available by the bottle or the glass. Open for lunch (11:30 A.M.–2:45 P.M.) and dinner (6:00–9:00 P.M.). After dinner, be sure to visit the workshops and retail stores (610–793–0949).

LODGING: Pennsbury Inn, 833 Baltimore Pike, Chadds Ford, PA 19317; (610) 388–1435. One of the things that makes this gracious bed-and-breakfast unique is the fact that its structure spans three centuries. Beautifully preserved are the original house, built in 1714 of Brandywine Blue Granite rubble stone; a 1750 stone addition with its hand-molded Flemish Bond Brick facade; a circa 1850 clapboard extension; and a garden-view dining area added in 1950. I particularly love the oldest section, with its original uneven floorboards, slanted doorways, "winder" staircase, and huge open fireplace in the parlor. If this appeals to you, too, ask for the Lafayette Room, with its toile balloon shades, drapery panels depicting the life of General Lafayette, and queen-size poster bed. In the nineteenth-century section is the popular Winterthur Room, a romantic hideaway with a wonderful view of the formal gardens from the Palladian window. Open year-round. Room rates range from $120 to $225.

Day 2 / Morning

Hit the road before daylight so that you can greet the sunrise from the basket of a hot-air balloon. **Lollipop Hot Air Balloons** (610–827–1610), headquartered in Chester Springs, has a convenient launch site only about twenty minutes away in Eagle, Pennsylvania. To get there, take Route 926 east less than 2 miles to where it intersects Route 52. Follow Route 52 north—about 3 miles up the road, Route 52 will become Route 100. Drive north on Route 100 about 10 miles until you reach Little Conestoga Road at the Eagle Tavern in the town of Eagle. Head toward the yellow blinking light, and turn right onto Park Road. Turn left into the first driveway at the real estate office. The balloon launch site is inside the white picket fence.

Like most other hot-air balloon companies, Lollipop offers flights at sunrise and sunset. The daybreak flight allows you to enjoy an aerial view in the cool of the morning when the only wildlife to be seen is of the four-legged variety. Lollipop offers flights lasting one-half hour ($95 per person) or a full hour ($165 per person). The entire experience will take about 2½ to 3 hours because, true to the centuries-old tradition of balloonists everywhere, every flight ends with a champagne (or soft drink) toast.

BREAKFAST: Pennsbury Inn. If you are in a hurry to continue your exploration of the surrounding countryside, Cheryl Grono will prepare a quick continental breakfast to get you on your way. If you want to ease your way into the day, however, she will serve you a hearty home-cooked breakfast in front of the fireplace in the Garden Room. Either is included with your room.

Back at the intersection of Routes 1 and 100, slowly begin to work your way through scenic, historic Chadds Ford. On Route 1, just south of Route 100, is the **Brandywine River Museum** (610–388–2700), a structure that began life as a nineteenth-century gristmill and is now a showcase for paintings by the Wyeth family—father Newell Convers (N.C.) and sons Jamie and Andrew—as well as other American artists. One of the most beloved paintings in the museum is Jamie Wyeth's tongue-in-cheek portrait of a pig. The popular porker is also the subject of a bronze statue that stands outside on the riverbank. Open 9:30 A.M.–4:30 P.M. daily. $6.00 for adults, $3.00 for seniors, students with ID, and children under six.

Exit the museum and walk through the cobblestone courtyard to a path that winds through the wildflowers to the beginning of a 1-mile-long river walk. In a nearby meadow you'll see a painstakingly authentic reproduction of a colonial-era barn that houses the headquarters, small museum, and gift shop of the **Chadds Ford Historical Society**. From "The Barn," continue along the path until you come to the **John Chads House** (610–388–7376), the wonderfully preserved eighteenth-century stone home and springhouse that belonged to the local ferryman, farmer, and innkeeper for whom the town was named. (If you're wondering where the extra "d" in Chadds Ford came from, the Historical Society surmises that it was simply a Victorian-era flourish added when the town was named.) For the same admission price, you can also visit the Barns-Brinton House (Route 1 and Chandler Road), a restored eighteenth-century tavern and residence. On weekends May through September from noon to 5:00 P.M., colonial-costumed guides bring history to life with demonstrations of domestic skills of the era, including baking in a beehive oven. Admission is $5.00.

Right across the street is **Chaddsford Winery,** 632 Baltimore Pike, Chadds Ford, PA 19317; (610–388–6221), the largest (in terms of volume) winery in Pennsylvania and one of the top ten on the East Coast. Located in a renovated seventeenth-century barn, the winery is open for tours, tastings, and sales seven days a week noon–6:00 P.M.; special events, including concerts, barrel tastings, and festivals, are held throughout the year.

Afternoon

LUNCH: Chadds Ford Tavern and Restaurant, Route 1 (1 mile south of the intersection of Routes 100 and 202), Chadds Ford, PA 19317; (610) 459–8453. When it was first built in the 1770s, this roadside tavern provided respite and refreshment to many of the famous generals who fought in the Battle of Brandywine. Beautifully restored, it is now a popular haunt for area artists (yes, that includes Wyeths) and other creative types. The moderate-to-expensive menu selections are eclectic and interesting, based mostly in American cuisine but influenced by the spiciness of Mexico, the elegance of France, and the gusto of Italy. Open daily for lunch and dinner.

Up and down Route 1 in Chadds Ford, you'll find all kinds of unique shops tucked in between the historic sites. The **Brandywine River Antiques Market** (610–388–2000), offers a wide assortment of antiques, furniture, and accessories. Right across the street (at the intersection of Routes 1 and 100) in the Chadds Ford Village & Barn Shops is the **Chadds Ford Gallery** (610–459–5510), which features investor-collector–quality art, including the largest selection of Wyeth reproductions anywhere. At the same intersection is **The Wooden Knob Antiques & Home Fashions** (610–388–3861), where you'll find furniture and decorative accessories from the 1800s and early 1900s.

Evening

DINNER: The Gables, 423 Baltimore Pike, Chadds Ford, PA 19317; (610) 388–7700. Intriguingly innovative, contemporary American menu with global inspirations in a setting of less-is-more elegance. Fish is a specialty here, the species and preparations varying with the seasons. Accompaniments such as wasabi mashed potatoes and saffron risotto are pretty special, too. Desserts, all made by the restaurant's pastry chef, also change regularly, but some examples have included raspberry bread pudding and Kahlúa mousse. Open for lunch (moderate to expensive) Tuesday through Sunday and dinner (expensive) Tuesday through Friday. Don't rush off after dinner—the bar is a nice place to relax after a busy day.

To get home, take Route 1 north. The return trip should take you a little over one hour.

There's More

Brandywine Battlefield Park, Route 1, Chadds Ford. On this battlefield, General George Washington and the Marquis de Lafayette took a united stand against the British. Although the battle was lost, a powerful alliance was forged, one that would eventually turn the tide of the war. You can tour General Washington's headquarters and Lafayette's quarters (for a nominal charge) and see the interpretive exhibits at the visitor center (free). Open Tuesday through Saturday 9:00 A.M.–5:00 P.M., Sunday noon–5:00 P.M.

Special Events

May. The Willowdale Gold Cup, Willowdale Steeple Chase, 101 East Street Road, Kennett Square; (610) 444–1582. Leaping horses, racing Jack Russell terriers, an antique-carriage parade, vendor and food tents, and children's activities. Admission charge. Proceeds benefit local environmental conservation efforts.

September. Mushroom Festival, Kennett Square; (610) 925–3373 or (888) 440–9920. A weekend of cooking demos, contests, and tastings; farm tours; art; antique cars; and dancing in the street.

Other Recommended Restaurants and Lodgings

Chadds Ford

Brandywine River Hotel, Routes 1 and 100; (610) 388–1200. Located in the heart of the historic district, this upscale country hotel features fireside Jacuzzi suites. Rates range from $125 to $169.

Cuisines, 200 Wilmington–West Chester Pike (Route 202 and Naamans Creek Road), Chadds Ford, PA 19317; (610) 459–3390. French, Italian, German, Spanish, Cajun, and Caribbean influences make for a delightfully diverse menu. Extensive foreign beer selection. Dinner only. Tuesday through Saturday 5:30–10:00 P.M., Sunday 4:00–8:00 P.M. Moderate to expensive.

Hedgerow Bed & Breakfast Suites, 268 Kennett Pike, Chadds Ford, PA 19317; (610) 388–6080. Three luxury suites with sitting room, private full bath, and separate bedroom(s). The Longwood Suite has a fireplace and a two-person Jacuzzi and is stocked with complimentary tea, coffee, soft drinks, and snacks. Rates are $135 to $170 and include a full breakfast.

Kennett Square

Half Moon Restaurant & Saloon, 108 West State Street; (610) 444–7232. Nineteen beers on tap and an adventurous menu that includes buffalo, elk, and venison, as well as traditional burgers. Mostly moderately priced.

West Chester

Dilworthtown Inn, 1390 Old Wilmington Pike; (610) 399–1390. For classic American steaks and chops, you won't find better. Alfresco dining available. Live music on weekends. Expensive.

Faunbrook Victorian Bed & Breakfast, 699 West Rosedale Avenue; (610) 436–5788. Gorgeous ironwork, porches, fountains, gardens, walks, fireplaces, brass beds, fireside gourmet breakfast. Rates range from $120 to $140 for the Master Suite.

For More Information

Brandywine Conference & Visitors Bureau; (800) 343–3983 or (610) 565–0833; www.brandywinecvb.org.

Chester County Conference and Visitor Bureau, 400 Exton Square Parkway, Exton, PA 19341; (800) 228–9933 or (610) 280–6145; www.brandywinevalley.com.

Chester County Historical Society, 225 North High Street, West Chester, PA 19380; (610) 692–4066.

Brandywine Valley, Delaware

Seat of an Empire

1 Night

Not to interfere with anybody's romantic aspirations, but in some cases, I think, separate vacations are best. Take, for instance, the Brandywine Valley. A great many people insist on combining the Pennsylvania and Delaware parts of this scenic and activity-packed area into one getaway. Admittedly, my initial impulse was to do the same thing. But after visiting Wilmington and the surrounding area, I realized that there's enough to see and do here to make it a wonderful escape destination of its own.

- [ ] Glorious Gardens
- [ ] Family Mansions
- [ ] Riverfront Resurrection
- [ ] Thoroughbred Racers

This is the heart of the empire built and ruled by the powerful duPont family. It is where they built a company that was destined to become a world giant and family mansions and exquisite gardens that were destined to become historic landmarks.

But even in Wilmington there was life before the duPonts. And there are still many colorful reminders of the city's pre-duPont past.

Of course, sight-seeing alone, even when the sights are as magnificent as these, does not a great escape make. Fortunately, Wilmington has a wealth of fun, games, and entertainment—ranging from golf to horse racing to opera—to keep sports aficionados, thrill seekers, and culture buffs happy, too.

Only 32 miles (forty to forty-five minutes driving time) south of Philadelphia on I–95, Wilmington is the nearest destination included in this book. But despite its proximity—or, perhaps, because of it—this small wonder right over the border is all too often underexplored and, as a result, underappreciated.

Day 1 / Morning

For your first stop, get off I–95 at exit 7B, get onto Route 52 north, and

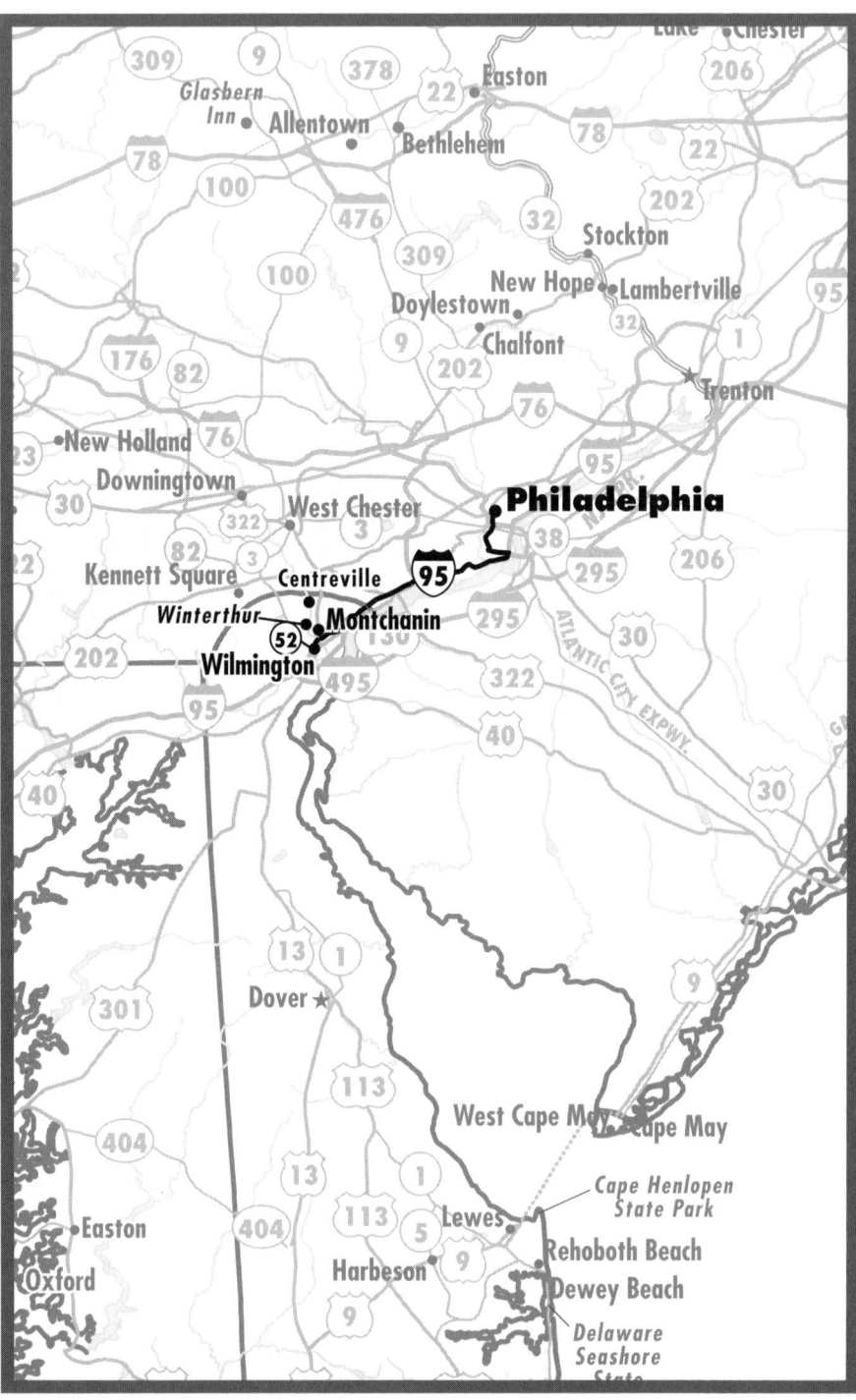

follow the signs 6 miles northwest of Wilmington to Winterthur.

One of the Brandywine Valley's premier attractions, **Winterthur, An American Country Estate** (800–448–3883 or 302–888–4600) is set on 965 acres where, almost half a century ago, Henry Francis duPont lived and indulged in his two greatest passions—horticulture and collecting early American decorative art. No matter what the season, duPont's sixty-acre garden of native and exotic plants will take your breath away. So will the period rooms and exhibition galleries that hold his collection of more than 89,000 objects, including Chippendale furniture, silver by Paul Revere, paintings by Gilbert Stuart, and a sixty-six-piece dinner service made for George Washington. Gardens and Galleries Tours cost $15.00 for adults, $13.00 for students and seniors, and $5.00 for children ages two to eleven. In-depth and specialized tours are also available. Open year-round 10:00 A.M.–5:00 P.M., Tuesday through Sunday; closed Mondays, except holidays.

Afternoon

L U N C H : The Garden Cafeteria, at Winterthur. One of the two very good dining options available at Winterthur, the Garden Cafeteria features individually themed food stations that offer everything from hearty hot stews and chilis to traditional deli fare to regional American down-home cookin'. The prices are inexpensive, so you can splurge a little on dessert, which usually includes homemade mousses, pies, cobblers, gourmet crepes, and chewy cookies.

For some insight into Wilmington's pre-duPont days, head down to the riverfront to the *Kalmar Nyckel* **Shipyard and Museum,** 1124 East Seventh Street, Wilmington, DE 19801; (302) 429–7447. Go east on Route 52 to I–95 south; get off at exit 6. Turn left onto Fourth Street and continue east under the railroad bridge to your first left-hand turn, which will be Swede's Landing Road; continue to the dead end at Seventh Street. Turn right.

The tall ship *Kalmar Nyckel* is a replica of the largest of the two Dutch warships that brought Delaware's first permanent settlers to the banks of the Christina River from Sweden in 1638. Crew members in period garb describe shipboard life in those early years. The shipyard recalls Wilmington's days as a major seventeenth-century shipbuilding center with exhibitions and live demonstrations. Open daily 10:00 A.M.–4:00 P.M. Sometimes the ship visits other cities and participates in tall-ship races, so to be sure it's in town when you are, call first. Admission is $5.00 for adults, $4.00 for children six to twelve.

Continue your tour of Wilmington's Swedish past with a visit to **Fort Christina** at the foot of Seventh Street adjacent to the shipyard (302–652–5629). You can read the history of the first Swedish settlers on brass plaques on the brick walls on either side of this historic park, then see the Rocks, the spot where the passengers of the *Kalmar Nyckel* disembarked in their new homeland. Some of their early log cabins remain as well. Nearby is **Old Swede's Church,** built in 1698, one of the oldest churches in America still used regularly for religious services. Famous and not-yet-famous artists from all over the country have painted the church, and many of their renditions are exhibited next door in **Hendrickson House.** Built in Pennsylvania in 1690 by settlers from the *Kalmar Nyckel* and relocated here in the 1950s, this old stone farmhouse also displays authentic furnishings and other artifacts from the period. A $2.00 admission covers all three sites. Open Wednesday through Saturday 10:00 A.M.–4:00 P.M.

Only blocks away from the waterfront, located in a Woolworth's Five & Ten from the 1940s, the **Delaware History Museum** (504 Market Street, Wilmington, DE 19801; 302–656–0637 or 302–655–7161) is as much fun on the inside as it looks on the outside. Three Art Deco galleries featuring changing interactive exhibits trace the history of Delaware through artifacts and relics such as costumes, toys, and decorative arts. Children will have a great time poking around in Grandma's Attic. A whimsical 9-foot-tall statue of George Washington makes sure you don't miss the gift shop, which offers a fine selection of Delaware handcrafted items. Open Monday through Friday noon–4:00 P.M., Saturday 10:00 A.M.–4:00 P.M. $4.00 adults, seniors $3.00, children two to eight $2.00.

Evening

DINNER: Krazy Kat's, Route 100 and Kirk Road at the Inn at Montchanin Village, Montchanin, DE 19710 (about 6 miles northwest of Wilmington); (302) 888–2133 or (800) COWBIRD. From Wilmington take Route 141 north until it intersects with Route 100; go north on 100 to Kirk Road. To name a fine dining restaurant Krazy Kat's takes either a great sense of humor or a really good reason. The owners of this very, very hot spot have both. If the outrageous decor with leopard skin–print chairs and jaguars on the charger plates doesn't make you smile, the portraits of the goofy military-clad cats (and a few dogs) that adorn the peach-colored walls will. According to owners Dan and Nancy "Missy" Lickle, she a direct duPont descendant, the name came from her grandmother, who used it as a term of affection when referring to a cat-adoring (and decidedly eccentric) tenant. Dinner entrees are priced mainly in the mid- to high twenties, but the food is superb and the setting is unique. It's an experience not to miss. The menu changes regularly, but the crab cake is a permanent favorite and there's usually a unique preparation of venison, ostrich, bear, wild boar, or other seasonal game. Desserts . . . don't get me started.

For an after-dinner treat, take in a show at the **Grand Opera House,** 818 Market Street Mall, Wilmington, DE 19801; (302) 652–5577 or (800) 37–GRAND. Located in a restored 1871 theater that once showcased the likes of "Buffalo Bill" Cody and John Philip Sousa, Delaware's center for the performing arts is now home to Opera-Delaware and the Delaware Symphony Orchestra. Box office is open Monday through Friday 10:00 A.M.–7:00 P.M., noon–5:00 P.M., Saturday and Sunday.

LODGING: The Inn at Montchanin Village, Route 100 and Kirk Road, Montchanin, DE 19710; (302) 888–2133 or (800) COWBIRD. (For directions, see Krazy Kat's.) The Lickles have transformed what was once a tiny nineteenth-century hamlet that was home to the workers at the duPont powder mills into an idyllic retreat that's close to all the city's attractions yet light years away from its busyness. A cluster of nine of the original stone, stucco, and wood buildings dating from 1840 to the 1900s has been painstakingly restored on the outside and updated on the inside to house thirty-seven guest units, each of which has been individually furnished with period pieces and reproductions. The independent spirit that makes Krazy Kat's so much fun is also very much in evidence here in the mixing of painted wooden wicker furniture with antiques and heirlooms. Room rates range from $150 to $185, suites from $225 to $375.

Day 2 / Morning

BREAKFAST: Delcastle Inn Restaurant, 801 McKennan's Church Road, Wilmington, DE 19808; (302) 994–4600. Fuel up for an early tee time at the Delcastle Golf Club with a three-egg cheese and local mushroom omelet or thick-cut Texas-style French toast (breakfast is served 7:00–11:00 A.M. daily). Inexpensive.

Although it's open to the public, the rolling hills and well-tended greens of the eighteen-hole, championship par 72 course at **Delcastle Golf Club** (302–995–1990) have the feel of a private country club.

Greens fees are $23 weekdays, $27 weekends and holidays, $17 after 2:00 P.M. weekdays ($18 weekends), seniors (sixty and over) and juniors (under eighteen) $16 weekdays, ladies $19 on Tuesday. Cart rentals are $8.00 for nine holes, $13.50 for eighteen holes. Private, semiprivate, and group lessons are available. An adjacent driving range has sixty-four tee stations as well as two large grass practice tees plus a challenging miniature golf course.

Afternoon

LUNCH: Riverfront Market, Market Street at the Christina River, Wilmington, DE 19801; (302) 425–4454. What was once a long-abandoned warehouse is now a lively market where local farmers and other food purveyors gather to sell some of the freshest produce, seafood, meats, and other elegant edibles around. Watch the on-site chef prepare your sushi at Mikimoto's. You might also catch the owner of Jeenwong Thai Cuisine handcrafting egg rolls and dumplings. P & S Ravioli has some inspired Italian-style sandwiches. Then there's the impossibly rich ice cream from Lockbriar Farms. Open 9:00 A.M.–7:00 P.M. Tuesday through Friday, 9:00 A.M.–6:00 P.M. Saturday.

To learn how and where the duPont legacy began, go 3 miles northwest of Wilmington via Route 52 north to Route 100 north, then to 141 north and follow the signs to the **Hagley Museum** (302–658–2400). Situated on 240 acres of trees and flowering plants along the banks of the Brandywine River, this is where the duPont family built its first American home and started its business with a black-powder mill. You can still visit the powder yards and Blacksmith Hill, where working exhibits and live demonstrations colorfully illustrate nineteenth-century working and home life. To see how the other half lived, visit Eleutherian Mills, the palatial Georgian-style residence built in 1803 by E. I. duPont that now contains antiques and memorabilia of five generations of the duPont family. Open mid-March through December daily 9:30 A.M.–4:30 P.M.; only weekends January through March. Guided tours weekdays at 1:30 P.M. $11.00 for adults, seniors and students $9.00, children six to fourteen $4.00.

Adjacent to the Hagley Museum entrance is the **Delaware Toy & Miniature Museum** (302–427–8697). If this absolutely charming museum doesn't make you feel like a kid again, nothing will. More than one hundred eighteenth- to twentieth-century dollhouses, furnishings, dolls, trains, boats, and planes from Europe and America tempt the child (or grown-up collector) in you to come and play. Other miniatures in ivory, silver, and porcelain as well as a wonderful collection of more than 700 tiny vases dating as far back as 600 B.C. will dazzle you. Open Tuesday through Saturday 10:00 A.M.–4:00 P.M., Sunday noon–4:00 P.M. Admission is $5.00 for adults, $4.00 for seniors, $3.00 for children twelve and under. (Babes in arms are free.)

Evening

DINNER: Buckley's Tavern, 5812 Kennett Pike/Route 52, Centreville, DE 19807; (302) 656–9776. This rustic restaurant and bar in a tiny village 5 miles north of Wilmington has been a Brandywine Valley landmark since the 1950s. Housed in a former early-nineteenth-century residence, Buckley's decor is colonial cozy, and its moderately priced menu makes good use of the seasonal bounty from nearby fields and waters. If you want to savor the area's famous fungi in all their glory, order the mushroom soup or mushrooms Wellington. Open for lunch and dinner.

To return to Philadelphia, simply head north on I–95. The return trip should take less than one hour.

There's More

Nemours Mansion and Gardens, Rockland Road between Routes 141 and 202, Wilmington, DE 19899; (302) 651–6912. This Louis XVI–style chateau set on 300 acres of splendid gardens and trees belonged to Alfred I. duPont and houses antiques and art dating from the fifteenth century. Open May to the end of December, tours are offered Tuesday through Saturday at 9:00 A.M., 11:00 A.M., 1:00 P.M., and 3:00 P.M.; Sunday 11:00 A.M., 1:00 P.M., and 3:00 P.M. Visitors must be at least twelve years of age. Admission is $12.

Bellevue State Park, 800 Carr Road (between Park and Silverside), Wilmington, DE 19809; (302) 577–3534. Fishing, game courts, picnicking, summer concerts, equestrian stables, gardens, and a picturesque pond on the former estate of the William duPont family. Tours of the preserved mansion, a replica of James Madison's home, Montpelier, are offered periodically.

Delaware Art Museum, 2301 Kentmere Parkway, Wilmington, DE 19732; (302) 571–9590. A permanent collection of works by leading nineteenth- and twentieth-century artists, including Winslow Homer, Thomas Eakins,

Howard Pyle, and three generations of Wyeths; pre-Raphaelite paintings and decorative arts. Open Tuesday, Thursday, Friday, and Saturday 9:00 A.M.–4:00 P.M.; Wednesday until 9:00 P.M.; Saturday and Sunday 10:00 A.M.–4:00 P.M. Admission is $7.00 for adults, seniors $5.00, students $2.50, and free for children six and under. Every Wednesday evening from 5:30 to 9:00 is Art After Hours night with special programs and free admission; also free Saturday 9:00 A.M.–noon.

Delaware Center for the Contemporary Arts, 200 South Madison Street, Wilmington, DE 19889; (302) 656–6466. Changing exhibits of cutting-edge works using all media and multimedia. Open Tuesday, Thursday, Friday, and Saturday 10:00 A.M.–5:00 P.M.; Sunday noon–5:00 P.M. $5.00 adults, $3.00 students and seniors.

Delaware Museum of Natural History, 4840 Kennett Pike, Wilmington, DE 19807 (5 miles northwest of Wilmington between Greenville and Centreville); (302) 658–9111. Delaware's only dinosaurs and other exhibits take you back in time and around the globe to learn about the past, present, and future of native and exotic mammals, fish, and birds. Monday through Saturday 9:30 A.M.–4:30 P.M., Sunday noon–4:30 P.M. Admission is $5.00 adults, $4.00 seniors, $3.00 children three to seventeen.

Delaware Park Racetrack, Delaware Park Boulevard, Wilmington, DE 19804; (302) 994–2521 or (800) 417–5687. Year-round Thoroughbred and harness racing. To get there from Wilmington, take I–95 south to exit 4B. Follow to second light and turn right onto Route 7 north. The entrance is 1½ miles on the left. From April to November you can enjoy live Thoroughbred racing. Every day (and Tuesday through Sunday nights) throughout the year, big-screen televisions in Delaware Park's big theaters and even more comfortable Race Book lounge simulcast races from top tracks around the world. First daily post time is 12:45 P.M. Free admission and parking as well as a beautiful wooded picnic grove and dining options ranging from concession stand to elegant fare.

Brandywine Zoo, 1001 North Park Drive, Brandywine Park, Wilmington, DE 19802; (302) 571–7785. A collection of about 150 animals from North and South America and temperate Asia ranges from river otters to Siberian tigers. Open daily year-round 10:00 A.M.–4:00 P.M. Admission is $4.00 for adults, $2.00 for seniors and children three to eleven.

Wilmington & Western Railroad, Greenbank Station, 2201 Newport Gap Pike, Wilmington, DE 19808; (302) 998–1930. Take a ride on an authentic late nineteenth-century steam train through the historic Red Clay Valley. Call for seasonal schedules and prices.

Bank One Center on the Riverfront, 800 South Madison Street; (888) 862–2787. Call for information on current exhibit.

Special Events

July. Delaware Handicap at Delaware Park Racetrack. The state's Grand Race of the Year, this more than century-old annual tradition features top horses and riders vying for hundreds of thousands of dollars.

Labor Day weekend. Annual Craft Festival at Winterthur. Held in association with the Pennsylvania Guild of Craftsmen, this two-day event features handmade jewelry, toys, stained glass, sculpture, furniture, wearable art, and other crafts created by more than 200 juried artisans from eleven states. Tickets are $8.00 per day in advance, $10.00 at the gate; children twelve and under are admitted free with an adult.

Other Recommended Restaurants and Lodgings

Wilmington

Brandywine Brewing Company, 3801 Kennett Pike, Greenville Center, DE 19807; (302) 655–8000. Award-winning handcrafted microbrews, signature corn chowder, and two or three fresh seafood specials each day. Lunch and dinner prices are generally moderate.

PUFF, Rockland Road and Route 100, Montchanin, DE 19710; (302) 658–0100. The name is an acronym for "Pick Up Fine Foods." This highly regarded gourmet take-out establishment housed in an 1889 railroad station adjacent to the Inn at Montchanin Village offers great sandwiches, homemade a la carte items, and cookies called "Oh Gods" that are perfect for picnics.

Columbus Inn, 2216 Pennsylvania Avenue (Route 52), Wilmington, DE 19806; (302) 571–1492. When "Buffalo Bill" Cody and Annie Oakley ate here, black-bean chili or the calypso spiced chicken breast stuffed with lobster, grilled corn, cabbage, and goat cheese probably weren't on the menu. What a shame. Moderate to expensive.

The Hop, 4542 Kirkwood Highway; (302) 633–1955. An inexpensive

1950s-style diner/restaurant that serves great homemade food, including a signature filet mignon sandwich and superbargain blue-plate specials, along with more than thirty soda fountain flavors.

Hotel du Pont, Eleventh and Market Streets; (800) 441–9019 or (302) 594–3100. Originally built in 1913, this historic 217-room hotel is still the epitome of elegance. Room rates range from $319 to $550. Special packages are available. The hotel's Green Room fine-dining restaurant has long been regarded as one of the Brandywine Valley's best.

For More Information

Greater Wilmington Convention & Visitors Bureau, 100 West Tenth Street, Suite 20, Wilmington, DE 19801; (302) 652–4088; www.wilmcvb.org.

Delaware Tourism Office, 99 Kings Highway, Dover, DE 19901; (866) 2–VISIT–DE (284–7483); www.visitdelaware.com.

Doylestown, Pennsylvania

Cultured Pearl

1 Night

Doylestown has long been a hotbed of creativity. In addition to being the home of prolific author James A. Michener, renowned librettist Oscar Hammerstein II, and horticulturist W. Atlee Burpee, the unique beauty of this village situated directly in the heart of Bucks County has been a muse for generations of writers, sculptors, painters, and other artists.

☐ Lakeside Serenity

☐ Soaring Castles

☐ Artistic Inspiration

And with its small-town charm and miles of carefully preserved natural splendor, it's no wonder. This is a place where one minute you can be marveling over the simple perfection of a wildflower and the next minute be awestruck by a thought-provoking piece of man-made art. It is a place where the day begins with the sweet sound of birdsong and ends with a stirring symphony.

There's an elegance and style here that is almost regal. In fact, one particularly inspired—and wealthy—local resident even built himself a kingdom of medieval-style castles (now superb museums) on a mile-long strip in the village.

Since its earliest days, when it was known as Doyl's Tavern (after innkeeper William Doyle, who set up his business there in the early 1700s), Doylestown has graciously shared its abundance of cultural and natural wonders with visitors. Only about one hour north of Philadelphia, it is a quick escape that can have a long-lasting impact on both body and soul.

Day 1 / Morning

From Philadelphia take the Schuylkill Expressway (I–76) west for 14 miles until you come to Route 23; take Route 23 west about 3 miles to Route 202. Take 202 east for about 18 miles straight into Doylestown. Driving time should be a little over 1½ hours.

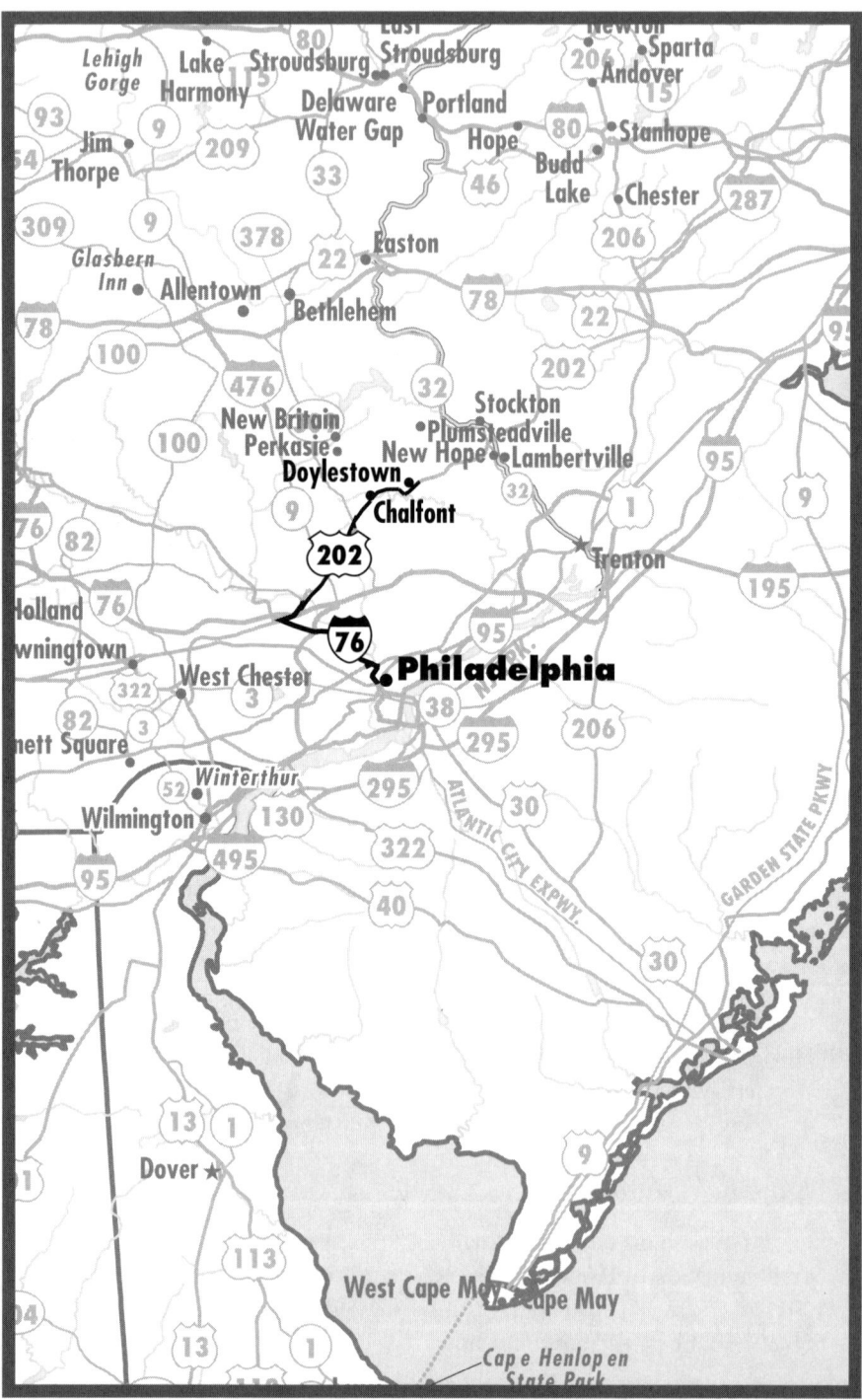

In downtown Doylestown, make your first stop **Lilly's** at 1 West Court Street (opposite the courthouse), Doylestown, PA 18901 (215–230–7883). For a memorable brown-bag lunch, owner Lilly Salvatore adds many thoughtful touches to her offerings, from black-bean salsa to a smoked turkey roll-up or horseradish mayo and roasted peppers to tender roast beef served on hand-sliced rye bread. Inexpensive. At night Lilly's magically becomes a full-service white-tablecloth bistro.

One of Doylestown's most illustrious and fascinating citizens was noted anthropologist, archaeologist, historian, ceramist, writer, and collector Henry Chapman Mercer. A leader of the twentieth-century Arts and Crafts movement, his castlelike home, museums, and tile works are some of the area's most identifiable landmarks. To get to the stretch of Route 313 known as the **Mercer Mile,** follow Court Street less than 1 mile to the first of Mercer's castles, **Fonthill Museum** (Route 313 and East Court Street, Doylestown, PA 18901; 215–348–9461). Unlike most structures, Mercer designed Fonthill from the inside out because, in addition to being his home, he intended it to house his vast collections of prints, decorative tiles, and other treasures gleaned from his travels around the world. Built entirely of hand-mixed concrete between 1908 and 1910, this dramatic structure now exhibits more than 900 of Mercer's personal treasures and has forty-four rooms, eighteen fireplaces, thirty-two stairwells, and 200 windows. Open year-round Monday through Saturday 10:00 A.M.–5:00 P.M., Sunday noon–5:00 P.M. Admission is $7.00 for adults, $6.50 for seniors, $2.50 for youths six to seventeen, and free for children under six.

Right next door is Mercer's **Moravian Pottery & Tile Works** (130 Swamp Road, Route 313, Doylestown, PA 18901; 215–345–6722), where artisans still use original formulas and methods to handcraft magnificent decorative tiles and mosaics. From the time it was opened in 1912, this facility has produced tiles that adorn buildings throughout the United States (including the halls of the state capitol) and around the world. Be sure to visit the adjacent **Moravian Tile Shop,** where the intricate works of art made on the premises are for sale. Open daily year-round 10:00 A.M.–4:45 P.M. Free; $3.50 adults, $3.00 seniors, $2.00 children for guided tour.

Afternoon

L U N C H : Enjoy your lunch at one of the picnic tables situated in a grove of trees outside the Moravian Pottery & Tile Works.

The third castle along the Mercer Mile is aptly named the **Mercer**

Museum (84 South Pine Street, Doylestown, PA 18901; 215–345–0210) and, like both of the other structures designed by this remarkable man, has an interesting story of its own. In 1897 Henry Mercer, always a collector of items that defined the everyday life of man through the ages, was searching in a junk dealer's barn when he came across a number of pre-1850 work-related implements that had been made obsolete by the Industrial Revolution. These items became the basis for a collection he called "The Tools of the Nation Maker," which grew to more than 50,000 antique objects representing sixty early American trades and Native American implements dating from 8,000 to 6,000 B.C. Open Monday through Saturday 10:00 A.M.–5:00 P.M., Tuesday until 9:00 P.M., Sunday from noon–5:00 P.M. Admission is $6.00 for adults, $5.50 for seniors, $2.50 for youths six and older, and free for children under six.

If making—or drinking—wine is one of your favorite hobbies, take a ride out into the nearby countryside to **Peace Valley Winery** (300 Old Limekiln Road, Chalfont, PA 18914; 215–249–9058), where you can pick your own fruit or simply pick up a bottle of the winery's award-winning reds or whites. To get there, take Route 313 northwest to New Galena Road (Ginger Bread Square is on the corner). Turn left and go 2 miles to Old Limekiln Road. Turn right and go 1 mile to the twenty-acre vineyard where owner Susan Gross grows more than two dozen varieties of grapes. During harvest time (September to mid-October) you can pick your own blue (Fredonia) or white (Niagara) grapes for at-home wine making. Susan also has a four-acre orchard of dwarf apple trees for making her—or your—spicy fall wines. Open Wednesday through Friday and Sunday noon–6:00 P.M., Saturday from 10:00 A.M. Hours are extended during harvest and Christmas seasons.

Evening

DINNER: Madam Butterfly, 34 West State Street, Doylestown, PA 18901; (215) 345–4488. Back in downtown Doylestown, right off Main near the courthouse, you can enjoy the freshest sushi, sashimi, and other traditional Japanese delicacies. The authentically prepared food is wonderful, from the cracklingly crunchy tempuras to the tender-crisp hibachi stir-fries. Prices run the gamut from inexpensive to expensive, depending on how hungry you are and whether you prefer to order a la carte. The restaurant doesn't have a liquor license, so be sure to bring your own sake or other wine.

After dinner, check in with the **Bucks County Symphony**

The Mercer Museum.

Orchestra (215–348–7321) to find out if they are having a concert tonight. These talented musicians, along with invited world-class guest soloists, have been bringing the classics to Bucks County for more than forty-five years. There are three subscription concerts in fall, winter (this is an afternoon concert), and spring, as well as various other events throughout the year. Most of the concerts take place at Central Bucks High School East, 2 to 3 miles southeast of Doylestown in the town of Buckingham. Call for ticket prices.

LODGING: Inn at Fordhook Farm, 105 New Britain Road, ½ mile from the center of Doylestown, PA 18901; (215) 345–1766. Take Court Street west to New Britain Road; turn right. There, surrounded by 200-year-old linden trees and nestled on sixty-plus acres of woodlands and meadows, you'll find this jewel of an inn. Built in 1750 and restored and remodeled 200 years later, this former home of horticulturist and self-made businessman W. Atlee Burpee (founder of the seed company) is now an elegant getaway owned by his grandchildren Blanche Burpee Dohan and Jonathan and Carole Burpee. The inn's guest rooms are decorated with a mixture of English and American antiques and family mementos. Make special note of the living-room fireplace inlaid with Henry Mercer's decorative tiles. Rates for rooms in the main house range from $195 to $350 per night weekdays, $295 to $395 weekends.

Day 2 / Morning

BREAKFAST: The Inn at Fordhook Farm. A full homemade breakfast is included with your room. Making the meal even more luxurious is the fact that you can savor it on heirloom china in the elegant dining room while admiring the view from the leaded bay windows.

Back to Peace Valley (see instructions for yesterday's trip to Peace Valley Winery, but instead of taking New Galena Road to Old Limekiln Road, turn left on Chapman Road) for a visit to the **Peace Valley Nature Center** (170 Chapman Road, New Britain, PA 18901, 3 miles north of Doylestown, west of Route 313; 215–345–7860). Start at the Solar Building with its interesting displays of local wildlife and plants. There's a "please touch" section for young ones, and you can pick up a map and schedules of guided nature walks. On this 300-acre protected property, you can find 14 miles of hiking trails through woods and fields filled with wildflowers, trees, butterflies, deer, and more than 250 species of birds. Open 9:00 A.M.–5:00 P.M. Tuesday through Sunday. The bird blinds and trails are open dawn till dusk.

Peace Valley Nature Center is actually part of 1,500-acre **Peace Valley Park,** where you'll find all-season water sports and activities tucked away in the wooded setting of **Lake Galena.** In season you can rent just about any kind of boat here, from paddle to sail. It is also a glorious spot for fishing and ice-skating. The park is open from dawn to dusk and there is no admission charge.

Afternoon

LUNCH: Ristorante Villa Capri, 51 West Court Street, Doylestown, PA 18901; (215) 348–9656. An unassuming pizzeria in front, this restaurant has a back dining room reminiscent of the garden of a gracious Italian villa, with white stucco walls, high-arched leaded windows, imported wrought-iron work, and pink-toned marble. This generous taste of Italy also extends to the lunch menu, which features inexpensive hot and cold sandwiches, pizzas by the slice or pie, and moderately priced homemade specialties, such as spaghetti a la carbonara, cannoli Florentine, and eggplant rolatini.

Another famous Doylestown must-see is the **James A. Michener Art Museum** (138 Pine Street, across from the Mercer Museum, Doylestown, PA 18901; 215–340–9800). Housed in an 1884 former prison are exhibits that trace local art from colonial times to the present, an outdoor sculpture garden, and a 22-foot semicircular mural. Works of national and international scope are also exhibited on a changing basis. Open Tuesday through Friday 10:00 A.M.–4:30 P.M., Saturday 10:00 A.M.–5:00 P.M., Sunday noon–5:00 P.M. Admission is $6.00 for adults, $5.50 for seniors, $3.00 for students, and free for children under six.

Before you head back home, take a little time to stroll the historic streets of downtown Doylestown, with its beautifully maintained colonial, Federal, and Victorian houses. The town also has some nice shops, including **Spirit Song** (17 West Court Street; 215–230–7311), a holistic gallery and shop featuring spirit-healing jewelry and art. At **Local Color** (21 East State Street, Doylestown, PA 18901; 215–230–4488), owner Helene Mullen fashions original designs from locally grown (whenever possible) dried flora. Feeling a little exotic? You'll find arrangements to suit you, too. For a custom arrangement, you can bring in a swatch of fabric or wallpaper and/or your own container. The shop itself is like a botanical garden, with trees and flowers all around. Mullen also sells antique and vintage collectibles.

To return to Philadelphia, follow Route 611 south all the way. The trip should take approximately one hour.

There's More

National Shrine of Our Lady of Czestochowa, 654 Ferry Road, Doylestown, PA 18901; (215) 345–0600. On exhibit at this Polish spiritual and pilgrimage center is a reproduction of a painting of the Virgin Mary that, according to legend, was created by St. Luke. Also on this 170-acre site is a church that can accommodate up to 1,800 and a smaller chapel with a seating capacity of 400. Open daily year-round; tours by request.

Pearl S. Buck National Historic Landmark, 520 Dublin Road, Hilltown Township (mailing address, Perkasie, PA 18944); (800) 220–2825 or (215) 249–0100. Located approximately ten minutes from Doylestown, this former estate of the late Nobel and Pulitzer Prize–winning author offers a guided tour of her circa 1835 farmhouse. A true reflection of the international scope of Buck's interests and tastes, the furnishings blend Chinese and nineteenth-century Pennsylvanian traditions of art and architecture. You may also enjoy the scenery from one of the walking trails. $6.00 adults, $5.00 seniors and students, $15.00 families (with children under eighteen), age six or under free.

Special Events

July and August. Brown Bag It With the Arts, Bucks County Courthouse Lawn, Doylestown, PA 18901; (215) 348–3913. Free music to eat lunch by every Wednesday at noon.

July and August. Free Concerts in the Park, Peace Valley Park, 230 Creek Road, New Britain, PA 18901; (215) 348–6114. Every Sunday.

September. Polish American Festival, National Shrine of Our Lady of Czestochowa, 645 Ferry Road, Doylestown, PA 18901; (215) 345–0600. Unlimited amusement rides as well as stage shows, polka party, arts and crafts, and lots of Polish and American delicacies (pierogies and hoagies do rhyme after all).

Other Recommended Restaurants and Lodgings

Doylestown

B. Maxwell's Restaurant & Victorian Pub, 37 North Main Street, Doylestown, PA 18901; (215) 348–1027. Its proximity to the courthouse, clubby atmosphere, and all-American fare make this a favorite lunch spot of local lawyers and other movers and shakers. Menu prices range from inexpensive to moderate.

Siam Cuisine at the Black Walnut, 80 West State Street, Doylestown, PA 18901; (215) 348–0708. Traditional French rack of lamb with herbs and mustard shares a sophisticated menu with Thai seafood ceviche. Expensive.

Coffee & Cream, 6 East State Street, Doylestown, PA 18901; (215) 348–1111. The aroma of freshly roasted and ground coffee is intoxicating from the minute you walk in the door of this cute coffee/ice-cream shop. Whether you take your brew hot or iced, make sure you also have a cookie, scone, or other freshly baked treat to go with it.

The Knight House, 96 West State Street, Doylestown, PA 18901; (215)

345–8746. New American cuisine infused with Asian, French, and other international influences. Seafood is a specialty, and the menu changes daily. The decor is casual-chic and the downstairs bar is a lively after-dinner spot. Expensive.

The Doylestown Inn, 18 West State Street, Doylestown, PA 18901; (215) 345–6610. Eleven guest rooms, each with jetted tub and minibar housed in a completely renovated circa 1902 building. Rates range from $135 to $220 in winter, $150 to $220 in spring.

Plumsteadville

Plumsteadville Inn, Route 611 and Stump Road, Plumsteadville, PA 18949 (4 miles north of Doylestown); (215) 766–7500. From its beginnings as a stagecoach stop in the mid–eighteenth century, this welcoming inn has been providing travelers with food, lodging, and boundless good cheer. Room rates are $79 Sunday through Thursday, $105 to $140 weekends; full breakfast included. The inn also has a splendid country dining room that serves continental fare.

For More Information

Bucks County Conference and Visitors Bureau, 3207 Street Road, Bensalem, PA 19020; (215) 639–0300; www.experiencebuckscounty.com.

Central Bucks Chamber of Commerce; (215) 348–3913.

Lancaster County, Pennsylvania

Back Roads through Long Ago

2 Nights

Along Route 30, the main road that goes straight through the heart of Lancaster, you'll see lots of neon lights, a Pennsylvania Dutch–themed amusement park, just about every outlet store you can think of, and horse-drawn buggies filled with waving tourists. This Lancaster often surprises visitors who have come to experience a different culture, a more basic way of life, and a quieter getaway. However, you can still find the Lancaster you seek, tucked away on green and rolling back roads and in small towns with names like Mount Joy, Lititz, Intercourse, and Bird-in-Hand that virtually radiate from the relative metropolis called Lancaster City.

☐ Cultural Crossroads

☐ Traditional Crafts

☐ Farm Food

If you choose to take these back roads, you will be immersed in another culture—actually, a variety of cultures. All of them have their roots in Switzerland where, in 1525, a group of Christians known as Mennonites, after their leader Menno Simons, broke away from the state church because of basic differences in their interpretation of Biblical teachings. In the late 1600s, a Swiss Mennonite named Jakob Ammann and his followers broke away and formed a separate sect, the Amish.

Persecuted in Europe, both groups sought religious freedom in Pennsylvania. And here they have peacefully coexisted ever since. But don't expect Lancaster to be a melting pot. Each group has retained its own strong and distinctive beliefs and customs (even though a third group called the Amish Mennonites has incorporated some of the teachings and practices of both). These differences give Lancaster County a character and flavor unlike any other place.

Day 1 / Morning

There are quicker ways to get to Lancaster County, which is about 1½

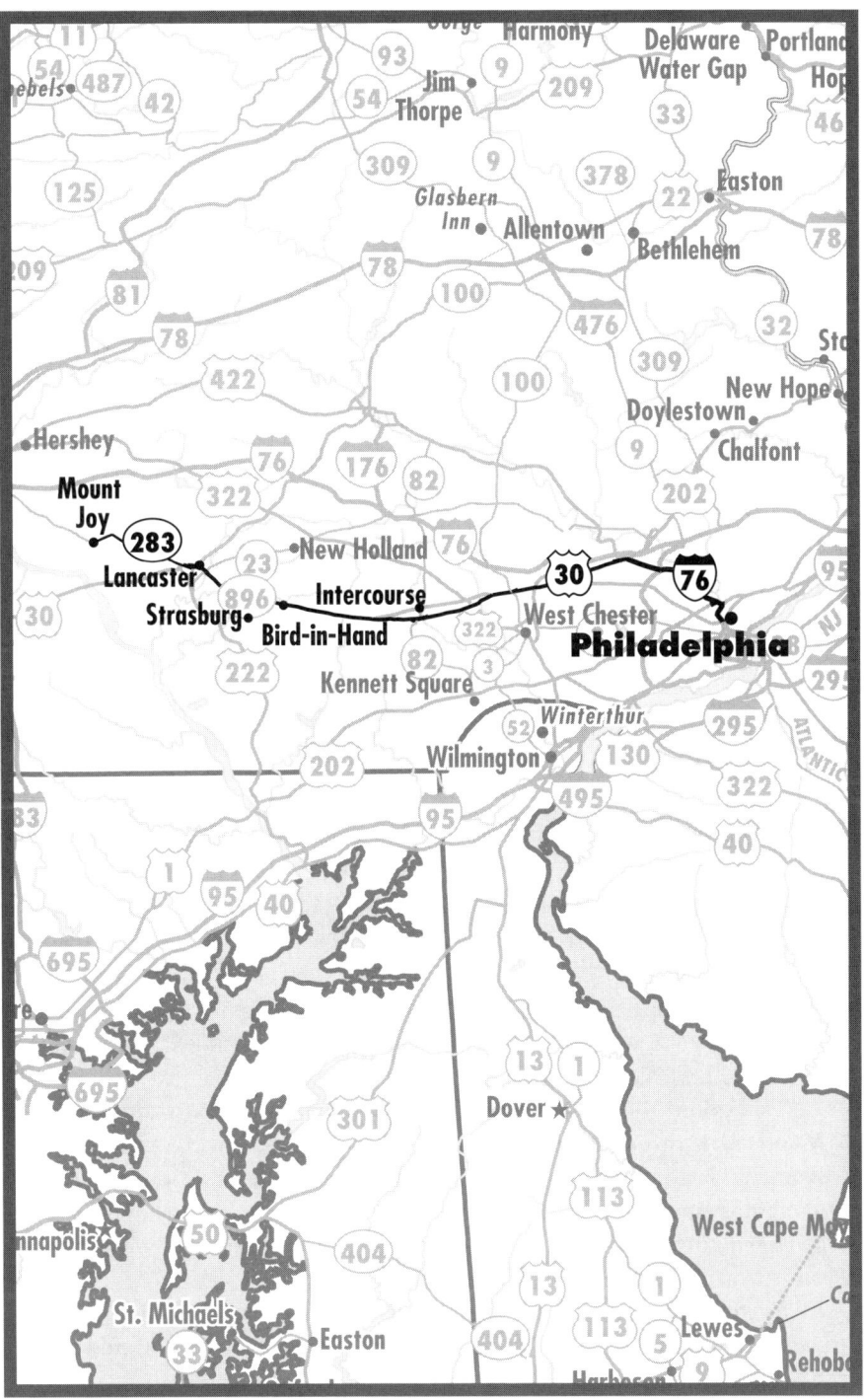

hours west of Philadelphia, but none so beautiful as via Route 30, with its gently rolling hills and cow-dotted farms. From Philadelphia, take the Schuylkill Expressway (I–76) to the King of Prussia/Route 202 south exit; go south on 202 to Route 30 west. Follow Route 30 west about 50 miles right into Lancaster.

Before you begin to explore the back roads of today's Lancaster County, a visit to the **Landis Valley Museum** (717–569–0401) will give you some insight into traditional Pennsylvania German (or Deutsch) life and culture. To get there, continue on Route 30 west until it intersects with Route 272 (Oregon Pike); take 272 north for about 2½ miles until you come to Landis Valley Road in Lancaster, PA 17601; (717) 569–0401. The largest Pennsylvania German folk museum in the state, this open-air complex features eighteen historic buildings, tens of thousands of artifacts, costumed interpreters, working craftspeople, and living farmsteads. Guided tours are available, or you can simply stroll around at your leisure. There's also a great museum shop that specializes in handcrafted items. Open Monday through Saturday 9:00 A.M.–5:00 P.M., Sunday noon–5:00 P.M. Admission is $9.00 for adults, $7.00 for seniors, $6.00 for children six to seventeen.

Afternoon

LUNCH: House of Clarendon, 201 West Walnut Street, Lancaster, PA 17603; (717) 290–7800. You probably wouldn't expect to find an authentic English tearoom right in the middle of Pennsylvania Dutch Country, but British-born baker Julie Bashore and her husband Bucky do high tea in high style. Opt for "Seven and a Surprise" ($15.95) and get a sampling of seven dessert and pastry items plus a "chef's surprise," which might be English sausage rolls, cream cheese and chive puffs, mini sandwiches, or another tantalizing tidbit. For $19.95, you'll get a selection of seven "Sweet and Savoury" treats. Tea is served Monday to Friday 1:00–2:30 P.M. or 3:00–4:30 P.M., Saturday noon–1:30 P.M. or 2:30–4:00 P.M.

To explore the back roads, you could pick up a free map at the **Mennonite Information Center** (2209 Millstream Road, right off of Route 30 in Lancaster, PA 17602; 717–299–0954). But it's a lot more fun, interesting, and educational to hire one of the center's guides to "backseat-drive" you in your own car to those off-the-beaten-tourist-path areas and sites.

As we rode past fruit orchards; fields of corn, tobacco, and alfalfa; working windmills and waterwheels, and one-room schoolhouses, our guide, a gentle Amish-Mennonite lady named Ada Fisher, described the customs, traditions, and daily routines that have defined the lives of the area's "plain people." She also asked us what our interests were so that she could individualize our tour.

Whatever you do, request a stop at **Mascot Roller Mills** to see a 1760 mill that is still used to grind corn for the local Amish community (open May through October weekdays and Saturday 9:00 A.M.–4:00 P.M. for free tours). As farmland has become increasingly scarce and expensive in Lancaster County, a number of the locals have become professional craftspeople and opened up workrooms and small businesses in the basements and barns of their homes. If you're interested, your guide will show you where to find the best furniture, toys, quilts, "quillows" (an ingenious combination quilt/pillow), and other beautiful handmade items. Then, of course, there are the multitude of roadside farm stands selling everything from fresh and pickled produce to homemade root beer to a mind-boggling array of baked goods.

Be sure to jot down the names and locations of any villages or shops you would like to revisit; it's easy to get confused when you're on your own. Remember, too, that almost all the Amish-run businesses are closed on Sunday. Guided tours from the Mennonite Information Center are available Monday through Saturday and cost $7.00 for a setup fee plus $9.50 per hour (minimum two hours) for your guide. It is important to keep in mind that even the Amish who own businesses are very private people and that their faith does not permit them to be photographed.

Late Afternoon/Evening

With all this wide-open space and clean air, the sunsets are truly something to see, especially from the vantage point of a hot-air balloon. The **U.S. Hot Air Balloon Team** (800–76–FLY–US) offers morning (during first two hours of daylight) and late afternoon (during last two hours of daylight) flights 365 days a year—weather permitting, of course. One of the most convenient departure points is at Rockvale Square (Routes 30 and 896). Go early and you can help the crew inflate your balloon and get some terrific preflight photos. $165 per hour.

DINNER: East of Eden Pub, 680 Millcross Road, Lancaster, PA 17601 (extension of Eden Road); (717) 299–0159. For dinner and a good night's rest (tomorrow is an early day), take Route 30 east to Route 23 east toward New Holland. In less than 1 mile turn right onto Eden Road (at the firehouse); in a little more than ½ mile you'll come to a bridge. Right across the bridge is this wonderful little restaurant that specializes in Old-World Austrian and German cooking. Be sure to try the sauerbraten, one of the schnitzel (veal) dishes, the spaetzle, or the Austrian bauernschmaus (roast pork, smoked pork, bratwurst, and smoked sausage with bread dumpling and sauerkraut). Mostly moderate prices. If the weather is nice, enjoy your meal in the riverside Biergarten.

LODGING: Gardens of Eden, 1894 Eden Road, Lancaster, PA 17601; (717) 393–5179. The name of this bed-and-breakfast would be just as appropriate even if it wasn't located on Eden Road. To get there from the pub, cross back over the bridge, then take a left onto the lane at the B&B sign and park below the stone wall. Situated on three and a half acres on the Conestoga River, the inn's lovingly landscaped exterior and antique-, folk-art-, and family heirloom–furnished interior make for a setting that is truly romantic. As soon as you meet innkeepers Bill and Marilyn Ebel, a historian/naturalist and floral designer, respectively, you can see that they have put a great deal of themselves into their home. In addition to three guest rooms in the 1867 main house, there is also a two-story cottage (actually a restored summer kitchen) on the grounds. Room rates range from $115 to $130. The cottage is $165 per night year-round. When you make your reservation at the Gardens of Eden, you can also ask the Ebels to arrange for a Dutch Country Tour with a guide from the Mennonite Center and/or a dinner at an Amish home (available on selected Saturday nights only).

Day 2 / *Morning*

If you are visiting the area on a Tuesday, Friday, or Saturday, rise and shine early so that you can rub elbows with the locals and get the freshest goodies at the **Central Market** (right off of Penn Square, Lancaster, PA 17603; 717–291–4739) located right in the heart of Lancaster City. One of the oldest publicly owned farmers' markets in the nation, Central Market has been a bustling center of commerce for local purveyors of produce, meats, cheeses, baked goods, and other foodstuffs since the 1730s. Open Tuesday and Friday 6:00 A.M.–4:00 P.M., Saturday 6:00 A.M.–2:00 P.M. Have an eye-opening cup of cappuccino (yes, cappuccino) and a just-baked sweet, but don't fill up too much because there's a gourmet meal waiting for you back at your bed-and-breakfast.

BREAKFAST: Gardens of Eden. In her studio Marilyn Ebel uses her own homegrown herbs and flowers to make beautiful decorative items. She also uses many of them to create culinary works of art (such as a lovely lavender syrup for pancakes) in her kitchen. Breakfast here is a hearty affair that usually includes fresh fruit and homemade muesli, an egg dish or other entree, and oven-fresh muffins or breads. In nice weather you can eat out on the screened-in porch overlooking the back garden.

And, speaking of gardens, be sure to ask Bill for the grand tour of the gardens that surround the inn. In spring and summer the Ebels' gardens are a profusion of colors and heady aromas from more than one hundred kinds of flowers, plants, trees, and shrubs, making this place a paradise, not only for guests, but for the more than sixty species of birds and other wildlife that frequently visit. And if you can't resist the lure of the adjacent river, the Ebels offer their guests the use of a canoe and rowboat.

If you equate Lancaster solely with plain people, you might be surprised by some of the colorful, and sometimes even funky, local folk art and carved furnishings on display at the **Heritage Center Museum** (13 West King Street, Lancaster, PA 17603; 717–299–6440), a complex of five historic buildings in downtown Lancaster. Open April through December Tuesday through Saturday 10:00 A.M.–5:00 P.M. Free.

Afternoon

Now it's on to more back-road adventures in two charming towns by the names of **Intercourse** and Bird-in-Hand. Head east on Route 30 until you get to Route 340 (also called Old Philadelphia Pike). At 3615 Old Philadelphia Pike (at Cross Keys Village Center, at the intersection of Route 340 and Route 772 east) in Intercourse, PA 17534, is **Intercourse Pretzel Factory** (717–768–3432), a must-stop for any aficionado of the fat, salty, delicious twists we think of as Pennsylvania Dutch pretzels. Soft, hard, stuffed (with jellies and cream cheese, sweet smoked bologna and onion relish, sausage and sauerkraut—you get the idea), covered in Wilbur's chocolate—this place makes them all by hand. This is truly an artisan shop where only about one hundred pounds of dough (1,800 pretzels) are produced at any one time, so if you want to see them made (the tour is free) and maybe get the chance to roll one yourself, call ahead for days and times.

LUNCH: **Stoltzfus Farm Restaurant,** Route 772, Intercourse, PA 17534; (717) 768–8156. About 10 miles east on Route 340, you'll come to the village of Intercourse (you'll pass right through Bird-in-Hand along the way, but don't worry, you'll be back). If you would like to hazard any theories on how this area got its name, remember you're in Amish country. Actually, the name is a reference to the fact that the village sits at the intersection, or intercourse, of two famous old highways, the King's Highway (now Route 340) and Newport Road (now Route 772). For a true taste of Pennsylvania Dutch cooking, go 1 block east on 772 to Stoltzfus Farm Restaurant, which serves honest country fare in the Amish farm homestead where owner Amos Stoltzfus grew up. The family-style meals (priced at $14.95 for adults, $6.95 for children four to ten) include such local favorites as homemade sausage, chicken and ham loaf, chowchow, apple butter, pepper cabbage, and other traditional "sweets and sours." Of course, there are also lots of freshly baked desserts—don't miss the shoofly pie. If you like the homemade sausage, you can buy some to take home at the family's own butcher shop right across the street in Cross Keys Village Center. Closed December through March.

The **People's Place** (3513 Old Philadelphia Pike, Route 340, Intercourse, PA 17534; 800–390–8436 or 717–768–7171) is a complex of galleries, museums, and shops with answers to many of the commonly asked questions about Amish and Mennonite beliefs and practices. Call for various attractions and admission prices. Open Monday through Saturday 9:30 A.M.–5:00 P.M., June through August until 8:00 P.M. One of its most popular features is the **People's Place Quilt Museum** (800–828–8218), where creators, collectors, and admirers can check out the beautiful collection of pre-1940 quilts. Admission is $5.00 for adults, $2.50 for children. At the **Museum Shoppe,** you'll find creations from more than 300 local crafters as well as an outstanding array of quilting fabrics, traditional and original patterns, and books. Open Monday through Saturday 9:00 A.M.–5:00 P.M.

No visit to Lancaster County is complete without a cone, sundae, or shake from **Lapp Valley Farms Ice Cream.** If you don't have time to visit the actual farm (located in nearby New Holland), there's a Lapp Valley Farms shop at **Kitchen Kettle Village** (3529 Old Philadelphia Pike, Intercourse, PA 17534; 800–732–3538 or 717–768–8261) where you can indulge in any of their twenty incredible flavors.

Legend has it that the name **Bird-in-Hand** originated when two surveyors laying out the Old Philadelphia Pike were deciding whether they would spend the night there or go on to Lancaster. "A bird in the hand is worth two in the bush," one supposedly said to the other. Whatever the

A local man and his son drive the back roads of Lancaster County.

derivation of its name, this picturesque village (about 3 miles west of Intercourse on Route 340) is renowned for its beautiful scenery. Another claim to fame is the **Bird-in-Hand Bake Shop** (542 Gibbons Road, Bird-in-Hand, PA 17505; 800–340–8558 or 717–656–7947). This family-owned and -operated bakery is a little bit out of the way (Route 340 to Beechwood Road, right onto Gibbons Road, next to the little red school-house), but the shoofly pies are the best, the cinnamon rolls irresistible, and the "whoopie pies" (two big moist cake-cookies sandwiched with thick white frosting) are the genuine article.

If you've been wondering how it feels to ride in the Amish family carriages you've been sharing the roads with throughout the county, take the twenty-five-minute, 2-mile tour offered by **Abe's Buggy Rides** (Route 340, ½ mile west of Bird-in-Hand; 717–392–1794). One of the oldest and most popular companies of its kind in the area, Abe's really does give you a unique back-roads experience. Open year-round, closed Sunday. $10.00 adults, $5.00 children twelve and under.

DINNER: Alois, 102 North Market Street, Mount Joy, PA 17552; (717) 653–2057. It's about 12 miles from Lancaster to Mount Joy taking Route 30 west to where it intersects with Route 283; then 283 west to Route 230. Go west on 230 to where it becomes Main Street in Mount Joy. One block off Main Street at 102 North Market Street you'll see a former brewery and Victorian hotel called Bube's. Inside are two beer-related museums, an art gallery, and three totally distinctive, absolutely wonderful restaurants. One of these is Alois, a truly romantic fine-dining spot with hand-stenciled walls and ceilings, imaginative decor, and small intimate dining rooms. Chef Ophelia Horn, who has cooked for presidents and other heads of state, matches the elegance of the restaurant with a luxurious six-course prix-fixe feast, including cocktails, appetizers, entrees, accompaniments, and desserts, that goes on for at least 2½ hours. Incredibly, the price for the whole experience is only $32 per person (not including tax and gratuity). After dinner, ask for a tour of the complex— it's an evening's entertainment all by itself. Alois is open for dinner Tuesday through Thursday 5:30–9:30 P.M., Friday and Saturday 5:00–10:00 P.M.

LODGING: Gardens of Eden.

Day 3 / Morning

BREAKFAST: Gardens of Eden.

For railroad enthusiasts, the little village of Strasburg is a must-see. To get there, pick up Route 222 in Lancaster and drive south for 5 miles until you reach Route 741; take 741 east for 4 miles into Strasburg. Before you begin your excursion into railroading past and present, pick up a walking tour map of the town's historic district available at many of the local shops. Take note of the many architecturally diverse eighteenth- and nineteenth-century log, brick, and stone houses and storefronts on its lovely tree-lined streets. Make sure you stop at **Eldreth Pottery** (246 North Decatur Street at Route 896, Strasburg, PA 17579; 717–687–8445), where you'll find salt-glazed pottery still being handcrafted and fired by a 500-year-old German process.

The first stop on your Strasburg railroading tour should be the **Railroad Museum of Pennsylvania** (Route 741 east of town; 717–687–8628). Colorful exhibits and illustrations follow the development of the railroad industry from the earliest steam locomotives to mid-twentieth-century technology. Open Monday through Saturday 9:00 A.M.–5:00 P.M., Sunday noon–5:00 P.M. (Closed Monday from November through April.) Admission is $6.00 for adults, $5.50 for seniors, $4.00 for youths six to twelve, free for children under six. Model-railroad fans of all ages will love **Choo Choo Barn, Traintown, USA** (Route 741 east, Strasburg, PA 17579; 717–687–7911), home of a detailed 1,700-square-foot miniature replica of Lancaster County, complete with seventeen operating trains, moving figures and vehicles, and handcrafted scenery. Open daily April to December. The Strasburg Train Shop is also here, with lots of neat stuff for your home layout.

The **National Toy Train Museum** (300 Paradise Lane, just north of Route 741, Strasburg, PA 17579; 717–687–8976), displays five huge operating layouts and hundreds of locomotives and cars dating from the late 1900s to the present. Open 10:00 A.M.–5:00 P.M. weekends in April, November, and December; daily May 1 through October 31. Admission is $3.00 for adults, $1.50 for children.

The main attraction here is the **Strasburg Rail Road** (Route 741 east, Strasburg, PA 17579; 717–687–7522), where an authentic vintage steam train will take you for a narrated forty-five-minute ride through the countryside and back in time. At the 1882 Victorian station, passengers can purchase tickets to ride in the plush interior parlor car (called Marian), the open-air observation car, or the beautifully restored standard wooden coaches. Train rides are available pretty much year-round and run every hour daily from March 30 to October 30. Fares start from $9.25 for adults, $4.75 for children three to eleven, and free for babies through age two. Reserved seats (when available) are $1.00 extra. Parlor car Marian and dining car seats are additional.

LUNCH: Lee E. Brenner Dining Car. Add an extra dollar to your fare and you can ride in this restored wooden dining coach and order a lovely lunch from the inexpensive to moderately priced menu. Try the home-made chicken corn soup (a local specialty) and a sandwich, chicken salad platter, or chicken Caesar salad. A $3.99 children's menu features the ever-popular hot dog or peanut butter and jelly. You'll think you're in Paradise . . . Paradise, Lancaster County, that is, which is where you will be before the train turns around for the return trip to Strasburg. Lunch in the Lee E. Brenner is available on all regularly scheduled hourly trains from March through December. An elegant—and more expensive—dinner menu is also available seasonally.

For your return trip to Philadelphia, take Route 896 north about 3 miles to Route 30. Retrace your trail home going east on Route 30 until you reach the Schuylkill Expressway (I–76). The entire trip should take about 1½ hours.

There's More

Covered Bridges. At one time there were 1,500 of them in Pennsylvania. Today 219 of them remain, 29 of which are located in Lancaster County. The Pennsylvania Dutch Convention and Visitors Bureau (800–PA–DUTCH) offers the free *Map and Visitors Guide* to the area, which gives directions to all the county's covered bridges.

DeMuth House & Tobacco Shop, 120 East King Street, Lancaster City, Lancaster, PA 17602; (717) 299–9940. If you're a fan of early-twentieth-century American modernist Charles DeMuth, you won't want to miss the twenty-five original drawings and paintings displayed in his home. The building also houses the nation's oldest tobacco shop (circa 1770). Open Tuesday through Friday 10:00 A.M.–4:00 P.M., Sunday 1:00–4:00 P.M. Closed January. Free.

Lancaster Museum of Art, 135 North Lime Street, Lancaster City, Lancaster, PA 17602; (717) 394–3497. A contemporary art gallery with a global perspective. Open Monday through Saturday 10:00 A.M.–4:00 P.M., Sunday noon–4:00 P.M. Free.

Fulton Opera House, 12 North Prince Street (corner of Prince and King Streets), Lancaster City, Lancaster, PA 17603; (717) 394–7133. Built in 1852 and named after inventor Robert Fulton (who was born in nearby Quarryville), this magnificently restored Victorian structure is the nation's oldest theater in continuous operation. George M. Cohan, Sarah Bernhardt, and Al Jolson played here. Today it is home to the Lancaster Symphony Orchestra, Fulton Academy Theatre, and the Lancaster Opera Company.

Wheatland, Route 23, 1120 Marietta Avenue, Lancaster City, Lancaster, PA 17603; (717) 392–8721. Built in 1828, this carefully restored example of Federal architecture was the home of James Buchanan, fifteenth president of the United States. Open daily, April through November 10:00 A.M.–4:00 P.M. Admission: adults $5.50, seniors $4.50, youths twelve and up $3.50, children six to eleven $1.75.

Hands-on House, 2380 Kissel Hill Road just off of Oregon Pike (Route 272), Lancaster City, Lancaster, PA 17601 (next to the Landis Valley

Museum); (717) 569–KIDS. Also known as the Children's Museum of Lancaster, this fun spot features eight play-and-learn areas including a corner grocery, a factory, a farm, and a spaceship designed for youngsters from ages two to ten and their parents to explore together. Open all year. Hours vary by day and season. Admission is $5.00 for children and adults.

Dutch Wonderland, 2249 Route 30 east, 4 miles east of Lancaster; (717) 291–1888. A family amusement park with rides, shows, and activities for all ages. Open June through August and selected days in April, May, September, and October. General admission (ages seven to fifty-nine) $25.95; three to six $20.95; seniors $18.95.

The Amish Village, Route 896, Strasburg, PA 17579; (717) 687–8511. See how the Amish have maintained their self-sufficient lifestyle for more than two and a half centuries. Visit an operating waterwheel, blacksmith shop, springhouse, one-room schoolhouse, smokehouse, and farm animals. You can picnic here, too. Open year-round. $6.50 for adults, $2.50 for children six to twelve.

Special Events

March or April. Annual Quilters' Heritage Celebration, Lancaster Host Resort, 2300 Lincoln Highway east, Lancaster, PA 17602; (717) 854–9323. Dazzling displays of award-winning quilts from all over the United States attract quilt aficionados from more than a dozen countries.

May. Annual Rhubarb Festival, Kitchen Kettle Village, Route 340, Intercourse, PA 17534; (800) 732–3538. Celebrate spring and pay homage to this noble plant and food source at a fun-filled festival featuring food, music, family festivities, and games—all centered around rhubarb.

July. Annual Pennsylvania State Craft Show, Franklin and Marshall College Alumni Sports and Fitness Center, 929 Harrisburg Pike, Lancaster, PA 17604; (717) 579–5997. More than 250 juried members of the Pennsylvania Guild of Craftsmen offer exhibits and demonstrations during this three-day event that has been a tradition for more than fifty years.

Other Recommended Restaurants and Lodgings

Lancaster

Kreider Dairy Farms Family Restaurant, Centerville Road and Columbia

Avenue, Lancaster, PA 17603; (717) 665–5039. An inexpensive fun family restaurant known for its hearty home cooking and luscious homemade ice cream.

Willow Valley Restaurant, 2416 Willow Street Pike, 3 miles south of Lancaster on Route 222, Lancaster, PA 17603; (800) 444–1714 or (717) 464–2711. Smorgasbord-style meals featuring meats fresh from their own butcher shop, homemade soups, and excellent desserts. The country fried chicken is a classic. Moderate.

Mount Joy

Groff's Farm Restaurant, 650 Pinkerton Road, Mount Joy, PA 17552; (717) 653–2048. Upscale Pennsylvania Dutch cooking has earned this restaurant national acclaim. You can order a la carte or family-style. Moderate to expensive. Open Friday, Saturday, and some holidays.

Rocky Acre Farm Bed and Breakfast, 1020 Pinkerton Road, Mount Joy, PA 17552; (717) 653–4449. Kid-friendly 200-year-old stone farmhouse with generous-size rooms, pettable animals, and lots of outdoor activities for families. Hearty farmer's breakfast included. Rates range from $95 per room (sleeps up to five people) to $149 for a two-bedroom apartment (sleeps seven).

Strasburg

Iron Horse Inn, 135 East Main Street, Strasburg, PA 17579; (717) 687–6362. The sign outside the door says NO DYSPEPTICS ALLOWED. So bring a good appetite and sense of humor when you visit this rustic-on-the-outside, casually elegant-on-the-inside spot for lunch or dinner. Moderate to expensive.

Strasburg Country Store & Creamery, 1 West Main Street, Centre Square, Strasburg, PA 17579; (717) 687–0766. From the moment you step inside, you can smell the waffles that are constantly being baked for cones and bowls to hold the store's fabulous homemade ice cream.

Limestone Inn Bed and Breakfast, 33 East Main Street, Strasburg, PA 17579; (800) 278–8392 or (717) 687–8392. Innkeepers Richard and Denise Walker are charming. And their 200-plus-year-old home with six guest rooms is a reflection of their personalities. Full breakfast is included. Rates range from $79 to $119 per night.

Red Caboose Lodge, Route 741 east, Strasburg, PA 17579; (717)

687–5000. Real railroad cabooses have been converted into motel rooms for couples and families. Prices vary by type of caboose, time of week, and time of year.

For More Information

Pennsylvania Dutch Convention and Visitors Bureau; (800) 324–1518 or (717) 299–8901; www.padutchcountry.com.

Harrisburg and Hershey, Pennsylvania

State Capital, World Capital

2 Nights

Only 13 miles apart in central Pennsylvania lie two capitals—one built on handshakes, the other on kisses. On weekdays, Harrisburg is a sea of suits bustling to and from meetings and sessions where laws are hammered out and enacted through processes that can run the gamut from filibuster to negotiation. In Hershey the atmosphere seems much more laid-back, but the chocolate perfume that fills the air is a sweet reminder that this town is hard at work producing confections for the world.

☐ Handshakes
☐ Kisses
☐ Skating Bears
☐ Senators at Bat

As industrious as both these capitals are, they know how to play as hard as they work. No matter what time of year you go, there's never a lack of fun, whether your idea of a good time is riverside recreation, sky-high amusement rides, or sports on the green, diamond, or rink. You can also have some truly painless learning experiences as you follow a law from proposal to enactment and see the chocolate-making process from the perspective of a cocoa bean.

This is a great family escape, especially in these hectic times when everyone seems to be on a different schedule and time together is at a premium. And, who knows, the kids might be so moved by this family bonding experience that they may shower you with kisses even sweeter than those that come in the silver foil wrappers.

Day 1 / Morning

Harrisburg is nearly two hours due west of Philadelphia. To get there, take the Schuylkill Expressway (I–76) west to the Pennsylvania Turnpike. You'll be on the turnpike for about 81 miles when you'll come to I–283. Go north on 283, then north again on I–83 for a total of about 6 miles. Then go west on Route 22 for about 3 miles into Harrisburg.

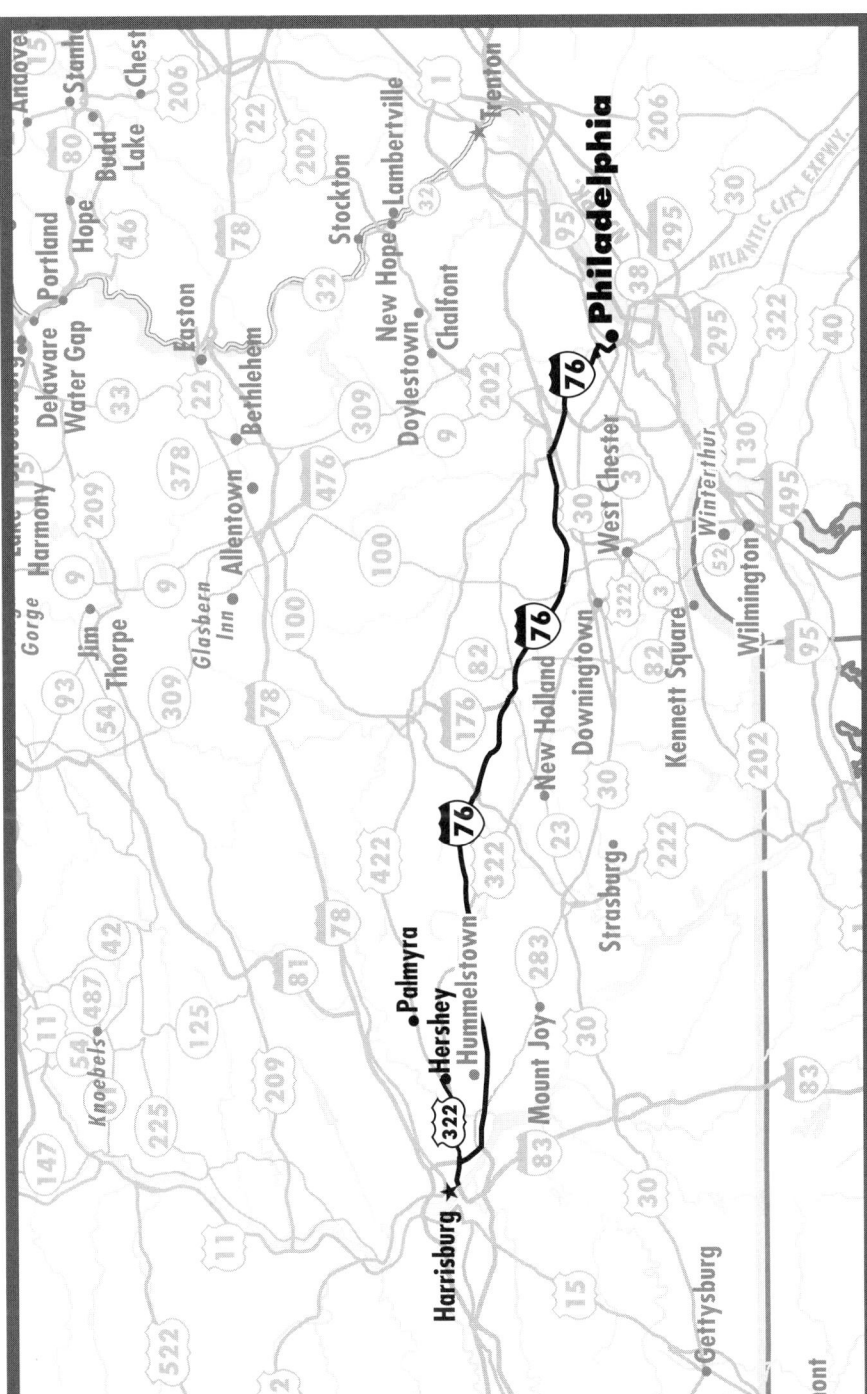

You can't miss the **State Capitol Building** at Third and State Streets (800–868–7672); it's the magnificent Italian Renaissance–style structure on top of the hill. This is a must-visit site not only because of its significance as Pennsylvania's seat of government, but also because it is one of the most awe-inspiring structures in the state, with its soaring 272-foot-high vaulted domes modeled after St. Peter's Basilica in Rome and its sweeping staircase inspired by the one at the Paris Opera. At its dedication in 1906, President Theodore Roosevelt called it "the handsomest building I ever saw." There are also splendid collections of art and sculpture, including dramatic wall murals and ceramic tiles created by Henry Mercer of Doylestown depicting Pennsylvania history and significant symbols. Free forty-minute guided and self-guided tours encompassing the rotunda, senate, house, and supreme court are available every half-hour Monday through Friday 8:30 A.M.–4:00 P.M., Saturday and Sunday at 9:00 and 11:00 A.M. and 1:00 and 3:00 P.M. only. After the tour, be sure to stop by the **Capitol Welcome Center,** a worthy destination on its own with eighteen interactive audiovisual exhibits on the history of Pennsylvania and the operation of its state government.

Afternoon

LUNCH: Broad Street Market, Third and Verbeke Streets in downtown Harrisburg, PA 17102; (717) 236–7923. From Tuesday through Saturday, you can join the locals for lunch at any one of the ethnic and eclectic food establishments housed in the two historic buildings that make up this complex. You'll find everything from Jamaican curried goat to Vietnamese soup, and from vegetarian and vegan specialties to a Pacific Rim cheeseburger! Prices are inexpensive, especially for a culinary trip around the world. On summer afternoons, there are free lunchtime music concerts at the market, too. Open Tuesday and Wednesday 9:00 A.M.–3:00 P.M., Thursday and Friday 7:00 A.M.–5:00 P.M., Saturday until 4:00 P.M.

With four floors of exhibits and activities, the **State Museum of Pennsylvania** (Third and North Streets across the street from the capitol, Harrisburg, PA 17108; 717–787–4980) traces the state's history and heritage, literally from the earth's beginning to the present, through archaeological artifacts, minerals, art, animal dioramas, and industrial and technological innovations. It has a wonderful planetarium, too. Open Tuesday through Saturday 9:00 A.M.–5:00 P.M., Sunday noon–5:00 P.M. Free.

In the spring, summer, and fall, the place to be on a beautiful afternoon is **City Island,** Harrisburg's playground located just offshore (1,000 yards) from the downtown area. You can get there by car over the Market Street Bridge or by foot or bike over the Walnut Street Bridge. Until 1987 this island in the Susquehanna River was merely sixty-three blighted acres of wasteland. Now it is a vibrant and growing recreation area with old-fashioned amusements, water sports, quaint shops, and fun-food concessions. Try the eighteen holes on the elaborately landscaped mini golf course at **Water Golf** (717–232–8533); open seven days a week from April through October. Prices are $5.00 for adults, $4.00 for seniors and children five to twelve, free for children four and under.

At **Riverside Stadium** the **Harrisburg Senators** Class AA minor league baseball team and affiliate of the Montreal Expos (717–231–4444) plays from April to September. Box seats are $8.00, reserved seats are $6.00, and general admission is $5.00 for adults and $3.00 for children under twelve and seniors over sixty. You can rent a paddleboat or other small craft if you want to ply the river under your own power, or you can board the *Pride of the Susquehanna* (717–234–6500), an authentic riverboat that offers forty-five-minute scenic cruises and two-hour dinner cruises from May to October. Cost for the forty-five-minute cruise is $4.95 for adults, $3.00 for children three to twelve, free for children two and under.

Evening

Here's a bit of local wisdom—the best scenic overlook, with the most beautiful views of the capitol, City Island, the parks, and other sites is from the cafeteria on the seventh floor of the Harrisburg Hospital on South Front Street. For dining, however, I would recommend the following spot.

DINNER: Passage to India, 525 South Front Street, Harrisburg, PA 17108; (717) 233–1202. If you like Indian food—or even if you've been dying for a chance to try it—this easygoing restaurant is just the place to enjoy a wide selection of authentic delights. Succulent tandooris, heavenly vegetarian creations, saffron-scented rice, mango-lassi shakes, and light-as-air native breads make it a delicious adventure. Prices are inexpensive to moderate. The all-you-can-eat lunch buffet ($7.99 weekdays, $9.99 Sunday) is a great bargain.

LODGING: The Hen-Apple, 409 South Lingle Avenue, Palmyra, PA 17078; (717) 838–8282.

On to Hershey and your night's lodging. From Route 22 in Harrisburg, drive 3 miles east until you come to I–83; take I–83 south for another 3 miles until you come to Route 322. As you approach Hershey, Route 322 will bear off toward Ephrata. Keep going straight—the road will now be called Route 422 and will go directly into town. The total trip should take somewhere under twenty minutes.

When you get to Hershey (you'll be on Chocolate Avenue), roll down your window and take a deep breath. On warm summer nights, you can smell heaven. And while the streets may not be paved with chocolate, they seem to be illuminated by it as giant Hershey Kisses perch on top of the streetlamps, their familiar white tags dancing in the breeze.

Your bed-and-breakfast is located in Palmyra, a tiny town right outside Hershey, so you still have about 2 miles to go before you sleep. Start counting the traffic lights when you get to the Hershey Motor Lodge on your right. At traffic light number six, you will pass the Hershey Chocolate Factory on your left; keep going until you come to light number eight, where you will turn right onto South Lingle Avenue—there will be a minimart with gas pumps on the opposite corner as you turn. Travel ½ mile on South Lingle until you come to a huge white house with a white retaining wall, a picket fence, and the welcoming glow of candles in the window.

The Hen-Apple, tucked away on a quiet residential street, is the home of Flo and Harold Eckert, and a wonderful, warm home it is. There's nothing stuffy about this 1825 Georgian-style farmhouse turned bed-and-breakfast with its lovely hand-stenciled walls and ceiling; lighthearted mixture of Victorian and country colors and furnishings; and mix of antiques, family heirlooms, and just plain fun stuff. The guest rooms range from whimsical to unabashedly romantic. The house is situated on two acres of greens and gardens—Flo's pride and joy—which explode in vibrant colors in spring and summer and provide fresh herbs for her cooking year-round. Room rates are $75 to $95 per night double occupancy. A very special continental breakfast (really, like most people's full breakfast) is served weekdays; an even more lavish spread is served on Sunday.

Day 2 /Morning

BREAKFAST: The Hen-Apple. Flo calls her breakfast continental, but don't expect merely toast and coffee. You can smell her fresh baking as soon as you get anywhere near the kitchen. She loves to whip up surprises (especially of the chocolate variety), so I won't give away any of her secrets. But come hungry. You won't want to miss a thing.

In 1894 a poor central Pennsylvania farm boy turned self-made businessman named Milton Snavely Hershey perfected a formula for smooth and creamy milk chocolate. From there he developed the Hershey Bar, which became an American icon and international industry. To accommodate his growing workforce, he also built a town.

Today much of the town's employment and a great many of its attractions continue to be linked, in one way or another, to the chocolate factory with the words HERSHEY'S COCOA formed in shrubbery on its front lawn. So it is only fitting that this is where we begin today's activities.

Although the factory tour at the **Hershey Chocolate World Visitor Center** (800 Park Boulevard, Hershey, PA 17033; 717–534–4900) is simulated, it's as close to the real thing as you're going to get. Like a theme-park ride, it is creative and colorful as you ride along in your own automated craft, sharing the journey of a cocoa bean from harvest to Hershey Bar and learning some of the secrets of chocolate making along the way. You'll be impressed to learn that Hershey's is the largest chocolate factory in the world, capable of making more than twenty-five million of its famous kisses each day in its more than two-million-square-foot facility. There's also a sweet little reward at the end of the tour. The tour is free, but for a $4.95 (adults), or $3.95 (children three to twelve) ticket, you can also see the **Hershey Really Big 3D Show**, a 30-minute interactive musical experience, in Chocolate World's 250-seat state-of-the-art theater. The largest part of the visitor center is devoted to sales of the products themselves, from the ubiquitous branded bars to the various members of the Reese's peanut butter branch of the family. Open seven days a week year-round; hours vary by month and season.

Once you've stocked up on your lifetime supply of chocolate, it's time to hit the teeth-clenching speed spirals, stomach-churning loops, and acrophobia-inducing heights of nearby **Hersheypark** (100 Hersheypark Drive, Hershey, PA 17033; 800–HERSHEY or 717–534–3900). With more than fifty-five rides and attractions, including a 90-foot-high, 360-degree looping steel coaster; a 100-foot-tall Ferris wheel; a superbig, superhigh water ride ominously named Tidal Force; and Storm Runner, a roller coaster with a 180-foot drop, there's plenty to keep the whole family amused for hours and dizzy for days. For kiddies (and those adults who find their rides more amusing), there are twenty just-the-right-size-and-speed rides, including one of the oldest operating carousels in America (circa 1919). Live entertainment; parades; seal, dolphin, and sea lion shows; and giant-size schmoozing Hershey Bar and Kiss–costumed characters round out the impressive array of attractions spread throughout this 110-acre park. May through September, gates open at 10:00 A.M.; days and hours vary by season. Regular admission (nine to fifty-four years old) is $35.95; for juniors (ages three to eight) and seniors (fifty-five and over) it is $19.95; free for children two and under.

Afternoon

LUNCH: Hershey Pantry, 801 East Chocolate Avenue, Hershey, PA 17033; (717) 533–7505. This is such a popular spot that lines frequently stretch out the door, so come early or late if you can. In this lace-trimmed tearoom environment, you might expect dainty portions. Far from it. The breakfasts, lunches, and dinners are beyond generous, the desserts big enough for four, and the prices inexpensive for daytime meals, mostly moderate for dinner.

After the wild rides of Hersheypark, it's a good time to seek a little serenity at **Hershey Gardens,** 170 Hotel Road, Hershey, PA 17033 (717–534–3492). It's only a short drive east on Hersheypark Drive to Hotel Road, where you'll turn left and follow the signs to the gardens. The centerpiece for this twenty-three-acre Eden, which was begun in 1937 for Milton Hershey, is its collection of 7,000 roses representing 275 varieties. This and other seasonal flowering annual displays make the gardens an inviting retreat from April to October. The **Butterfly House,** the largest indoor habitat of its kind in the state, features twenty-five different North American varieties of these colorful beauties (open mid-June to September daily 9:00 A.M.–6:00 P.M.), and the Children's Garden has nearly thirty themed gardens. Admission is $7.00 for adults (sixteen to sixty-one), $6.50 for seniors (sixty-two and over), $4.00 for youths (three to fifteen), free for children under three.

A worthwhile side trip will take you a short distance from Hershey Gardens to the old **Session House of Derry Presbyterian Church** (248 East Derry Road), a glass-enclosed 1732 cabin of hand-hewn logs that housed the first school ever to be held in this part of frontier America. Adjacent is a cemetery where the earliest grave is marked 1735 and where at least forty Revolutionary War soldiers are buried. To get there, take a right as you exit Hersheypark onto Hotel Road, then a left onto Front Street. Front Street will intersect Hersheypark Drive, but keep going straight—the road will now be called Park Avenue. When you reach the intersection of Park Avenue and East Derry Road, turn left.

For an unforgettable antiquing foray (or, more accurately, marathon) visit the more than 250 dealers at **Ziegler's in the Country** (Route 743, right off of Route 322, 3 miles south of Hershey, PA 17033; 717–533–1662) and its sister **Ziegler's Antique Mall** (717–533–7990) 3½ miles southeast on Route 743. No matter what age you are, you'll find lots of familiar collectibles from your childhood—and depending on what age you are, they may be classified as antiques or as "vintage" items. Visit both locations for maximum impact and selection of everything from home furnishings and garden fountains to matchbooks and Pez dispensers to baseball cards and Bobbsey Twins books.

DINNER: **Catherine's at Spinner's,** 845 East Chocolate Avenue, Hershey, PA 17033; (717) 533–9050. If you're looking for a romantic dinner spot, this is it. Intriguing appetizers might include roasted fennel pierogies and mussels with hazelnut butter. The sophisticated entrees might include a signature creation of beef tournedos stuffed with crabmeat and sun-dried tomato pesto; boneless chicken breast filled with lobster and brie; and New York strip steak with baby grapes topped with cabernet sauce and Roquefort cheese. Expensive.

While some small towns roll up their sidewalks and go to sleep soon after dark, Hershey isn't one of them. From October through mid-April the **Hershey Bears,** one of the nation's oldest continuously operating American Hockey League teams, plays its home games at **Giant Center,** 950 West Hersheypark Drive, Hershey, PA 17033 (717–534–3911).

LODGING: Hen-Apple.

Day 3 / Morning

BREAKFAST: Hen-Apple.

Before you leave Hershey, treat yourself to one more chocolaty indulgence—one that will really make you feel good because it's totally noncaloric. At the **Spa at the Hotel Hershey** (100 Hotel Road, Hershey, PA 17033), you can immerse yourself from head to toe in such sweet sensations as the signature whipped cocoa bath, chocolate fondue wrap, cocoa butter scrub, and chocolate mud hydrotherapy. A wide range of other non-chocolate-based treatments is also available, including manicures, pedicures, massages, facials, and hair and makeup services. Treatment prices range from $25 for a Hershey Rain Shower to $145 for a stone, cocoa, or deep tissue massage. Spa packages begin at $115 for 1½ hours to $340 for five hours. Day spa guests may also participate in a variety of fitness services, including classes in yoga, tai chi, and aerobics, nature walks, personal training sessions, and fitness assessments, to name a few. Call for hours and reservations; (717) 520–5888.

Afternoon

LUNCH: Breads N' Cheese of Hershey, 243 West Chocolate Avenue, Hershey, PA 17033; (717) 533–4546. This cozy European-style bakery and cafe serves great homemade soups, quiches, specialty pocket sandwiches, and salads, as well as oven-fresh desserts to die for. Take home some of the twenty-five styles of freshly baked breads, international cheeses, and pâtés. And did I mention pastries? Inexpensive.

To return to Philadelphia, take Route 743 for 1 mile south to Route 322; travel east on 322 for 14 miles until you come to Route 72. Go south on 72 for 2 miles until you come to the Pennsylvania Turnpike. Take the turnpike going east for 61 miles until you get to the Schuylkill Expressway (I–76); then head east on the expressway for 22 miles into Philadelphia.

There's More

The Whitaker Center for Science and the Arts, 222 Market Street, Harrisburg, PA 17101; (717) 214–ARTS. More than 200 interactive exhibits focus on a range of scientific disciplines and subjects, while live theatrical performances bring facts and theories to life. IMAX theater admission is separate. Monday through Saturday 9:30 A.M.–5:00 P.M., opens Sunday at 11:30 A.M. Adults, $7.75; seniors and students, and children $6.25.

Fort Hunter Mansion and Park, 5300 North Front Street, Harrisburg, PA 17110; (717) 599–5751. Restorations, exhibits, and demonstrations bring the nineteenth century to life at this wonderful mansion situated on thirty-five acres of parkland on the banks of the Susquehanna River. The park is open daily 8:00 A.M.–dusk. Mansion tours May through December Tuesday through Saturday 10:00 A.M.–4:30 P.M., Sunday noon–4:30 P.M. Admission is $4.00 adults, $3.00 seniors, and $2.00 students.

West Hanover Winery, 7646 Jonestown Road, Harrisburg, PA 17112; (717) 652–3711. You could visit this winery in the hills just for the scenery, but don't forget to taste some of owner George Kline's unique blueberry, sour cherry, berry, and apple varieties. Open Tuesday through Thursday noon–6:30 P.M., Friday noon–8:00 P.M., Saturday noon–5:00 P.M.

Hershey Museum, 170 Hersheypark Drive, Hershey, PA 17033; (717) 534–3439. Through photographs, artifacts, and colorful exhibits, this museum chronicles Milton Hershey's struggle to establish his chocolate business and build a town. Included are his extensive collections of Pennsylvania German and Native American art and artifacts. Open 10:00 A.M.–5:00 P.M. Labor Day to Memorial Day; until 6:00 P.M. Memorial Day to Labor Day. Admission for adults (sixteen to sixty-one) is $6.50; for seniors (sixty-two and over), $6.00; for youths (three to fifteen), $3.00.

Hershey Theatre, 15 Caracas Avenue, Hershey, PA 17033; (717) 534–3405. From September through April, concerts, dance programs, Broadway musicals, and classic dramas starring national and world headliners perform in this exquisite venue with its sculpted, painted, gold, and tile ceilings; marble walls; Italian lava rock floors; and formal arches. The box office is open Monday through Friday 10:00 A.M.–5:00 P.M. (10:00 A.M. to curtain time on performance days).

Hershey Symphony, (717) 522–8449. This excellent orchestra performs October through May at the Hershey Theatre. Tickets are $12.00 for adults, $10.00 for senior citizens, and $5.00 for students.

ZooAmerica North American Wildlife Park, Park Avenue, Hershey, PA 17033; (717) 534–3860 (Route 743, between Chocolate Avenue and Hersheypark Drive). Originally begun in the early 1900s to display Milton Hershey's private animal collection, this totally redesigned, eleven-acre walk-through sanctuary brings together mammals, reptiles, birds, fish, and plants from all over the continent. Open year-round, hours vary seasonally. If you purchase the one-price admission plan from Hersheypark, you can simply cross the bridge inside the park. Otherwise, admission is $7.00 for persons thirteen and over, $6.50 for seniors, $5.75 for children three to twelve, and free for children under two.

Trolley Works, Chocolate and Cocoa Avenues, Hershey, PA 17033; (717) 533–3000. See the sights of the town from an old-fashioned trolley complete with singing conductor. Tours depart every fifteen minutes from the front of Hershey's Chocolate World. Tickets are $9.95 for adults, $9.45 seniors, $5.95 for children three to twelve, and free for children two and under. Seating is limited, so you might want to make advance reservations during peak summer and Christmas seasons.

Golf. Call 800–HERSHEY for information about the town's one eighteen-hole and two nine-hole public golf courses. The Hotel Hershey also has two eighteen-hole private courses for guests.

Special Events

January. Pennsylvania Farm Show, Farm Show Complex, Harrisburg, PA 17110; (717) 787–5373. Since 1851, this annual five-day showcase of farm animals, equipment, food, agricultural demonstrations, and hundreds of exhibits has been drawing visitors from all over the East Coast. Free.

March. Pennsylvania National Arts and Crafts Show, Farm Show Complex, Harrisburg, PA 17110; (717) 796–0531. Demonstrations and original contemporary and traditional crafts by more than 320 of the nation's finest juried artisans from more than thirty-five states.

July. American MusicFest, City Island, Harrisburg, PA 17101; (717) 255–3020. The largest celebration of its kind in the region, featuring four days of food, rides, concerts, jet-ski and boat races, Civil War reenactments, and a huge fireworks show. July Fourth weekend.

September. Kipona Celebration, Riverfront Park and City Island, Harrisburg, PA 17101; (717) 255–3020. One of the oldest inland water-front festivals in the nation, with race competitions, food, arts and crafts, theater, concerts, games, and rides. Labor Day weekend.

October. Antique Auto Club of America Fall Meet and Flea Market, Hersheypark, Hershey, PA 17033; (717) 534–1910. This annual event attracts antique- and classic-car collectors and aficionados from all over the world.

October. Hersheypark Balloon Fest, near Hershey's Chocolate World, Hershey, PA 17033; (800) HERSHEY. Dozens of hot-air balloons fill the sky as the crowd below enjoys pay-as-you-ride amusements and hayrides, live entertainment, demonstrations, craft vendors, and lots of food. Free admission.

October. Pennsylvania National Horse Show, Farm Show Complex, Harrisburg, PA 17110; (717) 975–3677. One thousand horses and top international riders compete for prestigious titles and large cash awards.

Mid-November to late December. Hersheypark Christmas Candylane, Hersheypark, Hershey, PA 17033; (717) 534–3900. No admission charge. Pay-as-you-ride amusements, live reindeer, and a million twinkling lights.

Other Recommended Restaurants and Lodgings

Hershey

Carla's Cucina, 1144 East Chocolate Avenue, Hershey, PA 17033; (717) 534–2099. Italian fare in a pretty and lively setting. Specialties include pizzas and chicken cerubi (in Marsala wine with mushrooms, peppers, and hot Italian sausage). Prices range from moderate to expensive.

Spinner's Inn, 845 East Chocolate Avenue, Hershey, PA 17033; (717) 533–9157. This inn offers reasonable prices and some very nice amenities such as a heated pool, game room, and free continental breakfast. Rates range from $49 to $89 off-season, $69 to $159 peak season.

Hotel Hershey, Hotel Road, Hershey, PA 17033; (717) 533–2171. This is a beautiful full-service resort hotel with elegantly appointed rooms, indoor and outdoor swimming pools, whirlpool, sauna, exercise room, tennis courts, cycling and nature trails, tobogganing, and cross-country skiing. Room rates range from $99 to $329, depending on the season. Meal plans and special package plans are also available.

Milton Motel, 1733 East Chocolate Avenue, Hershey, PA 17033; (717) 533–4533. This family-run operation is a very happy medium between the anonymity of a chain and the intimacy of a bed-and-breakfast. Heated pool, discounted Hersheypark tickets, and free coffee in the morning. Prices (double occupancy) range from $49 off-season to $149 in season, $99 to $299 for suites.

Pinehurst Inn Bed & Breakfast, 50 Northeast Drive, Hershey, PA 17033; (717) 533–2603. This beautiful brick home was built in 1930 by Milton Hershey. Summer rates with private bath are $85 per night, $75 in fall and winter.

Harrisburg

Raspberries, Harrisburg Hilton, 1 North Second Street, Harrisburg, PA 17101; (717) 237–6419. Bountiful breakfast, lunch, and dinner buffets are real bargains.

Arches Restaurant, 4125 North Front Street (at exit I–81), Harrisburg, PA 17110; (717) 233–5479. Casual breakfasts, lunches, and dinners with a river view. Continental dinner menu specializes in fresh seafood, veal, and prime rib. Inexpensive breakfasts, moderate to expensive lunches and dinners.

Zephyr Express, 400 North Second Street, Harrisburg, PA 17101; (717) 257–1328. Casual California-style cuisine with gourmet pizzas, pastas, and specialty sandwiches. Inexpensive.

Campgrounds. Hershey Highmeadow Camp, 1200 Matlock Road, Hummelstown, PA 17036; (717) 566–0902. Nearly 300 open and shaded sites and rental cabins on fifty-five beautiful acres with many amenities. Free shuttle service to Hershey attractions, access to all Hershey golf courses, and other exclusive benefits. Prices vary by time of year and type of camping facility.

For More Information

Hershey Capital Region Visitors Bureau; (800) PA-PULSE or (717) 231–7788; www.hersheycapitalregion.com.

Hershey Information Center; (800) HERSHEY (recorded message); www.800hershey.com.

Gettysburg, Pennsylvania

Eloquent Fields, Memorable Addresses

2 Nights

Before the summer of 1863, no one could have guessed that this little rural south-central Pennsylvania town would become a focal point and gathering place for generations of historians, students, military leaders, armchair generals, and visitors from around the world. It was a chance encounter that brought General Robert E. Lee's 75,000-man Army of Northern Virginia and General George Meade's 97,000-man Army of the Potomac together for three days of pitched battle that would decimate both forces and prove to be the turning point of the Civil War.

- ☐ Living History
- ☐ Spirited Evenings
- ☐ Civil War Antiques

As a town, Gettysburg has accepted its permanent place in history—as well as in the international spotlight—with grace, dignity, and a commitment to preserving the memories and humanity of the people who lived, fought, and died here. With monuments, museums, reenactments, and the telling of stories that have been passed down through local families for as many as six generations, this town has prevented the events of those three days in July from becoming merely forgotten statistics in some dusty history book. But the most compelling storyteller of all is the battlefield itself. In speaking so honestly and accurately about war, it presents the most powerful argument for peace.

Peak tourist months for Gettysburg are April through October; it is quietest in January and February. Locals suggest coming in November, when most sites are open and a number of special annual events take place.

HELPFUL HINTS: Unless you're a Civil War scholar, you may want to brush up on your history before your visit to Gettysburg. I recommend reading Michael Shaara's book *The Killer Angels,* or viewing the 1993 film *Gettysburg* or the Battle of Gettysburg segment of Ken Burns's *Civil War* series, both of which are available on video.

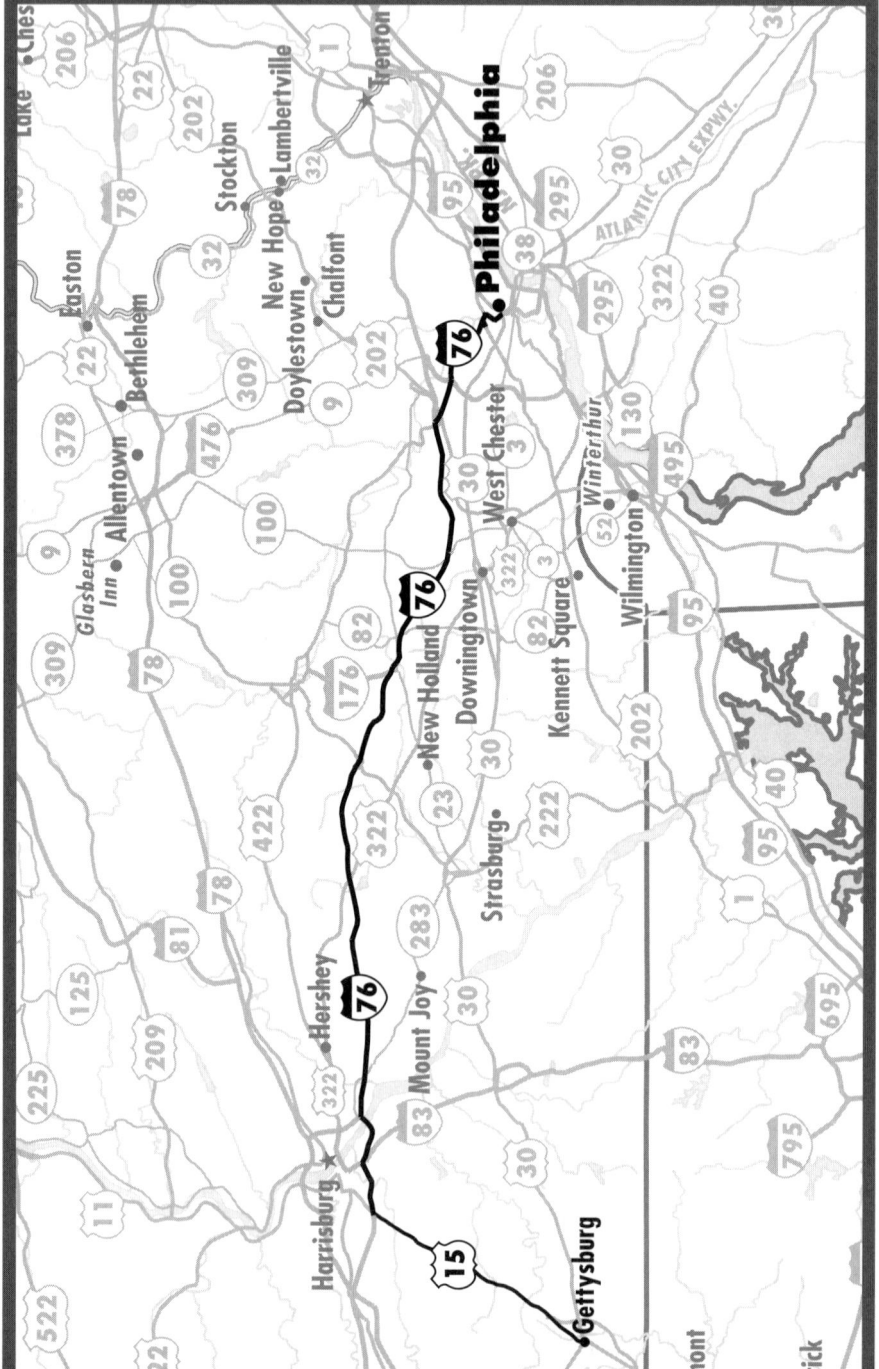

Day 1 / *Morning*

It takes about 2¾ to 3 hours to get to Gettysburg from Philadelphia. The quickest way is to take the Schuylkill Expressway (I–76) 22 miles west to the King of Prussia entrance to the Pennsylvania Turnpike. Travel west on the turnpike for about 92 miles to exit 236 (Gettysburg/Route 15); go south on Route 15 until you come to Route 30 west. Take Route 30 west for about 2 miles into Gettysburg.

The Battle of Gettysburg was not confined to the surrounding fields. Some of the heaviest fighting occurred right in the heart of town. For some insight into the lives of the people who lived with the battlefield in their backyard (and sometimes on their own doorsteps), pick up a self-guided walking tour map at the **Gettysburg Convention and Visitors Bureau,** located at 31 Carlisle Street, Gettysburg, PA 17325; (717–334–6274 or 800–337–5015). In addition to open-to-the-public sites, the map offers information on the historic background of many privately owned buildings that were transformed into makeshift hospitals and people who were literally and figuratively caught in the crossfire between the Union and Confederate troops. Signs throughout the town also mark the spots where incidents of interest and import took place. The Gettysburg Convention and Visitors Bureau is open 8:30 A.M.–5:00 P.M.

At 309 Baltimore Street stands a former family residence that was occupied by Confederate sharpshooters during some of the battle. Today the restored and authentically furnished **Schriver House** (717–337–2800) is an example of the powerful impact the war had on the everyday citizens who found themselves caught in the middle. Open April through October Monday through Saturday 10:00 A.M.–5:00 P.M., Sunday noon–5:00 P.M.; November through March, Friday through Monday noon–5:00 P.M. Admission $5.75 for adults, $3.95 for children six to twelve.

Amazingly enough, the bloody fighting that raged throughout the town claimed only one civilian casualty—a nineteen-year-old woman named Mary Virginia "Jennie" Wade. As you tour the **Jennie Wade House** (758 Baltimore Street, Gettysburg, PA 17325; 717–334–4100) with its hundreds of bullet and shell holes, the Talking Soldier tells of her tragic death after being hit by a stray bullet while baking bread for the Union Infantry. Open daily spring and fall 9:00 A.M.–5:00 P.M., until 9:00 P.M. in summer. Admission is $5.95 for adults, $3.50 for children.

While you're in the area, make sure you stop at **Dirty Billy's Hats** (430A Baltimore Street, Gettysburg, PA 17325; 717–334–3200), where

Hollywood comes when it needs authentic reproductions of historic headwear from any time in history. That's Billy's work you saw in the movie *Gettysburg*. If you don't find what you're looking for at the shop or in his catalog, Billy can probably handcraft the hat of your dreams from a photo within four to six weeks. Open Friday through Monday 11:00 A.M.–6:00 P.M.

Afternoon

L U N C H :   The Pub & Restaurant, northwest corner of Lincoln Square, Gettysburg, PA 17325; (717) 334–7100. Grab a seat by a window so that you can watch the action on the square as you enjoy one of the menu's many burger, chicken breast, or deli sandwich variations, salads, or soups. A favorite local spot for lunch or dinner. Inexpensive.

Half a block south of Lincoln Square at 30 Baltimore Street, Gettysburg, PA 17325, is the **Antique Center of Gettysburg** (717–337–3669), one of the largest and most comprehensive antiques stores in the area with one hundred showcases displaying all manner of collectibles, including Native American and Western artifacts, international militaria from all wars, and Abraham Lincoln memorabilia. Open Monday, Wednesday, Thursday, and Saturday 10:00 A.M.–6:00 P.M., Friday until 8:00 P.M., Sunday noon–6:00 P.M.

From the square, travel 8 blocks west on Route 30 (Chambersburg Street) to **Lee's Headquarters and Museum** (717–334–3141), on historic Seminary Ridge. From this strategically situated house (then a private home owned by noted statesman Thaddeus Stevens), General Robert E. Lee and his staff developed battle plans for the three-day struggle. Today it is filled with an extensive collection of Confederate and Union military and medical equipment, period artifacts, and rare photos and documents. If you really want to immerse yourself in history, the second floor is available for overnight accommodations. Open mid-March through mid-November, daily 9:00 A.M.–5:00 P.M.; extended summer hours. Admission: adults $2.00; children six and older $1.00; free for children under six.

About 1 mile from Lincoln Square along Route 134 south is the entrance to the **Gettysburg National Cemetery** (97 Taneytown Road, adjacent to the National Park Service Information Center; 717–334–1124). Here rest nearly 7,000 of Gettysburg's esteemed dead spanning two centuries, including 3,500 from the Civil War and more than 3,300 American soldiers and dependents from subsequent wars. Stop by the information center for an excellent self-guided walking tour map and visit the site (marked by a monument) where President Abraham Lincoln delivered his famous address. The Soldier's National Monument, surrounded by its huge semicircle of graves, silently pays tribute to those who sacrificed their lives. Open dawn to dusk.

Next door to the main entrance of the cemetery is one of the town's oldest, yet still most consistently popular, attractions, the **Hall of Presidents** (Baltimore Street, Gettysburg, PA 17325; 717–334–5717). Here, painstakingly detailed wax figures of all the American presidents, beginning with George Washington, take turns telling in their own words the story of how this nation developed over the centuries. Be sure to take note of the magnificent background murals, painted by contemporary artist Charles Morganthaler. Also on display is the famous Smithsonian Collection of America's First Ladies, dressed in reproductions of their inaugural gowns. Open spring and fall daily 9:00 A.M.– 5:00 P.M., summer until 9:00 P.M. $5.95 for adults, $3.50 for children.

For some of the finest Civil War art, visit **Gallon Historical Art** (9 Steinwehr Avenue, Gettysburg, PA 17325; 717–334–0430), where the complete works of renowned Gettysburg artist-in-residence Dale Gallon are on display, and original oil paintings and limited-edition prints are available for sale. Open 10:00 A.M.–8:00 P.M. Friday and Saturday, until 5:00 P.M. Sunday through Thursday in-season; 10:00 A.M.–4:00 P.M. off-season.

Evening

DINNER: Blue Parrot Bistro, 35 Chambersburg Street, Gettysburg, PA 17325; (717) 337–3739. Enjoy continental fare in an easygoing setting at one of the hottest restaurants in town. Among the specialties on the moderately priced menu are a Bistro Mixed Grill with French pork chop, venison steak, and lamb chop topped with white-wine shallot demi-glacé; sautéed crab cakes with ginger lime sauce; and roasted summer vegetables served over garlic polenta. It's open for lunch, too.

Obviously, Gettysburg is a town deeply devoted to preserving and paying tribute to the memory of Abraham Lincoln. But if you really want to get an idea of what the flesh-and-blood man was like, stop at **The Battle Theater** (571 Steinwehr Avenue, Gettysburg, PA 17325; 717–334–6049) to see if you can catch a performance of *Mr. Lincoln Returns to Gettysburg.* This forty-five-minute, live one-man show stars James A. Getty, a nationally acclaimed actor who has been portraying the president throughout the United States and Canada since 1977. Performances are offered on a seasonal basis; reservations are recommended.

LODGING: Doubleday Inn, 104 Doubleday Avenue, Gettysburg, PA 17325; (717) 334–9119. To get to your lodging (the only bed-and-breakfast on the Gettysburg battlefield) from Lincoln Square, take Carlisle Street north to Lincoln Street; turn left on Lincoln. Make a right onto Cottage Avenue, which becomes Mummasburg Road in 1 block. From Mummasburg Road make a left onto Doubleday Avenue (National Park Service Auto Tour Stop No. 3). You'll drive past some monuments and the inn will be on your left. This beautiful 1929 home is situated on Oak Hill, where during the first day of battle, a seriously outnumbered Brigadier General Abner Doubleday (the same man who, for many years, was believed to have invented baseball) held off Confederate forces, allowing the Union troops to regroup and gain a stronghold position in the field.

Today the inn offers a panoramic view of the town and battlefield. Innkeepers Charles and Ruth Anne Wilcox have furnished their home in an English country style accented with Civil War–era antiques, art, and memorabilia. On selected evenings the Wilcoxes invite a local historian to entertain guests with historically accurate wartime accounts and lively discussions. Rates range from $95 (shared bath) to $130 (private bath). A full breakfast is included. Note: Early-to-bedders should be aware that the floorboards in this charming old house may groan underfoot a bit, but the ambience, amenities, and warm hospitality more than make up for a few night noises.

Day 2 / Morning

BREAKFAST: Doubleday Inn. When was the last time you had breakfast by candlelight? The experience is delicious, just like the caramel (or apple) French toast, sausage and egg casserole, or other house specialties that are cooked up by your hosts.

There are many ways you can tour the **Gettysburg National Military Park** (aka the Battlefield). A number of them are discussed in the "There's More" section of this chapter. One great way is to ask your innkeeper to arrange for a tour in your own car with a licensed battlefield guide at the wheel ($40 for one to six persons in a vehicle, $60 for seven to fifteen persons). I was lucky to get lifelong Gettysburg resident Terry Fox, who knows all the dates, names, and statistics you can handle, as well as the kind of colorful tidbits of information and local lore that add so much to a tour.

Before you embark on your field trip, I strongly recommend that you take advantage of the orientation activities and programs offered at the **National Military Park Visitor Center** (717–334–1124). For no charge you can see one of the world's largest collections of artifacts at the center's **Gettysburg Museum of the Civil War.** The 3-D Electric Map presents a thirty-minute light-and-sound show illustrating troop movement from the first volley to the final retreat. Shows every day, 8:15 A.M.–4:25 P.M. Admission: $4.00 for adults, $3.00 for seniors and youths seven to sixteen, and free for children under seven. At the nearby **Cyclorama Center,** you'll see a 360-foot-long circular oil-on-canvas painting (circa 1884) depicting Pickett's charge, accompanied by a stirring sound-and-light show. Admission is $4.00 for adults, $3.00 for children seven and up; under seven free.

Gettysburg National Military Park looks very much like it did in 1863. As you travel from site to site with such infamous names as Little Round Top, the Devil's Den, and the Angle, you will encounter the same farms, orchards, fences, and rock walls that the soldiers did on those three infamous days in July. More than 51,000 soldiers were killed, wounded, or missing in action during the fighting, and today more than 1,400 monuments, markers, and memorials mark the spots on the 6,000-acre battlefield where they fought and fell. A particularly poignant stop is the **Eternal Light Peace Memorial,** where thousands gathered in 1938 to watch a former Union soldier and a former Confederate soldier come together to light the symbolic eternal flame.

Afternoon

LUNCH: Head left on Chambersburg Street to Route 30 west then 1½ miles on Route 30 to **Herr Tavern & Publick House** (900 Chambersburg Road, Gettysburg, PA 17325; 717–334–4332). Known for its Reuben sandwiches (everything from the corned beef to the dressing is homemade) on marble rye, this circa 1828 dining spot also offers fine American cuisine (expensive) for dinner along with very nice bed-and-breakfast lodging.

Head to the Gettysburg National Military Park Visitor Center, approximately 1 mile south of town on Taneytown Road (SR 134) and Steinwehr Avenue (US 15 business route) to catch the shuttle to the **Eisenhower National Historic Site,** the only private home ever owned by our thirty-fourth president and his wife, Mamie. During his two terms as president, Dwight D. Eisenhower used his Gettysburg farm for weekend retreats (it sometimes even served as the temporary White House). After his retirement he and Mamie moved here permanently and stayed until their deaths. The preserved farm, furnishings, and personal belongings honor and offer insight into the lives of this renowned couple. Open daily April through October 9:00 A.M.–4:00 P.M., closed Monday and Tuesday November through March. Admission is $7.00 for adults, $4.00 for youths thirteen to sixteen; $3.00 for children six to twelve.

Back in the downtown area, stop in at **Moonacre Ironworks & the Gettysburg Candle Shop** (62 Chambersburg Street; 717–337–9200) and try the devious little handmade wrought-iron puzzles with such ominous names as Satan's Stirrup and Blackbeard's Revenge. For something a little more traditional, see what seasonal delights crafters Dick and Carol Cole have whipped up for their **Fiddle Faddles Folk Art and Primitives** shop (54 Chambersburg Street; 717–334–8270).

Evening

DINNER: Dobbin House Tavern, 89 Steinwehr Avenue, Gettysburg, PA 17325; (717) 334–2100. Built in 1776 as a private family home, this building became one of the first stops north of the Mason-Dixon line on the Underground Railroad (the crawl space where the runaway slaves hid is part of the tiny free museum upstairs). It was also a hospital for soldiers from both the North and South after the nearby battle. Over 200 years later, the Dobbin House looks much the same, with its original native-stone walls, seven fireplaces, and hand-carved woodwork. Even the china and flatware used in the restaurant exactly match fragments unearthed during reexcavation of the cellar. Entrees range from moderate to expensive.

Many of the locals believe that the spirits of those who died on the Gettysburg Battlefield still roam the streets and haunt the houses by night. The **Ghosts of Gettysburg Candlelight Walking Tours** (271 Baltimore Street, Gettysburg, PA 17325; 717–337–0445) are based on generations-old accounts and tales dug up (so to speak) by Mark Nesbitt, author of the extremely popular *Ghosts of Gettysburg* series. Call for descriptions and times. Tours cost $6.00 to $6.50 for adults, free for children under seven. For hauntings of the indoor variety, head for the Farnsworth House (401 Baltimore Street; 717–334–8838). Descend the staircase into the stone cellar that is the **Civil War Mourning Theatre,** where you will listen to ghostly storytellers speak of restless souls and unexplainable phenomena. Call for times. $6.00 for adults, free for children.

LODGING: Doubleday Inn.

Day 3 / Morning

BREAKFAST: Doubleday Inn.

If the mention of another museum makes the kids groan, they'll change their tune when you take them to **Boyd's Bear Country,** located just south of town at 75 Cunningham Road, Gettysburg, PA 17325 (717–630–2600). It's promoted as "The World's Most Humongous Teddy Bear Store and Free Museum," and at 120,000 square feet and featuring some 70,000 bears, hares, moose, mice, cats, and other critters in five stories of elaborately designed displays, that may be an accurate description.

The free museum takes a tongue-in-jowl look at Boyd's Bear history. But the real attractions here are the teddy tableaux, including an "Enchanted Faerie Forest"; the hamlet of "Bearly Built Villages" with its 8-foot-tall mountain and working Lionel train display; "Kringle's Yuletide Hideaway"; and a life-size dollhouse. For some hands-on fun, there's a Make 'N Take Craft Center, where kids can dress and accessorize their own bear or, in season, families can create a country wreath. Open daily 10:00 A.M.–6:00 P.M.

LUNCH: Whether you've worked up a grizzly bear–size hunger or the cubs are just clambering for a little nibble, Boyd's has an eating option to appease any appetite. **Willie B. Bacon's Feed Truck** offers a wide variety of deli sandwiches, soups, stuffed potatoes, and salads. For a family-style meal, **Rufus, Dufus, and Daryl's Dinner Hall** serves comfort food with all the fixings. **The Patchbeary Fruit & Orchard Shack** whips up smoothies, fresh-fruit cups, homemade seasonal fruit cobblers, ice cream, and a heavenly caramel apple dessert topped with hot caramel and whipped cream. And **Sweetie Pie's Bearkery** brews mom-and-dad pleasing espresso drinks. All are inexpensive to moderately priced.

There's More

Battle Reenactments, Call for specific locations; (717) 338–1525. Major reenactments of encampments and battles, performances of period music, and demonstrations on domestic arts are highlights of this three-day event in July. Admission. Children get a reduced rate and youngsters under six are free. There are also numerous living-history events and demos at various sites throughout the year.

Historic Tours, 55 Steinwehr Avenue, Gettysburg, PA 17325; (717) 334–8000. Two-hour dramatized audio battlefield tours in a classic 1930s Yellowstone Park bus. $16.95 for adults, $11.00 for children.

Gettysburg Bicycle and Fitness, 307 York Street, Gettysburg, PA 17325; (717) 334–7791. Rent a built-for-comfort bike with distance-calculating handlebar-mounted computer to tour the battlefields. Rates are $7.00 hourly, $25.00 daily.

Battlefield Horseback Tour, National Riding Stable, Artillery Ridge Camping Resort, 610 Taneytown Road, Route 134, Gettysburg, PA 17325; (717) 334–1288. Two-hour tour on horseback and one-hour trail rides with a trail master for accomplished riders or novices are available. Call for times and prices.

Gettysburg Scenic Rail Tours, 106 North Washington Street, Gettysburg, PA 17325; (717) 334–6932. A variety of different options for seeing the countryside by rail, including the unique Fire Hall Dinner Trains, which take you on a 34-mile trip through the Blue Ridge Mountains and conclude with a chicken barbecue or ham dinner in a local fire hall. Call for schedules and rates.

Gettysburg Village Factory Stores, 1863 Gettysburg Village Drive, Gettysburg, PA 17325; (717) 337–9705. Bargain shopping meets entertainment at this seventy-plus-store complex modeled after a nineteenth-century "Main Street." Among the heavy hitters here are Adidas, Gap Outlet, Jones NY, KB Toy Liquidator, Pfaltzgraff, Vitamin World, and Zales Jewelers. For family fun, there are historic character greeters and street performers and music in the bandstand on weekends.

Land of Little Horses, Knoxlyn Road, 3 miles west of Gettysburg on Route 30, Gettysburg, PA 17325; (717) 334–7295. Animal lovers will find more than one hundred miniature horses and other fuzzy and furry friends to admire, applaud, and pet at this unusual attraction. Performances, nature areas, carriage museum, snack bar, petting farm, and menagerie. Open seven days a week, 10:00 A.M.–5:00 P.M. Memorial Day through August 30. Call for off-season hours. Admission is $7.00.

Habitat, 1–5 Steinwehr Avenue, Gettysburg, PA 17325; (717) 334–1218. Comprises three charming shops housed in adjacent historic buildings. **Habitat for Gifts** has rooms devoted to local crafts, Christmas collectibles,

Gettysburg is famous for its battlefield reenactments.

kitchen accessories, and cat-fancier delights, to name a few. ***Camelot for Kids of All Ages*** offers two floors filled with all manner of Gettysburg souvenirs, from caps and mugs to miniature cannons. And ***Stonehams Armory*** features replica weapons from the Civil, Revolutionary, and Indian Wars; Civil War books and art reproductions; and Pennsylvanian pottery and pewter ware.

Camping, Gettysburg KOA Campground, 20 Knox Road, Gettysburg, PA 17325; (717) 642–5713. Quiet wooded accommodations for tents and RVs with full-hookup sites, laundry and game rooms, heated pool, playground, and other amenities.

Artillery Ridge Camping Resort, 610 Taneytown Road, Gettysburg, PA 17325; (717) 334–1288. Tent and RV accommodations with hookups, free twenty-four-hour hot showers, laundry room.

Special Events

(Unless otherwise indicated, the contact telephone number for the following events is 800–337–5015.)

May. Annual Gettysburg Spring Bluegrass Festival, Granite Hill Campground, 6 miles west of Gettysburg on Route 116. Nonstop music from some of the country's best bluegrass music performers in a beautiful country setting.

May. Annual Gettysburg Outdoor Antique Show, downtown Gettysburg. More than 175 dealers from thirteen states line the downtown streets.

May. Annual Memorial Day Parade and Ceremonies. One of the oldest (more than 130 years) Memorial Day observances in the United States with a big parade and ceremony in Gettysburg National Cemetery.

June or July. Gettysburg Civil War Collectors Show. Sponsored by the Gettysburg Battlefield Preservation Association and held annually the last weekend in June, this event features original Civil War art, personal effects, weapons, documents, and books.

June/July. Gettysburg Civil War Heritage Days. Held annually the last weekend in June and first week in July, this event commemorates the Battle of Gettysburg with living-history encampments, battle reenactments, band concerts, Fourth of July program, and lectures series.

August. Gettysburg Annual Fall Bluegrass Festival; (717) 642–8749. Held annually the fourth weekend in August or the weekend before Labor Day. (See Spring Bluegrass Festival in May.)

September. Eisenhower World War II Weekend, Eisenhower National Historic Site. A living-history encampment featuring Allied soldiers, tanks, and military vehicles. Held annually the third weekend in September.

November. Anniversary of Lincoln's Gettysburg Address, Gettysburg National Cemetery. An annual observance with a wreath laying, celebrity speakers, brief memorial services, and other special programs sponsored by the Lincoln Fellowship of Pennsylvania. Always on November 19.

November. Remembrance Day. Held in conjunction with the Lincoln observance, this event honors those who died in the Civil War and other American conflicts. The day is marked with a parade and other special events throughout the town. Sponsored by the Sons of Union Veterans.

GETTYSBURG, PENNSYLVANIA 203

Other Recommended Restaurants and Lodgings

Cashtown

Historic Cashtown Inn, 1325 Old Route 30; (800) 367–1797 or (717) 334–9722. Commandeered by Confederate General A. P. Hill as his headquarters during the battle, this 1749 inn now serves such specialties as bourbon walnut beef medallions, seafood trilogy, and pesto scallops. Moderate. Overnight accommodations are also available.

Gettysburg

Gettysbrew Restaurant & Brewery, 248 Hunterstown Road (less than 2 miles from the square), Gettysburg, PA 17325; (717) 337–1001. During the war this was the site of one of the largest Confederate field hospitals. Now it is a lively place to bring the family for lunch or dinner. Try the signature beer-simmered sausage platter (varieties change daily). Other specialties that have appeared on the moderately priced, seasonal menu include smoked salmon and mushroom bisque, sandwiches on piegga bread (a honey-kissed focaccia), and horseradish chicken.

Historic Farnsworth House Restaurant & Inn, 401 Baltimore Street; (717) 334–8838. Authentically restored circa 1810 dining rooms decorated with oil paintings of Generals Meade and Lee, photos by renowned Civil War photographer Mathew Brady, and artifacts. Specializing in period fare such as game pie, peanut soup, and spoon bread. Children's menu. Moderate. Overnight accommodations (some haunted) are also available.

James Gettys Hotel, 27 Chambersburg Street; (717) 337–1334. This restored two-century-old hotel offers eleven amenity-filled suites from $125 to $145. Winter rates are also available.

Gettystown Inn, 89 Steinwehr Avenue; (717) 334–2100. An authentic Civil War–era home overlooking the site where Lincoln delivered his Gettysburg Address. Amenities include old-fashioned beds, hooked and Oriental rugs, and nineteenth-century antiques. Includes a full breakfast at the 1776 Dobbin House next door. Rates, including tax, range from $95 to $165 double occupancy.

Inns of the Gettysburg Area; (800) 587–2216 or (717) 624–1300. This bed-and-breakfast association is composed of twenty of the area's historic accommodations, all located within minutes of the battlefield. You tell them your specifications, they'll offer a variety of choices and let you know which ones are available on the dates you specify.

Gaslight Inn Bed & Breakfast, 35 East Middle Street; (717) 337–9100. Stately three-story brick house with elegantly appointed rooms (all with private baths, most with fireplaces) and old-fashioned front porch. Rates range from $120 to $175 per night in season, from $100 midweek in winter.

For More Information

Gettysburg Convention and Visitors Bureau; (800) 337–5015; www .gettysburgcvb.org.

New York City, New York

Delicious to the Core

2 Nights

Like a huge Great Dane, New York City can bowl you over with its expanse and unbridled energy. From the moment you merge into the crush of humanity that, day and night, flows up and down its sidewalks and, at a decidedly slower pace, its streets, you become part of that energy, too, as you eagerly make your way to one adventure after another.

☐ A Whole Lot of Everything . . .

☐ and More

Thanks to a brilliant marketing campaign, many people have come to think of New York as "the Big Apple." But a tour group I know of more aptly describes the city as "the Big Onion," made up of layers and layers of zesty flavors. Whether you choose to devour New York in big, random bites or to methodically savor it one delectable layer at a time, a three-day escape to this fabulous town is just enough to whet your appetite.

Day 1 / Morning

New York City is 98 driving miles and about two hours (due to almost certain traffic delays) northeast of Philadelphia. Quite frankly, the easiest and most efficient way to get to New York is by train, either on Amtrak (800–USA–RAIL) or the more economical SEPTA (215–580–7800). Once you arrive in the city, you can get around the way the locals do—on foot or via taxi (quick and reasonably priced) or by bus or subway (if you are comfortable with the routes). If you truly can't bear to be without your car, go east on Race Street across the Ben Franklin Bridge; continue east for 4 miles on I–676. When you come to I–76; go east for 2 more miles to I–295. Go north on 295 for 1 mile and you'll come to Route 168; go east for 2 miles to the New Jersey Turnpike. Take the turnpike north 62 miles, which will take you back onto I–95. Travel 19 miles north on 95 to Route 1/Route 9, which will take you into Jersey City. Go east on Route 78 (Twelfth Street) to the Holland Tunnel.

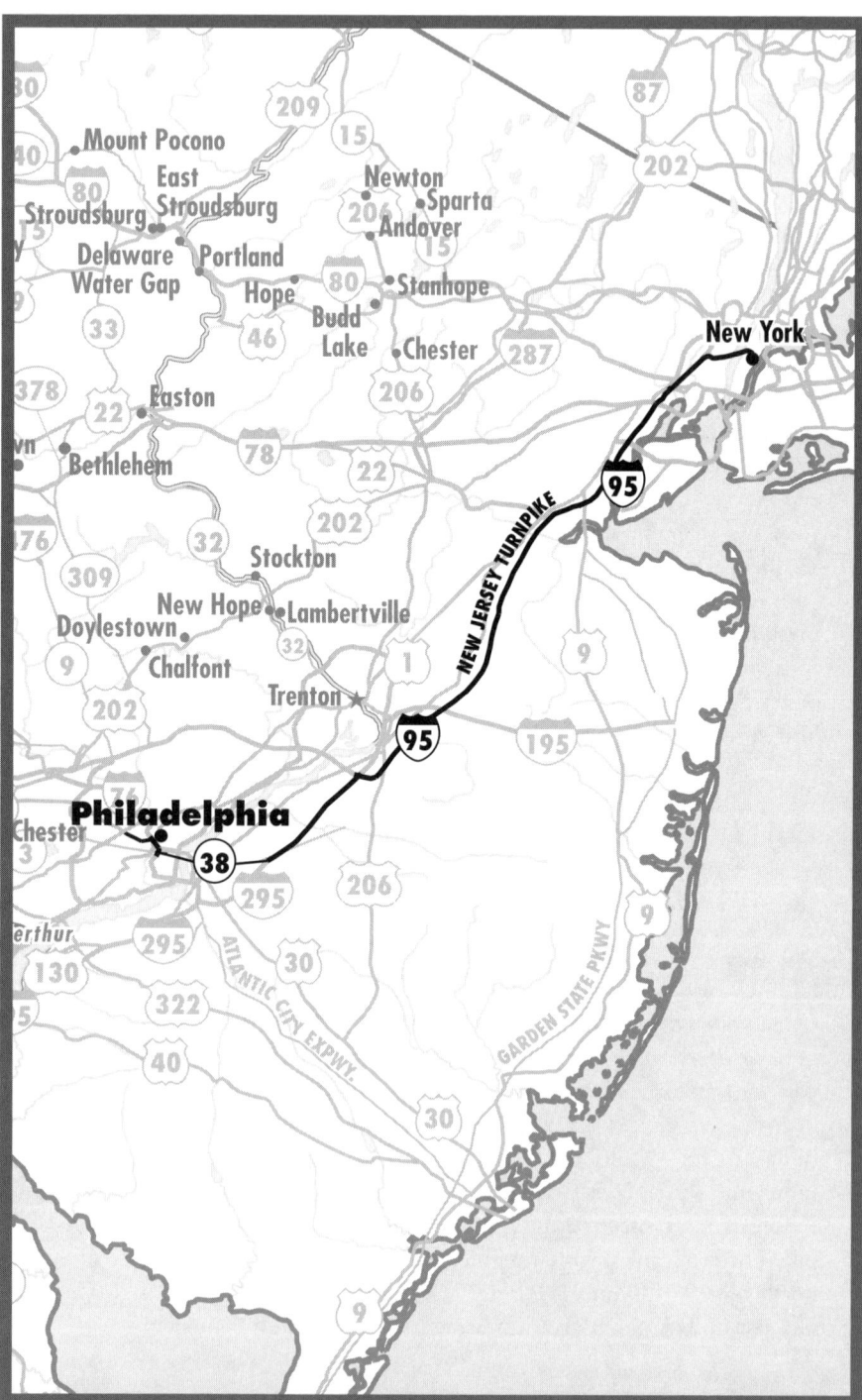

Afternoon

After you emerge from the tunnel, go straight until you come to Beach Street; make a slight right-hand turn onto Beach Street. Then turn left onto Greenwich Street. Go north on Greenwich for about a block until you come to Franklin Street. You are now in the heart of **TriBeCa** (Triangle Below Canal), bordered by Chambers and Lafayette Streets and the Hudson River, an interesting mix of old warehouses and new office buildings, artists' lofts, and ultratrendy eateries.

LUNCH: One of the trendiest of these eateries is **TriBeCa Grill** at 375 Greenwich Street, New York, NY 10013, at the corner of Franklin (212–941–3900). Owned by actor Robert De Niro and renowned chef/restaurateur Drew Nieporent, this hot spot set in a converted coffee factory serves an ever-changing menu of American cuisine with pronounced international accents. Like many of the city's better-known restaurants, this one can be pricey, even at lunch. For around $20 you can get the prix fixe lunch, which includes salad or soup, one of two entree selections, and dessert.

If you travel east from the restaurant a few blocks, you'll bump into Broadway. Take Broadway down to **Battery Park,** located at Manhattan's southern tip, where you'll pick up the **Statue of Liberty/Ellis Island Ferry** (212–269–5755). One round-trip ticket price for the ferry is $10.00 for adults eighteen and over, $8.00 for seniors, $4.00 for children three to seventeen (free for children under three). The ferry will take you to both Liberty Island and Ellis Island.

Few pieces of art have touched as many lives and elicited as wide a range of emotions as *Liberty Enlightening the World,* the 151-foot-tall statue presented as a gift from France in 1886. Although the Statue of Liberty, including the American Museum of Immigration located in its base, was closed to the public after September 11, 2001, it was scheduled to reopen in the summer of 2004. Call (212) 363–3200 for the most up-to-date information.

Located a few hundred yards north of the Statue of Liberty is **Ellis Island,** the "island of hope, island of tears" where more than twelve million immigrants were processed during the largest human migration in modern history, between 1892 and 1954. Interactive displays and exhibits of artifacts, photos, taped reminiscences, films, oral histories, and music give a human face to the immigrant experience. Scan the more than 500,000 names inscribed on the **American Immigrant Wall of Honor** and you'll find George Washington's great-grandfather, Myles Standish, Priscilla Alden, and perhaps one of your own ancestors. A genealogy facility called the **American Immigration History Center** helps families trace their own family trees through state-of-the-art computer technology.

Both Liberty Island and Ellis Island are open seven days a week, 9:00 A.M.–5:00 P.M., with extended hours in summer. For recorded information call (212) 363–3200.

Monday through Saturday between 3:30 and 5:30 P.M., it's officially teatime on Manhattan's chic Upper East Side and, specifically, at **Payard Patisserie & Bistro,** 1032 Lexington Avenue, New York, NY 10021, between Seventy-third and Seventy-fourth Streets (212–717–5252). If you like, you can order your tea (or coffee) at the espresso bar and select a la carte from the dazzling array of single-serving pastries and other confections displayed in the glass cases out front. Or you can have the full royal treatment with a $21 or $26 fixed-price extravaganza.

Evening

On Friday and Saturday evenings, the **Metropolitan Museum of Art** (1000 Fifth Avenue at Eighty-second Street, New York, NY 10028; 212–535–7710) stays open until 8:45 P.M., giving you plenty of time to tour its fabulous exhibits spanning 5,000 years and the world. Return to ancient times at the Egyptian Temple of Dendur and pass through the Moon Gate into a serene Chinese garden. Check out the knight-wear at the medieval armor exhibit and three centuries of fashion at the Costume Institute. The Roof Garden offers exhibits of contemporary sculpture along with a sensational view of the city. For the ultimate late-night experience, savor a cocktail and some wonderful live music on the balcony of the Great Hall. The museum opens daily (except Monday) at 9:30 A.M. Closing hours are Sunday and Tuesday through Friday at 5:30 P.M., Saturday at 9:00 P.M. Admission is $12.00 for adults, $7.00 for seniors and students, free for children under twelve with an adult.

DINNER: Union Square Cafe, 21 East Sixteenth Street, New York, NY 10003; (212) 243–4020. You'd better have a reservation if you plan to dine here because this pretty spot seems to be everybody's favorite. It will be well worth your while for the inspired menu, which changes regularly with the availability of fresh ingredients and the imaginative impulses of the chef. The unpretentious atmosphere and gracious service make you feel welcome, no matter how busy the restaurant gets. Expensive.

The Metropolitan Museum of Art.

LODGING: Fitzpatrick Grand Central, 141 East Forty-fourth Street at Lexington Avenue, New York, NY 10017; (800) 367–7701 or (212) 351–6800. There's a little bit of Ireland in midtown Manhattan at this exquisitely intimate boutique hotel. Everything from the bedspread fabrics to the little bottles of water in the minifridge is imported from the Emerald Isle. At the end of each day, you'll find on your pillow a bedtime story taken from the *Book of Ancient Legends.* Room rates, double occupancy, begin at $239; $199 July through September.

Day 2 / *Morning*

BREAKFAST: Chelsea Market, 75 Ninth Avenue, New York, NY 10011, between Fifteenth and Sixteenth Streets. Cross over Broadway to the west side of town; then head south on Ninth Avenue. Still revered as the site where the first Oreo cookie was made, this circa 1840 National Biscuit Company (Nabisco) factory is now home to a new generation of great cookie bakers as well as vendors of all kinds of other good stuff from live lobsters to Thai to potpies. And since the market opens early (around 7:00 A.M. weekdays, 10:00 A.M. weekends), this is a great place to build your own breakfast feast. Start at **Ronnybrook Farm Dairy** (212–741–6455) for some rich organic yogurt. Next stop, **Manhattan Fruit Exchange** (212–989–2444) for some additional nutrients; and finally, **Amy's Bread** (212–462–4338) for some oven-fresh scones, brioche, muffins, or a true Parisian repast of one-half baguette with butter, coffee or tea, and jam ($3.75). Chelsea Market closes at 7:00 P.M.

Go east to Fifth Avenue, then south until you come to **Washington Square Park** and the **Washington Arch,** a 77-foot-high George Washington inaugural bicentennial monument regarded as the official entrance to **Greenwich Village.** Bordered by the Hudson River, Houston (pronounced *How*-stun) Street, West Broadway, and Fourteenth Street, the Village has been a gathering place for artists and rebels for more than one hundred years. You can still experience some of that electricity today in the music clubs along **Bleecker Street** and in the multimedia exhibits at the **Guggenheim Museum SoHo,** 575 Broadway at Prince Street, New York, NY 10128; (212) 423–3500. Open Thursday through Monday 11:00 A.M.–6:00 P.M. Free.

If Greenwich Village lit the spark of innovation, then **SoHo** has turned it into a bonfire. Beginning south of Houston Street (hence its name) and bounded by Canal, Lafayette, and Sixth Streets, this neighborhood of 1850s cast-iron warehouses is filled with galleries and small ethnic shops selling everything from Tibetan singing bowls to African tribal art and foods from crepes-to-go to Peruvian seven-flavor chicken. For a comprehensive multicultural walking, tasting, and discovery exploration of both neighborhoods, take Foods of New York's **"Greenwich Village: Off the Beaten Path"** tour (212–239–1124) any Tuesday through Sunday ($36.50). During this three-hour excursion, you will learn about life, history, and culture in the Village dating back 150 years. You'll stroll through an old Italian neighborhood with its mom-and-pop shops, restaurants, a speakeasy from the Roaring Twenties, early-nineteenth-century architecture, hidden gardens, and music and poetry venues.

Afternoon

LUNCH: Although international cuisine is fast becoming part of the

American mainstream, immigrants from around the world have been contributing their own distinctive flavors to the New York food experience for the past two centuries. Included in your Food of New York tour of Greenwich Village will be samplings of specialties from seven unique shops and food purveyors, some of which have been doing business in the area for more than one hundred years.

Head back up to Midtown for the rest of the grand tour (the one the natives take their friends on) of Manhattan island, its three rivers, seven major bridges, five boroughs, and more than twenty-five famous landmarks on a three-hour, full-island **Circle Line Cruise,** Pier 16, South Street Seaport, New York, NY 10038; (212) 748–8782. Included is a spin around the harbor at forty-five mph on the *BEAST* speedboat ride. Tickets cost $33 for adults, $28 for senior citizens, and $18 for children twelve and under. Cruises are offered daily.

Evening

DINNER: Carmine's, 200 West Forty-fourth Street, New York, NY 10036; (212) 221–3800. Everything here is bigger than life, especially the blackboard menu with its close to forty entree selections of Italian and American specialties ranging from pasta served more than twenty different ways to four different preparations of porterhouse steak. Food is served family-style, so plan to share. Portions are gigantic, enough to feed a family of four. If you still have leftovers, take home a doggie bag to make sure you save room for dessert. Expensive—but the per person price really isn't when you share.

With all those twinkling lights and architecturally compelling theater buildings, you simply can't ignore **Broadway's theater district.** Just on the Great White Way between West Forty-first and West Fifty-fourth Streets alone there are almost three dozen theaters featuring new and classic musicals, comedies, and dramas. To find out what's playing, call the Broadway Line toll-free at (888) BROADWAY (locally 212–302–4111) or New York City On Stage hot line at (212) 768–1818.

For a little après-theater sweet, go north on Broadway to 154 West Seventieth Street, New York, NY 10023, where **Cafe Mozart** (212–595–9797) is waiting to dazzle you with an unbelievable array of French, Italian, Viennese, and American-inspired desserts and soothe your spirits with live classical music. The choices are endless . . . and torturous. Prices are moderate.

LODGING: Fitzpatrick Grand Central.

Day 3 / Morning

BREAKFAST: Zoë, 90 Prince Street, New York, NY 10012, between Mercer and Broadway; (212) 966–6722. Weekend brunch at this very hot restaurant costs about $20 and features three delectable courses. There's also an a la cart menu that usually features a yummy version of stuffed French toast and a changing selection of interesting breakfast and lunch fare, such as pizza *al uovo* (with rosemary potatoes, cheese, pancetta, and truffled eggs) or house-smoked salmon. Moderate to expensive.

At Central Park West and West Seventy-ninth Street, New York, NY 10024, is the **American Museum of Natural History** (212–769–5100), a collection of works by and about the world's premier and most prolific artist—Mother Nature. You can trace the evolution of vertebrate life through the world's largest collection of fossils, including dinosaurs (about one hundred), ancient fishes, and mammals, and discover the intricacies of our interdependence with our floral, furred, finned, and feathered planet-mates. There's also a wonderful air-and-space exhibition, including a planetarium. The museum is open seven days a week, 10:00 A.M.–5:45 P.M. Sunday through Thursday and until 8:45 P.M. Friday and Saturday. Basic admission is $12.00 for adults, $9.00 for seniors and students, and $7.00 for children. Planetarium and IMAX shows are additional.

Afternoon

Central Park (212–794–6564) is where New York comes to play. Feeding time for the sea lions is only one of the many delights at the **Central Park Wildlife Conservation Center**—aka the zoo—at 830 Fifth Avenue, off Sixty-fourth Street, New York, NY 10021; (212) 861–6500. Here more than two dozen species of animals live and play in natural habitats. Admission is $6.00 for adults, $1.25 for seniors, $1.00 for children three to twelve, and free for children under three. Open seven days a week 10:00 A.M.–4:30 P.M. You can also rent a rowboat for paddling ($10.00 first hour), a bike for pedaling ($9.00 to $15.00 per hour), or even take a one-hour gondola ride ($30.00) at **Loeb Boathouse on the Lake,** Seventy-second and Fifth Avenue; (212) 517–3623. Available March through October, 10:00 A.M.–5:00 P.M. seven days a week. One dollar buys a ride atop one of the antique carved horses on the 1908 **carousel.** And we haven't even touched on all the free stuff you can do at the park such as enjoying the free warm weather concerts (212–360–3444) and following the age-old tradition of climbing the statues of Alice in Wonderland and Hans Christian Andersen.

Evening

LATE LUNCH/EARLY DINNER: Carnegie Deli, 854 Seventh Avenue, Fifty-fourth and Fifty-fifth Streets, New York, NY 10019; (212) 757–2245. Don't even think of leaving New York without a trip for one of this deli's world-renowned pastrami sandwiches or, perhaps, a bowl of matzo-ball soup. Scan the wall of fame and see which celebrities share your devotion to deli. For dessert, there's real New York strawberry cheesecake. Moderate. No credit cards. Open seven days a week from 7:00 A.M. until 4:00 the next morning.

To return home, go south to Thirty-fourth Street, then west on Thirty-fourth through the tunnel. Continue to Route 495 until it intersects with I–95. Go south on I–95 for 25 miles until you come to the New Jersey Turnpike. Go southwest on the New Jersey Turnpike 52 miles and exit at Route 168. Retrace the rest of the route from day one.

There's More

City Pass. One ticket good for admission to the Empire State Building Observatory and NY SkyRide, Intrepid Sea-Air-Space Museum, American Museum of Natural History, Museum of Modern Art, Guggenheim Museum, and Circle Line Sight-seeing Cruises. $45 for adults, $39 for youths thirteen to eighteen. Pick up at first attraction visited.

Big Apple Greeter, 1 Centre Street, New York, NY 10007; (212) 669–2896. New York volunteers will introduce you to little-known places and local favorites on personalized, one-on-one tours. Most incredible is the fact that this service is absolutely free

Big Onion Walking Tours, 476 Thirteenth Street, New York, NY 11215; (212) 439–1090. Two-hour weekend ethnic neighborhood walking tours led by guides who hold advanced degrees in American history from Columbia or New York Universities. Every weekend and holiday year-round. $12 adults, $10 seniors and students.

Madame Tussaud's, New York, 234 West Forty-second Street, New York,

NY 10036; (212) 512–9600. This is truly a star-studded experience, featuring nearly 200 "wax portraits" of the famous and infamous from the worlds of entertainment, government, society, and history spanning more than two centuries. Open daily 10:00 A.M.–8:00 P.M. Monday through Thursday, 10:00 A.M.–10:00 P.M. Friday through Sunday. $25 for adults and children thirteen and over, $19 for children four to twelve, and $22 for seniors.

United Nations, First Avenue at Forty-sixth Street, New York, NY 10118; (212) 963–8687. Multilingual forty-five-minute to one-hour guided tours offered daily (except Saturday and Sunday in January and February) 9:15 A.M.–4:45 P.M. Tours include the General Assembly, council chambers, and works of art from member nations. Admission is $10.50 for adults, $8.00 for seniors, $7.00 for students, $6.00 for children grades one through eight.

NBC Studio Tour, 30 Rockefeller Plaza, New York, NY 10112; (212) 664–7174. A one-hour-and-ten-minute guided behind-the-scenes sneakpeak at your favorite programs. Daily. Hours vary seasonally; reservations are recommended. $17.75 adults, $15.25 seniors and children (six through sixteen); children under six not admitted.

Special Events

June, July, August. Shakespeare in the Park, Delacorte Theater, Central Park; (212) 539–8500. Founded by Joseph Papp, these spectacular free summer productions of Shakespeare and other works are performed in an open-air amphitheater.

November. Annual Thanksgiving Day Parade. Begins at Central Park West at Seventy-seventh Street, continues down Broadway to Macy's Herald Square (Thirty-fourth Street), and finishes at Seventh Avenue.

December. Ice-skating at Rockefeller Center, Fifth Avenue between Forty-ninth and Fiftieth Streets; (212) 332-7654. Daytime and evening skating mid-October through April. Rentals available.

December. Lighting of the Christmas Tree, Rockefeller Center; (212) 698–2950.

Other Recommended Restaurants and Lodgings

New York City

Hotel Wales, 1295 Madison Avenue (at Ninety-second Street), New York, NY 10128; (212) 876–6000. This beautifully restored late-nineteenth-century boutique hotel is located in the Carnegie Hall section of the Upper East Side. Continental breakfast each morning, tea and twenty-four-hour cappuccino and tea bar. Room rates range from $199 to $750.

Hotel Wolcott, 4 West Thirty-first Street, New York, NY 10001, between Fifth and Broadway; (212) 268–2900. Ornate architecture, gilded and mirrored lobby, crystal chandeliers, and wrought-iron railings in a budget-priced hotel? Yes, and clean, comfortable rooms as well for $110 to $170 double occupancy. Convenient midtown location makes the United Nations, Broadway theaters, shopping, and other major attractions easily walkable.

Grand Central Oyster Bar, Grand Central Station, Forty-second Street, New York, NY 10017, between Vanderbilt and Lexington Avenues; (212) 490–6650. A little pricey, but where else can you dine on more than thirty types of oysters and other fresh seafood in the splendor of one of New York's most famous landmarks?

Cowgirl Hall of Fame, 519 Hudson Street at Tenth, New York, NY 10014; (212) 633–1133. Whimsical Western-style decor and good chuck-wagon grub (for example, "chicken-fried" chicken and catfish po'boys) at moderate prices.

For More Information

New York Convention & Visitors Bureau, 810 Seventh Avenue, New York, NY 10019, between Fifty-second and Fifty-third Streets; (212) 484–1200; www.nycvisit.com.

Baltimore, Maryland

City of Firsts

2 Nights

According to *The World Book Dictionary,* the word *rampart* is defined as a wide bank of earth, often with a wall on top, built around a fort to help defend it: *O'er the ramparts we watched* . . .

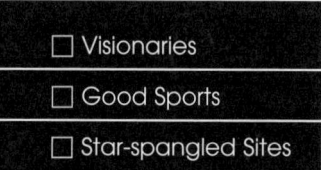

☐ Visionaries

☐ Good Sports

☐ Star-spangled Sites

OK, that's settled. I thought we should get that out of the way before visiting the home of Fort McHenry and the flag that inspired a certain lawyer named Key to wax poetic on a mid-September dawn almost two centuries ago. Well, the flag is *still* there, bigger than life (although with thirty-five additional stars and two fewer stripes), flying o'er the ramparts. And the city of Baltimore is still inspiring poets as well as painters, sculptors, and other artists, artisans, and innovators.

Perhaps that's why Baltimore's history is filled with so many firsts, including the first use of an umbrella in the United States (1772)—as well as the establishment of the first umbrella factory (1828). Baltimore also claims the building of the first passenger railroad train ("Tom Thumb" in 1830) and the manufacture of such necessities of life as ice cream (1851) and bottle caps (1892).

Baltimore is also a city of first-class historical, recreational, and cultural attractions. Ringing its lively harbor are some of the finest—and some of the funkiest—museums, shops, and dining spots you'll ever find in one place. But don't stop there. Beyond the waterfront are the city's distinctive neighborhoods, each with its own colorful personality, individual history, particular style of hospitality, and delicious flavors.

Day 1 / Morning

Baltimore is only 93 miles southwest of Philadelphia. But, realistically, the drive takes about two hours. The most straightforward route for getting there is to take the Schuylkill Expressway (I–76) to I–95. Travel south on 95 for 87 miles to Route 895 south and the Harbor Tunnel. From the tunnel, take Route 40 west straight into Baltimore. As most visitors do,

follow the signs to the Inner Harbor and park your car for the day. One convenient spot is in the lot directly across from the main entrance to the American Visionary Art Museum (800 Key Highway), where you can park all day for $3.00. At the harbor you'll spot signs for **Ed Kane's Water Taxi** (800–658–8947 or 410–563–3901), which for a flat rate of $6.00 for adults, $3.00 for children under ten, offers an all-day ticket for transportation to fifteen landings and thirty-five of the city's major attractions.

Everyone knows about the Wright Brothers' flight into fame from Kitty Hawk, North Carolina, in 1903. But, in reality, the first manned aircraft flight—in a hot-air balloon—had already taken place almost 120 years before in the outskirts of Baltimore! So what better way to celebrate the city's heritage than floating 450 feet above the Inner Harbor in the tethered gondola of the **HiFlyer Balloon at Port Discovery** (Intersection of Baltimore and President Streets, Baltimore, MD 21202; 410–949–2FLY), where you can savor the view from the city's highest public observation point. Day and evening fifteen-minute flights are available daily; call for seasonal hours. Tickets are $12.00 for adults, $8.50 for children three to twelve.

Port Discovery (35 Market Place, corner of Market and Lombard Streets, Baltimore, MD 21202; 410–727–8120) calls itself the "kid-powered museum." And that's quite an accurate description, with three floors of interactive exhibits (designed in collaboration with Walt Disney Imagineering) to educate and entertain the entire family. Young ones can give their brains and bodies a real workout as they solve mysteries, create art, "star" in their own TV shows, and travel back in time to ancient Egypt. Open daily; call for seasonal hours. Tickets are $11.00 adults, $10.00 seniors, $8.50 children three to twelve.

Afternoon

LUNCH: Chiapparelli's Restaurant, 237 South High Street, Baltimore, MD 21202; (410) 837–0309.

Just east of Inner Harbor (a ten-minute walk or quick water-taxi ride away) is the picturesque neighborhood known as **Little Italy,** and you're just in time for lunch. Like warm, generous family homes, the restaurants of Little Italy welcome you with irresistible aromas and an abundance of Old- and New-World specialties. You can find fancier restaurants in Little Italy, but none is better than Chiapparelli's. It's a favorite of the locals, renowned for its made-on-the-premises ravioli and other luscious pastas. Of course, this is

Maryland, so you know there's great seafood on the menu. Also chicken and veal in a constantly changing array of classical and original presentations. Desserts are definitely homemade. Moderate to expensive.

Your water-taxi ticket also covers ground transportation (which you'll pick up at Landing No. 4) to the **Fort McHenry National Monument and Historic Shrine** at the end of Fort Avenue, Baltimore, MD 21230 (410–962–4290). Even if its ramparts hadn't been mentioned in America's most patriotic paean, this star-shaped brick fortress, originally built during the Revolution and in use through World War II, would be a site worth seeing.

Begin at the visitor center, where a film dramatization of the day- and nightlong bombardment by the British will prepare you for a tour of this formidable fort that includes restored powder magazines, guardrooms, officers' quarters, and barracks. The grounds are open daily 8:00 A.M.–5:00 P.M. (the visitor center, until 4:45 P.M.) with extended hours in summer. Entrance fee is $5.00 for adults seventeen and over; children sixteen and under are admitted free.

Take the water taxi across the harbor to the **National Aquarium in Baltimore** (Pier 3, 501 East Pratt Street, Baltimore, MD 21202; 410–576–3800), where more than 10,000 creatures are on display in naturalistic habitats representing environments ranging from Maryland's own mountain ponds to the Atlantic coral reef to a tropical rain forest. In the Marine Mammal Pavilion, you can watch a dolphin show or come face to face with sharks. The upper level Rain Forest is home to all kinds of creatures from monkeys to brightly colored birds. Call for seasonal hours. Admission is $15.50 for adults, $12.50 for seniors, $7.50 for children three to eleven, and free for children under three.

Back across the harbor is the **American Visionary Art Museum** at 800 Key Highway, Baltimore Inner Harbor, Baltimore, MD 21202 (410–244–1900). The 55-foot-high, multicolored, wind-powered whirligig outside in the central plaza should be your tip-off that this is not your traditional art museum. Inside its seven galleries are displayed the works of self-taught *visionary artists*—ordinary people from farmers to housewives to the homeless who are "inspired by the fire within" to express themselves in media ranging from painting and sculpture to tattoos and toothpicks. If you need some quiet time to adjust to this unusual experience, take a few moments to mellow out in the Wildflower/Sculpture Garden with its woven tree-limb meditation chapel/nondenominational wedding altar. Open Tuesday through Sunday 10:00 A.M.–6:00 P.M. Admission for adults is $9.00; $6.00 for children, students, and seniors.

Evening

DINNER: Pisces, Hyatt Regency Baltimore on the Inner Harbor, 300 Light Street, Baltimore, MD 21202; (410) 605–2856. Actually, the whole name of this restaurant is Pisces, A Seafood Place. Ah, but it's not just *any* seafood place. Not only does this rooftop dining spot offer one of Baltimore's most breathtaking views, its constantly changing menu is always filled with innovative preparations of your shelled and finny favorites. For purists, there's the "Ultimate Raw Bar" featuring oysters, clams, crab claws, and shrimp. And you can have your fresh fare prepared broiled, sautéed, grilled, or blackened if you wish. But for a real seafaring adventure, try one of the chef's originals, such as grilled squid with herb and avocado butter, smoked salmon with potato and apple pancake and Dijon crème fraîche, shrimp battered crab claw . . . or whatever new delight he has dreamed up by the time you visit. Expensive.

After dinner, walk over to the wooden finger piers in front of the Maryland Science Museum for one of the weekend calypso and reggae cruises aboard **Clipper City** (410–931–6277), a replica of one of the famous tall ships that plied the waters of the East Coast from 1854 to 1892. Not your ordinary sight-seeing excursion, this is a three-hour floating party with live music, dancing, and a cash bar. The reggae cruise sails from 8:00 to 11:00 P.M. Friday and Saturday; tickets are $20 per person. *Clipper City* also offers two-hour sailing tours of the Inner and Outer Harbor daily ($12.00 for adults, $4.00 for children) and a three-hour brunch sail on Sunday ($30); call for schedules.

LODGING: Celie's Waterfront Bed & Breakfast, 1714 Thames Street, Fell's Point, Baltimore, MD 21231; (410) 522–2323. Celie's is located right across the water from Inner Harbor in the heart of one of the nation's oldest surviving maritime communities, the 1730 village of **Fell's Point.** To get there by car, take Pratt Street east to President Street; turn right onto President Street and follow it to Fleet Street. Turn left onto Fleet Street and go 8 blocks to Ann Street. Turn right onto Ann Street and travel 3 blocks to Thames Street. Make a left onto Thames Street to no. 1714 in the middle of the block; Celie's is the gray building with the rose trim.

Don't let the big iron gate at the door intimidate you. This three-story, seven-room bed-and-breakfast is a charmer. The cheerful antique-appointed rooms, some with fireplaces and/or whirlpools, are filled with sunshine from overhead skylights and windows that open onto the private garden, atrium, and harbor. There are flowers everywhere—from those growing in the colorful window boxes to the garden-fresh blooms that adorn each guest room. Double occupancy rates for rooms with courtyard or harbor-front views are $129 to $239. Continental breakfast is included.

Day 2 / *Morning*

BREAKFAST: Celie's Waterfront Bed & Breakfast. Not only does Celie's provide you with a hearty buffet spread of fresh fruits, breads, cereals, and gourmet coffees and teas, it also offers a variety of beautiful settings in which to enjoy your repast. My favorite is the roof deck, with its sweeping views of the Baltimore skyline and Inner Harbor. When the weather is cool, there's usually a warming fire in the dining room.

Aside from its cobblestone streets and more than 350 original examples of eighteenth- and nineteenth-century architecture, Fell's Point is known for its wide array of art galleries and antiques and specialty shops. **Angeline's Art Gallery & Boutique** (1631 Thames Street/Brown's Wharf, Baltimore, MD 21231; 410–522–7909) specializes in paintings, jewelry, curios, and sculptures by local and national artists, including owner Angeline V. Culfogienis herself. **Another Period in Time** at 1708 Fleet Street, Baltimore, MD 21231 (410–675–4776) is an antique collector's nirvana, with fifteen different dealers of everything from art to toys to sports memorabilia under one roof. And if you want to know "who done it," ask at **Mystery Loves Company** (1730 Fleet Street, Baltimore, MD 21231; 410–276–6708), a bookstore specializing in new and used mysteries and first editions.

Take the car back to the downtown area. But instead of making your left-hand turn at Pratt Street, continue north to Fayette Street. Turn left on Fayette and take it to Amity Street. Turn right onto Amity.

Master of the macabre, Edgar Allan Poe left a trail of houses and haunts that stretch from Boston to Richmond (including Philadelphia, of course). One of the most significant was his aunt Maria Clemm's house at 203 North Amity Street, Baltimore, MD 21223, where he lived from 1832 to 1835 and began his writing career. Today the **Edgar Allan Poe House & Museum** (410–396–7932) has one of the most extensive collections of artifacts around, along with exhibits and a fine video presentation. Open Tuesday through Saturday 10:00 A.M.–5:00 P.M., Sunday 11:00 A.M.–5:00

P.M. Admission $6.00 adults, $5.00 seniors and students.

Two years after his 1847 death in Baltimore, Poe's permanent address became the **Westminster Burying Grounds & Catacombs** at Fayette and Greene Streets (410–706–2072). To get there from the Poe house, go south on Amity Street to the end of the block. Turn left onto Lexington to the first traffic light, which is Fremont. Turn right onto Fremont and follow it for 2 blocks south to Baltimore Street. Turn left at Baltimore and go 3 blocks to Paca. Make a left at Paca, go 1 block and turn left onto Fayette Street; the next street you will come to is Greene. Immediately on your left at the corner you will see Westminster Hall and the grave site of Edgar Allan Poe. Poe was originally buried in an unmarked grave behind the church until 1865, when a local schoolteacher organized a campaign encouraging children to donate their "pennies for Poe" to pay for his reburial in the family plot and a fitting monument to mark his resting place. The cemetery is open to the public from 8:00 A.M. until dusk.

Afternoon

LUNCH: Lexington Market, 400 West Lexington Street, Baltimore, MD 21201; (410) 685–6169. From the corner of Fayette and Greene, it's only 1 block north and about 2 blocks east to the oldest city market in the United States, where more than 140 merchants sell all kinds of fresh produce, baked goods, and local meats. Monday through Saturday 8:30 A.M.–6:00 P.M.

You may have noticed that I haven't yet referred you to a place to feast on genuine Maryland crab cakes. Some of the best and most famous are served right here at **John W. Faidleys Seafood** (201 North Paca, Baltimore, MD 21201; 410–727–4898). An all-lump crabmeat cake sells for $12.95; with two sides it's $16.95. Faidleys also sells uncooked and pre-browned crab cakes for take-home and can continually replenish your supply through its mail order service!

Turn left at the corner of Monument and Eutaw Streets, then right at Mulberry Street. Follow Mulberry east to North Charles Street; turn left. At North Charles and Mt. Vernon Place, you will see the 178-foot-high white marble column that was the first architectural monument (begun in 1815) built in honor of George Washington. At the **Washington Monument** (410–396–1049) there's a ground-floor museum and, if it's open (hours vary), for a small donation, you can climb the 228 steps to the top for a fabulous view of the city. Open Wednesday through Sunday 10:00 A.M.–4:00 P.M.

Baltimore's Mt. Vernon neighborhood is a cultural hot spot for lovers of music, art, and architecture.

Aside from the monument, this urban oasis of nineteenth-century homes and beautifully landscaped parks called **Mount Vernon** is also a well-known cultural destination. The **Walters Art Museum** (600 North Charles Street at Mount Vernon Square, Baltimore, MD 21201; 410–547–9000) exhibits more than 30,000 objects, including Oriental art, Fabergé, and Lalique, spanning fifty-five centuries and four continents. Open Tuesday through Sunday 10:00 A.M.–5:00 P.M. (until 8:00 P.M. first Thursday of every month). Admission is $8.00 for adults, $6.00 senior citizens, $5.00 college students, $5.00 young adults (eighteen to twenty-five), and free for children seventeen and under.

While you're in the neighborhood, you may want to check if there is a performance scheduled at the world-famous **Peabody Conservatory of Music,** 1 East Mt. Vernon Place, Baltimore, MD 21201 (410–659–

8100, ext. 2). The conservatory presents operas, orchestra concerts, and other special events. Ticket prices range from $18.00 to $35.00 for adults, $10.00 to $18.00 seniors, and $8.00 to $12.00 students. If you would rather see a good play, **Center Stage,** the state theater of Maryland, at 700 North Calvert Street, Baltimore, MD 21202 (410–332–0033), offers a six-play mainstage season series of original and classic comedies, dramas, and musicals from September to June for ticket prices ranging from $25 to $60.

Evening

DINNER: John Steven Ltd., 1800 Thames Street, Fell's Point, Baltimore, MD 21231; (410) 327–5561. Weather permitting, dine alfresco in the courtyard at this very, very charming restaurant. The internationally inspired menu contains some interesting surprises, such as the safari burger made from 100 percent ostrich meat; spicy Cajun crawfish pie; and seafood-packed Baltimore bouillabaisse. Entrees range from $12.95 to $22.50 for steak and crab cake.

LODGING: Celie's Waterfront Bed & Breakfast.

Day 3 / Morning

BREAKFAST: Celie's Waterfront Bed & Breakfast.

You'll be heading toward home today, but there are a few major stops you'll be making before your escape comes to an end. Take the car and head back toward the Inner Harbor. This time make your left-hand turn at Lombard Street, then a left onto Howard Street. Another left onto Camden Street will take you to **Oriole Park at Camden Yards** (333 West Camden Street, Baltimore, MD 21201; 410–685–9800), home of Baltimore Orioles baseball and one of the most famous ballparks in the country. If there's a home game scheduled for today or tonight, grab a ticket for a real old-fashioned "take me out to the ball game" experience at this natural Maryland bluegrass stadium modeled on the ones Babe Ruth and the gang used to play in. Ticket prices range from $9.00 for bleachers to $45.00 for a club box. By the way, if you happen to miss baseball season, the Baltimore Ravens football team now has its own field at M&T Bank Stadium (1101 Russell Street, Baltimore, MD 21230), near Camden Yards. For information call (410) 261–RAVE.

Afternoon

L U N C H : **ESPN Zone,** 601 East Pratt Street at the Power Plant, Inner Harbor, Baltimore, MD 21202; (410) 685–ESPN. Can't get enough of sports? ESPN Zone features dining experiences in a simulated television studio set or in front of a 16-foot video wall that shows all sports all day. The moderately priced menu features everything from burgers and ribs to salmon and rigatoni to filet mignon. Indulgent yet irresistible desserts include the signature chocolate-chip cookie sundae served in a skillet.

To work off those calories (or at least try to fool your brain into thinking that's what you're doing), go score some points at the ESPN Zone's pay-as-you-play **Sports Arena.** This 10,000-square-foot entertainment area has more than 150 interactive baseball, football, basketball, and golf-oriented games and attractions, including state-of-the-art sports simulators and video games. Restaurant hours are daily 11:30 A.M.–11:00 P.M.

Before you leave Baltimore, take about an hour for a tour across the Seven Seas and back hundreds of years at **"PassPort Baltimore, Voyages of Discovery"** right next door to ESPN Zone at 621 East Pratt Street (The Pier 4 Building), Baltimore, MD 21202; (410) 468–0700. Time Elevator, a 4-D theater combining film, motion platforms, and special effects, puts you right in the midst of history from before the American Revolution to the present day. The Oceanarium takes you on an underwater voyage from the Inner Harbor through the oceans of the world with panoramic screens, special effects, surround-sound audio, and motion-based seating. Open seven days; hours vary seasonally. Tickets are $11.95 for adults, $10.95 seniors and military, $8.95 children (five through twelve).

To return to Philadelphia, head east on Pratt Street to Charles Street; turn right onto Charles and right again at Conway Street. Turn left in front of the ballpark, onto I–395. Stay toward the right; you'll be exiting almost immediately onto I–95 north. Pass through the toll tunnel and take I–95 north all the way back home. The trip should take about two hours.

There's More

The Baltimore Zoo, Druid Hill Park, Baltimore, MD 21217; (410) 396–7102. Wilderness and farmland habitats are home to more than 2,000 animals from around the world. Open daily 10:00 A.M.–4:00 P.M., extended summer weekend hours. Admission is $11.00 for adults, $9.00 for seniors and $7.00 for children.

Baltimore Harbor Pass. This three-day pass provides discounts on admission to the National Aquarium in Baltimore, Port Discovery, Maryland Science Center and to the World Observation Level at Baltimore's World Trade Center, Baltimore Orioles games, Ed Kane's Water Taxi, ESPN Zone, "PassPort, Voyages of Discovery," and other attractions, accommodations, shopping, and dining spots. Order in advance by calling (877) BAL-TIMORE or through the Web site www.baltimore.org. You can also pick up the pass at the Baltimore Area Convention and Visitor Association's Connect Baltimore ticketing and reservation service located on the west shore of the Inner Harbor. $35 for adults, $25 children three through twelve.

Maryland Historical Society, 201 West Monument Street; Baltimore, MD 21201; (410) 685–3750. Among the more than 100,000 artifacts pertaining to Maryland's history housed here are Francis Scott Key's original manuscript of "The Star-Spangled Banner" and the nation's largest collection of nineteenth-century silver. Open Wednesday through Sunday 10:00 A.M.–5:00 P.M. Admission is $8.00 adults, $6.00 children thirteen to seventeen and seniors.

Baltimore Maritime Museum, Pier 3, Pratt Street, Inner Harbor, Baltimore, MD 21202; (410) 396–3453. Three historic ships (including the only one to survive the attack on Pearl Harbor), a lighthouse, and other exhibits and hands-on activities provide a wealth of maritime history. Open daily 10:00 A.M.–5:00 P.M. in summer; call for off-season hours. Admission is $4.00 for adults, $3.00 for seniors and children three to seventeen and students.

Baltimore Museum of Art, 10 Art Museum Drive, North Charles Street at Thirty-first Street, Baltimore, MD 21218; (410) 396–7100. More than 100,000 objets d'art ranging from ancient mosaics to renowned contemporary works, including a whole wing devoted to post-1945 art. Open Wednesday through Friday 11:00 A.M.–5:00 P.M., Saturday and Sunday 11:00 A.M.–6:00 P.M. Admission is $7.00 for adults, $5.00 for seniors, children under eighteen free. Free for everyone first Thursday of each month (11:00 A.M.–8:00 P.M.)

Maryland Science Center, 601 Light Street at Key Highway, Inner Harbor, Baltimore, MD 21202; (410) 685–5225. Three floors featuring a science arcade filled with hands-on activities, an IMAX theater, a planetarium, and live images from the Hubble telescope. Open 10:00 A.M.–5:00 P.M. Tuesday through Friday, 10:00 A.M.–6:00 P.M. Saturday, noon–5:00 P.M. Sunday. Combo admission (one IMAX film, exhibits, and planetarium is $15.50 for adults, $14.50 for seniors, and $10.50 for children three to twelve.

Babe Ruth Birthplace and Orioles Museum, 26 Emory Street (2 blocks from Camden Yards), Baltimore, MD 21223; (410) 727–1539. Exhibits in this 12-foot-wide row house where George Herman Ruth was born chronicle his life and career and feature Orioles memorabilia. Open daily April through October 10:00 A.M.–5:00 P.M. (7:00 P.M. on Orioles home game nights); November to March 10:00 A.M.–4:00 P.M. Admission is $6.00 for adults, $4.00 for children five to sixteen, and free for children under five.

National Museum of Dentistry, 31 South Greene Street, Baltimore, MD 21201; (410) 706–0600. If you think a museum devoted to teeth sounds as if it would be about as much fun as a root canal, you haven't seen the feats of an iron jaw performer, a tooth jukebox, and George Washington's not-so-wooden teeth. Open Wednesday through Saturday 10:00 A.M.–4:00 P.M., Sunday 1:00–4:00 P.M. Admission is $4.50 for adults, $2.50 for seniors and students.

Special Events

May. Preakness Celebration and Race, Pimlico Race Course, Northern Parkway, Baltimore, MD; (410) 542–9400. This weeklong festival leading up to the running of the Preakness Stakes, the middle jewel in the prestigious Triple Crown, features hot-air balloons, parades, and lots of other pre-race hoopla.

Memorial Day Weekend through Labor Day Weekend. Free Summer Concert Series, Harborplace Amphitheatre; (800) HARBOR–1 or (410) 332–4191. Every Friday, Saturday, and Sunday.

July. Artscape. The nation's largest arts festival showcases local and regional literary, visual, and performing arts; art car parade; headliner musicians; and more. Call (888) BALTIMORE for more information.

September. A Star-Spangled Weekend, Fort McHenry; (410) 962–4290. Annual commemoration of the bombardment and the writing of "The Star-Spangled Banner" includes military encampments and reenactments, a concert by the U.S. Army Field Band and Soldiers Chorus, and fireworks.

September. Baltimore Book Festival. A huge celebration of the literary arts featuring readings by well-known authors, children's writers, and storytellers; author signings; and entertainment. Call (888) BALTIMORE for more information.

Other Recommended Restaurants and Lodgings

Fell's Point

Admiral Fell Inn, 888 South Broadway, Baltimore, MD 21231; (410) 522–7377. You'd never know this elegant European-style inn was once a seaman's hostel and, later, a YMCA. Among the amenities are beautiful Federal period–style furnishings, an on-premises gourmet restaurant, and an English-style pub. Rates range from $145 off-season, to $235 peak season.

Baltimore

Abacrombie Badger Bed & Breakfast, 58 West Biddle Street, Baltimore, MD 21201; (410) 244–7227. Located in the heart of Baltimore's cultural center, this enchanting 1880s town house has an engaging personality all its own. Continental breakfast is included. Rates for double occupancy range from $115 to $155 per night.

M & S Grill, 1006 Harborplace, 201 East Pratt Street, Baltimore, MD 21202; (410) 547–9333. Comfort food, including pot roast, roasted chicken, and pasta, with a view. Moderate prices for lunch and dinner.

For More Information

Baltimore Visitor Center, 301 East Pratt Street, Baltimore, MD 21202; (800) 282–6632 or (410) 837–4636. Open daily 9:00 A.M.–5:30 P.M.

Baltimore Area Convention & Visitor Association; (877) BALTIMORE (225–8466); www.baltimore.org.

Maryland Office of Tourism Development; (800) MD–IS–FUN, (800) 634–7386; www.mdwelcome.org.

Washington, D.C.

Monumental Decisions

2 Nights

You might not normally think of Washington, D.C., as a free-and-easy kind of town. But it can be if you know where to look … and how to get around.

Free—as in no charge—is the admission price for visiting a wide range of Washington's top attractions, including the Folger Shakespeare Library, Kenilworth Aquatic Gardens, National Arboretum, National Gallery of Art, National Geographic Society, U.S. Holocaust Memorial Museum, and all fourteen Smithsonian Institution museums. Now that doesn't mean you can leave the credit cards at home. D.C.'s outstanding hospitality of the food-and-lodging variety is far from free. But many of its most outstanding attractions—and hidden treasures—are.

☐ President's Residence

☐ International Neighborhoods

☐ Smithsonians Galore

Day 1 / Morning

Washington, D.C., is 144 driving miles south of Philadelphia. However, you will be driving on the outskirts of several heavily trafficked cities, so expect to be on the road about three hours. Take the Schuylkill Expressway (I–76) east to I–95 south 88 miles to I–895 south through the Harbor Tunnel to I–295 (Baltimore–Washington Expressway). I–295 turns into I–95 again and continues south to I–495 (the Beltway). Go west on 495 to exit 30 and head south on Route 29 for about 15 miles. Route 29 will become Sixteenth Street and will take you to the intersection of Sixteenth and H Streets, 2 blocks from the White House.

Once in the city, your focal point should be the U.S. Capitol.

HELPFUL HINTS: As in many other major downtown areas, parking in D.C. can be a pain in the neck. To save yourself time, aggravation, and more than a few bucks, use the Metro as your main source of touring transportation. It's convenient, clean, and safe, and an all-day Tourist Pass costs $6.00 (202–637–7000). Metro maps are available at stops and all over town.

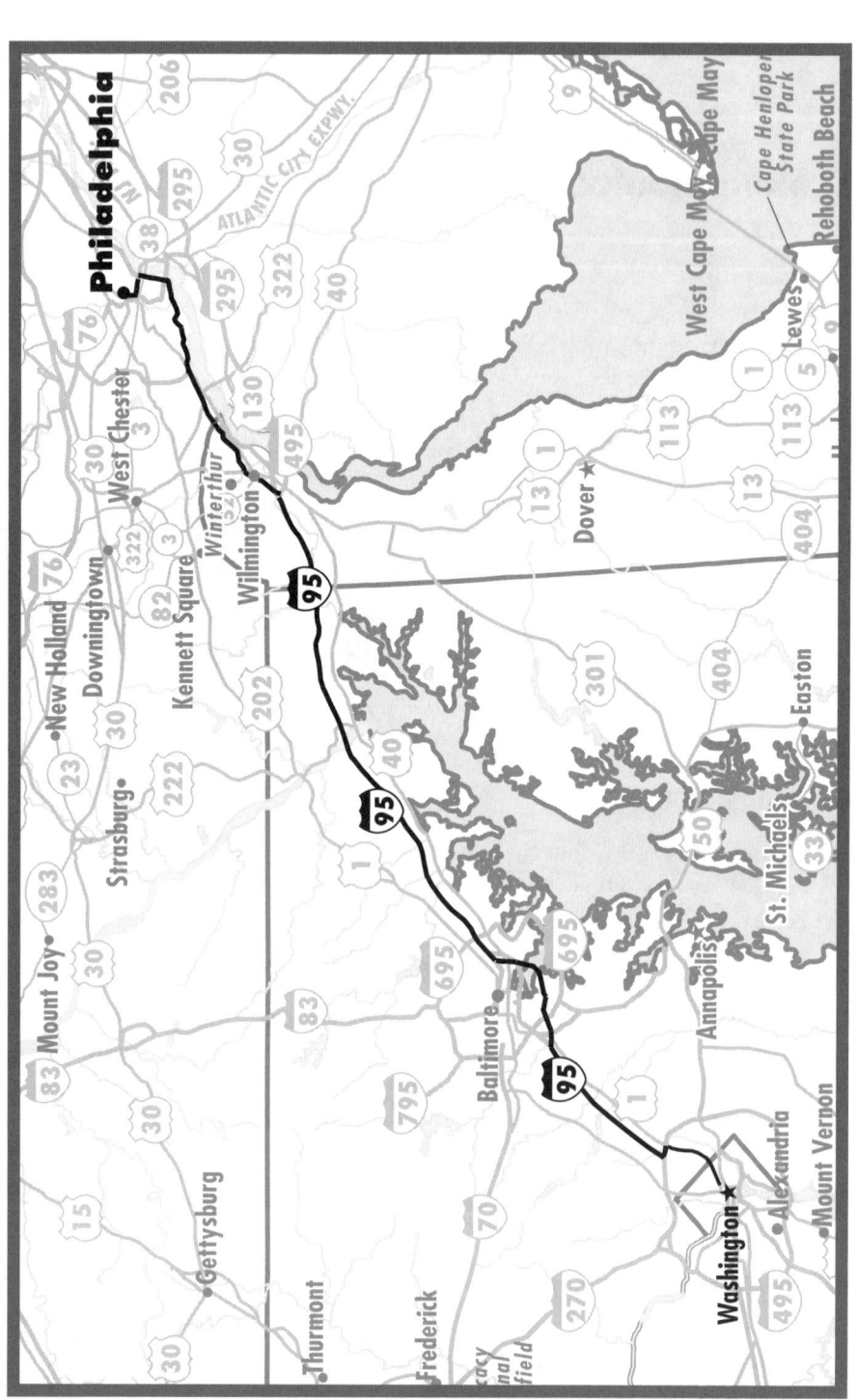

If you insist on driving, keep in mind that radiating out from the Capitol are four quadrant designations. The divider streets are North Capitol, South Capitol, and East Capitol Streets and the National Mall. Numbered streets run north-south, with addresses getting higher the farther away you go from the Capitol; east-west streets are named for letters in alphabetical order.

Afternoon

LUNCH: Two Quail Restaurant, 320 Massachusetts Avenue NE, Washington, DC 20002, about 4 blocks north of the Capitol; (202) 543–8030. Three town houses on historic **Capitol Hill** have been joined together and furnished with big, overstuffed library chairs, floral drapes, all kinds of pictures, and other homey touches to create a slightly funky, totally charming dining spot. The $9.95 prix fixe lunch is always a good buy with its choice of soup or salad and imaginative variations of chicken, pasta, and fish.

In D.C. the **Smithsonian Institution** operates fourteen art, history, and science museums and galleries in addition to the National Zoo. From the Capitol it's an easy walk due west on the **National Mall** to nine of them. Each is unique and all of them are wonderful. So how do you make up your mind which one (or ones) you will visit during this brief foray to our nation's capital? Head straight for **The Castle,** the can't-miss-it regal piece of 1855 architecture that graces 1000 Jefferson Drive SW, about midway between the Capitol and the Washington Monument. The Castle (202–357–2700) is the official visitor center for the Smithsonian where you can pick up brochures, maps, and other information as well as see a twenty-four-minute video overview of all the other museums and galleries in the complex. All of the Smithsonians are free and open daily 10:00 A.M.–5:30 P.M. unless otherwise noted.

The largest and most visited of the Smithsonians—and, in fact, of all the museums in the world—is the **National Air and Space Museum,** Independence Avenue between Fourth and Seventh Streets SW, Washington, DC 20560; (202) 357–1686. You can actually trace the history of aviation just by viewing its star-studded lineup, including the Wright Brothers' 1903 *Flyer,* Charles Lindbergh's *Spirit of St. Louis,* the *Apollo 11* command modules and rockets, and the Skylab orbital workshop. Other highlights include more than fifty interactive stations, a planetarium, and an IMAX theater (202–357–1686). Museum admission is free; there is a nominal charge for admission to the IMAX theater.

Inside the National Air and Space Museum.

By this time you're probably ready for some outdoor fun. But it's hard to tear yourself away from all of the fascinating educational and historical attractions Washington has to offer. No problem! Head to the west end of the Mall to the body of water called the Tidal Basin. Get a rental at **Tidal Basin Pedal Boats** (Ohio Drive and Tidal Basin NW; 202–484–0206) and have some fun floating in the shadow of the majestic marble-columned rotunda of the **Thomas Jefferson Memorial** (202–426– 6841) under the watchful eye of the 19-foot-tall bronze statue of our third president. Pedal boats are available seven days a week, March through September, 10:00 A.M.–6:00 P.M. Rental rates are $8.00 for a two-person boat, $16.00 for a four-person one. The Jefferson Memorial is open daily, 8:00 A.M.–midnight.

Evening

Get ready for an international evening visiting two of D.C.'s most colorful neighborhoods. Travel west on Massachusetts Avenue until you come to Dupont Circle; about 6 blocks past the circle is **Embassy Row,** where you can take a minitour of the world just by taking a stroll down the street. Nearly 150 countries are represented in Washington by embassies and chanceries. The majority of them are located here in these tree-shaded, late-Victorian mansions that can be easily identified by the national flags, coats-of-arms, and other accoutrements they proudly display.

On to **Adams Morgan,** a little United Nations unto itself with its multi-ethnic sights, sounds, and flavors. To get there, take Massachusetts Avenue going east until you intersect with S Street. Make a left onto S, go 3 blocks to Connecticut Avenue, and turn left. In 2 blocks Connecticut Avenue will intersect in a V-shape with Columbia Road. Follow Columbia Road about 3 blocks into Adams Morgan.

In this neighborhood of colorful wall murals and eclectic art and music, you will find boutique shops of just about every nationality selling a wide range of wares, from beaten metal jewelry to authentic garb from Africa and other faraway places. Restaurants and sidewalk cafes tempt you with a multitude of accents, including Vietnamese, Brazilian, Hindi, Cajun, Caribbean, French, and Italian.

DINNER: The Grill from Ipanema, 1858 Columbia Road NW, Washington, DC 20009; (202) 986–0757. If the name doesn't make your taste buds start to samba, the Brazilian menu surely will. Start with a refreshing caipirinha, a native drink made with a powerful sugarcane liquor called cachaca, freshly squeezed limes, and sugar, or a non-alcoholic Guarana, a soft drink made with the berries of a fruit found only in the Amazon. A must-try is the rich stew of black beans, dry beef, pork, sausage, and smoked meat called feijoada. It's the national dish of Brazil created by Africans who arrived in the country between the sixteenth and nineteenth centuries. Moderate prices.

Any Friday or Saturday evening, you can enjoy the wry topical insights of a group of former congressional staffers-cum-musicians/political-satirists called **Capitol Steps** in the **Amphitheater of the Ronald Reagan Building and International Trade Center** (1300 Pennsylvania Avenue, Washington, DC 20004; 202–312–1555). Tickets are $31.50 and can be purchased in advance through Ticketmaster.

LODGING: Latham Hotel, 3000 M Street NW, Georgetown, Washington, DC 20007; (800) 368–5922 or (202) 726–5000. With its elegantly appointed lobby, spacious rooms, and gracious staff, the Latham offers a combination of comfort, luxury, and personal attention that is indicative of the fine European accommodations on which it is modeled. It is also home to one of Washington's most celebrated fine-dining restaurants, Citronelle. Deluxe rooms range from $139 to $245. Special winter discount packages may be available.

Day 2 / Morning

BREAKFAST: The Diner, 2453 Eighteenth Street NW, Washington, DC 20009; (202) 232–8800. This real old-fashioned eatery located in Adams Morgan lives up to its name, with hearty, low-priced omelets, pancakes, and other morning fare served up hot and fresh round the clock.

Head into downtown D.C. by going east on M Street to Pennsylvania Avenue. Make a right onto Pennsylvania and follow it to the White House.

If you want to tour the **White House** (1600 Pennsylvania Avenue NW, Washington, DC 20502), you must submit your request to your state's member of Congress up to six months in advance of the desired date. If your request can be accommodated, you will be notified one month prior to that date of your inclusion in a self-guided group tour. Tours are usually scheduled Tuesday through Saturday 7:30 A.M.–11:30 A.M. Seasonal White House Garden Tours may also be offered (call for dates and ticket information). All visitors should call the twenty-four-hour visitors office information line at (202) 456–7041 to determine if any last-minute changes have been made in the tour schedule.

Whether or not you take one of the inside tours, a stop at the **White House Visitor Center** at the southeast corner of Fifteenth and E Streets is definitely worthwhile. Open seven days a week from 7:30 A.M. until 4:00 P.M., the Visitor Center features a thirty-minute video as well as displays and information on many aspects of the White House, including its architecture, furnishings, first families, social events, and relations with the press and world leaders. The White House Historical Association also sponsors a sales area.

On-street parking is not available near the White House, so public transportation is usually a less frustrating alternative. The closest Metrorail stations to the White House are Federal Triangle (blue and orange lines), Metro Center (blue, orange, and red lines), and McPherson Square (blue and orange lines).

If you're one of those people who thinks that making money is what life is all about, take a stroll down by the Tidal Basin to the **Bureau of Engraving and Printing** (Fourteenth and C Streets SW, Washington, DC 20228; 202–622–2000) and get a few pointers from the pros. Each year, more than $100 billion in currency is printed here, with new bills (along with postage stamps and other important stuff) being produced at the rate of 8,000 sheets per hour—make sure you warn the kids not to try this at home. Exhibits at the **Visitor Center** trace the history of money from pieces of eight to our present currency. Open for guided tours Monday through Friday 10:00 A.M.–2:00 P.M. (evening tours available June through August). Peak season tickets are available from 7:30 A.M. Closed Federal holidays.

Afternoon

Head back to Georgetown and park at the hotel. Then walk across the street to **Miss Saigon** (3057 M Street NW, Washington, DC 20007; 202–333–5545) for a selection of delectable Vietnamese specialties to go. The restaurant is particularly well known for its sweet yet tongue-tingling clay pot–cooked caramel meat and seafood. For vegetarians, there's also a faux duck meat and vegetable sauté that could easily pass for the real thing. Inexpensive to moderate.

With lunch in hand, stroll the few blocks to **Washington Harbor** to rent a canoe at **Thompson Boat Center,** 2900 Virginia Avenue NW, Washington, DC 20037; (800) 654–6308 or (202) 333–9543. This is the best (and one of the only) means of transportation for getting to **Theodore Roosevelt Island** (703–289–2530), a beautiful eighty-eight-acre wilderness preserve in the Potomac between Georgetown and Virginia dedicated to one of America's most ardent environmentalists. Wandering the 2 miles of footpaths, you may very well find yourself alone (except for the 17-foot bronze statue of our twenty-sixth president) to commune at will with the abundant trees, wildflowers, and wildlife.

LUNCH: Picnicking is permitted at Theodore Roosevelt Island if you don't mind eating on a bench or bringing along a blanket to spread out on the grass.

On your return to Georgetown, head north on Rock Creek Parkway until you come to the **Arlington Memorial Bridge.** With the Lincoln Memorial on one side and the Arlington House (also known as the Robert E. Lee Memorial and Custis-Lee Mansion) on the other, this bridge was viewed as a symbolic post–Civil War link between the North and South. Cross to the Virginia side and you'll come to **Arlington National Cemetery,** once the estate where General Robert E. Lee and his family lived. It's now the final resting place for presidents, astronauts, and some 200,000 U.S. soldiers who fought in battles from the American Revolution to the Gulf Wars. At the main entrance you will see the new **Women in Military Service for America Memorial** and the **Visitor Center,** where you can pick up free maps and information. There is a nominal fee for parking.

Admission is free if you choose to explore the site on foot, but you also have the option of boarding a Tourmobile ($6.00 for adults, $3.00 for children three to eleven) for a narrated highlights tour that includes the **Kennedy Grave Sites,** the ceremonial changing of the guard at the **Tomb of the Unknowns,** the **Shuttle** *Challenger* **Memorial,** the **Iwo Jima Statue,** and **Arlington House.** At the south end of the cemetery is an area known as **Freedman's Village,** once a village for fugitive and liberated slaves, now the burial place of more than 3,800 of those who lived there during and after the Civil War. Arlington National Cemetery is open to visitors 365 days a year 8:00 A.M.–7:00 P.M. April 1 through September 30, and until 5:00 P.M. October 1 through March 31.

To get back into downtown Washington, cross the bridge to Constitution Avenue, then turn right onto Constitution Avenue.

By late afternoon the traffic in downtown Washington usually begins to thin out a bit, which means that your chances of finding a parking space increase and the lines at even the most popular monuments dramatically decrease. More than just another 555-foot-tall marble obelisk, the **Washington Monument** (National Mall at Fifteenth Street NW, Washington, DC 20001; 202–426–6841) has many stories to tell. Each of its 193 commemorative stones has a history of its own. Once inside, it's only a seventy-second elevator ride to the top and a panoramic view of the city you'll find nowhere else. Admission is free, but you will need a timed ticket, distributed on a first-come, first-served basis from 9:00 A.M. to 4:30 P.M. from a kiosk between Fourteenth and Fifteenth Streets on Jefferson Drive.

At the west end of the Mall at Twenty-third Street NW, the seated marble statue of our sixteenth president looks out over the capital from its columned Greek temple inscribed with the immortal words of his own Gettysburg and Second Inaugural Addresses. The **Lincoln Memorial** (202–426–6841) is open daily 8:00 A.M.–midnight. Free.

Evening

Every evening year-round at 6:00 P.M., you can see a free hour-long live musical and/or dance performance at the **Millennium Stage** in the grand foyer of the **John F. Kennedy Center for the Performing Arts,** 2700 F Street NW, Washington, DC 20566; (800) 444–1324 or (202) 467–4600. On stage (actually a specially built platform) you might see musicians representing genres from classical to jazz to folk, dancers from toe to tap, or even storytellers. No tickets are required. The Kennedy Center complex features five theaters and is home to the National Symphony Orchestra, the Washington Opera, and the American Film Institute.

DINNER: **Filomena,** 1063 Wisconsin Avenue NW, Georgetown, Washington DC 20007; (202) 33–PASTA. You can't miss Filomena's when you're walking down Wisconsin Avenue—not with its two "pasta mamas" merrily working in the front window. The Italian garden–like dining room with its statuary, bold displays of flowers, and softly glowing antique gas lamps is romantic. Presidents dine here, in a little area reserved for VIPs who might need a little special protection. But when it comes to service, the same gracious hospitality is extended to all. Resist filling up on the home-baked focaccia with pesto butter because the Italian regional entrees are enormous. Complimentary after-dinner decanters of sambuca and amaretto are accompanied, in the Italian tradition, by three coffee beans— one each for love, wealth, and health. Moderate to expensive.

LODGING: Latham Hotel.

Day 3 / *Morning*

BREAKFAST: **Martin's Tavern,** 1264 Wisconsin Avenue NW, Georgetown, Washington, DC 20007; (202) 333–7370. Weekend brunch here has been a D.C. tradition for generations. Since it opened in 1933, Martin's has been a regular stop for a wide variety of movers and shakers from presidential to media types. There's something for everyone from the basic ham-eggs-potatoes purist to the luxury seekers' lump-meat crab cakes. Inexpensive to moderate.

If you can possibly plan your Washington quick escape for a weekend when historian, author *(The Burning of Washington)*, and tour guide extraordinaire **Anthony Pitch** is scheduled to lead one of his Sunday two-hour walks through Georgetown, for heaven's sake do it! And be sure to arrive at the R Street steps to Georgetown Library at the corner of Wisconsin Avenue at 11:00 A.M. sharp because, as Pitch will show you, there's much more to this historic neighborhood than its profusion of great restaurants and glitzy shops. A master storyteller with a huge storehouse of facts at his fingertips, he will regale you with stories of the noted and the notorious who have always populated Georgetown and of the soap operas that continue to play out behind the elegant front doors of its town homes. Among the highlights are residences of past and present literary lights, politicos, suspected spies, even the neighborhood Mata Hari. Cost is $15.00 per person. For a schedule of Pitch's tours, call (301) 294–9514.

Afternoon

Head back to the National Mall area one last time. A few blocks north of the mall between the Capitol and the White House is **Ford's Theater** (511 Tenth Street NW, Washington, DC 20004; 202–347–4833 or 800–899–2367), where you can take in a matinee or evening performance of a new musical or original production in the restored setting of one of America's most infamous sites. It's kind of eerie to sit in this theater and look up at the bunting-draped presidential box with its empty chairs. It's even eerier to go down to the basement museum (free admission) where John Wilkes Booth's gun, Abraham Lincoln's bullet-torn coat, and other artifacts from that fateful night in April 1865 sit silently on display. Theater performance prices range from $27 to $40; tours (daily 9:00 A.M.–5:00 P.M.) are free.

After the shooting, Lincoln was carried to the **Petersen House** across the street (516 Tenth Street NW, Washington, DC 20004; 202–426–6924), where he died at 7:22 the next morning. Outside the house is a tree that visitors have turned into a makeshift memorial by covering its trunk with pennies. Open daily 9:00 A.M.–5:00 P.M. Modest admission fee.

Evening

DINNER: Georgia Brown's, 950 Fifteenth Street NW, Washington, DC 20005; 202–393–4499). For some real Southern comfort, don't miss the Low-Country South Carolina fare. Specialties include buttermilk-fried chicken, Carolina gumbo, catfish, and pecan-crusted lamb chops served with such down-home go-withs as fried green tomatoes, dirty rice, hoppin' John, and, of course, grits. Mostly moderately priced. Sunday gospel or jazz brunch, too.

To return to Philadelphia, go north on Route 29 about 15 miles, past Walter Reed Hospital; then get on the Beltway going east at exit 28 AB and stay on until exit 27 (I–495). Take I–495 north to I–95. Take I–95 north all the way to Philadelphia. The trip should take about three hours.

There's More

Tourmobile Sightseeing Trams, (888) 868–7707 or (202) 554–5100. For a single ticket price ($20 for adults, $10 for children three to eleven), you can hop on and off all day at twenty-five stops convenient to more than forty major historic sights and attractions (including Arlington National Cemetery). Twlight tours are also available.

Ticketplace, Old Post Office Pavilion (ground floor), 1100 Pennsylvania Avenue NW, Washington, DC 20004; (202) 842–5387. Selling half-price day-of-show and full-price advance tickets for sixty of Washington's cultural institutions and theaters. Discount tickets for Sunday and Monday are sold on Saturday.

National Museum of American History, Fourteenth Street and Constitution Avenue NW, Washington, DC 20560; (202) 357–2700. Edison's phonograph, the original star-spangled banner, and Fonzi's jacket—all in one place! And let us not forget that famed statue with the head of George Washington and the body of an Arnold Schwarzenegger look-alike. Free. Open daily 10:00 A.M.–5:30 P.M.

National Zoological Park, 3000 block, Connecticut Avenue NW, Washington, DC 20008; (202) 673–4800. Home to 5,000 animals from around the world and Amazonia, a re-created microcosm of the world's largest rain forest. Open daily 10:00 A.M.–4:30 P.M.; until 6:00 P.M. May through mid-September. Free admission.

U.S. Capitol, Capitol Hill, First Street between Constitution and Independence Avenues; (202) 547–1500. Open Monday through Saturday, 9:00 A.M.–4:30 P.M. Guided tours every fifteen minutes until 3:45 P.M. Free.

Special Events

Late March to mid-April. Cherry Blossom Festival, various locations; (202) 547–1500. Each year Washington celebrates the blossoming of its 6,000 Japanese cherry trees with a parade, crowning of the Cherry Blossom Festival Queen, sports activities, and arts-and-crafts shows. Free.

April. Annual White House Easter Egg Roll, White House South Lawn and Ellipse; (202) 456–2200. Children of all ages are invited to participate in this day of fun and entertainment.

December. National Christmas Tree Lighting Pageant of Peace, the Ellipse; (202) 619–7222. The celebration includes seasonal music and caroling. Nightly choral performances and special programs until New Year's Day. Free.

Other Recommended Restaurants and Lodgings

Washington, D.C.

Georgetown Inn, 1310 Wisconsin Avenue NW, Washington, DC 20007; (202) 333–8900. The first guests when this hotel opened in 1962 were the Duke and Duchess of Windsor, followed by Charles Lindbergh, Pearl Buck, and all of the Apollo astronauts. Colonial warmth, European style. Deluxe rooms range from $139 to $245.

Hay-Adams Hotel, Sixteenth and H Streets NW, Washington, DC 20006; (202) 638–6600. Right across Lafayette Square, this small, intimate hotel is a feast of architectural delights. Room rates are $269 weekdays, $300 weekends.

Kinkead's, 2000 Pennsylvania Avenue NW, Washington, DC 20006; (202) 296–7700. Adapting international dishes to American ingredients and taste is the hallmark of this very popular restaurant. Expensive.

Old Ebbitt Grille, next to the White House; (202) 296–7700. D.C.'s oldest saloon (1856) has fed numerous presidents and is a regular haunt of White House staffers. The menu features good crab cakes, mussels, and an oyster bar paired with oyster-friendly wines. Moderate.

Red Sage, 605 Fourteenth Street NW, Washington, DC 20005; (202) 638–4444. The creative hand of superchef Mark Miller is evident in a menu featuring smoked and roasted meat, game, seafood, and poultry among the house specialties.

Morrison-Clark Historic Inn, Massachusetts Avenue and Eleventh Street NW, Washington, DC 20001; (202) 898–1200. Beautiful, gracious, romantic—this circa 1864 boutique hotel comprises two separate historic town houses. It is also the only inn located in the nation's capital to be listed on the National Register of Historic Places. Throughout its history, the inn has also been a preferred spot for luncheons and teas hosted by First Ladies. Deluxe room rates range from $175 to $239.

For More Information

Washington, D.C., Convention & Tourism Corporation; (202) 789–7000; www.washington.org.

Washington, D.C., Chamber of Commerce Visitor Information Center, Ronald Reagan Building and International Trade Center, 1300 Pennsylvania Avenue, Washington, DC 20004; (202) VISIT–DC; www.dcvisit.com.

Alexandria and Mount Vernon, Virginia

George's Beloved

2 Nights

George Washington may have slept in a lot of places, but he always came home to his "beloved Alexandria." Who could blame him? For more than 250 years this lovely city on the Potomac has been capturing the affections of Americans with its timeless beauty and vibrant personality.

☐ Presidential Party Place

☐ Torpedo on Target

☐ Lively Nights

In Old Town Alexandria, today and yesterday happily coexist—sometimes in a single building. On gas-lantern-lit cobblestone streets named for international and American royalty, you can admire three centuries of architecture ranging from the modest to the magnificent. Then only a block or two away, find yourself in a modern mecca of top-shelf shopping and dining.

There has rarely been a dull moment here from its days as a busy eighteenth-century seaport to its role as a tinderbox for revolution and a somewhat reluctant defender of the capital during the Civil War. You can immerse yourself in all of that history by day. At night, however, Alexandria becomes a real party town, with an energy reminiscent of New Orleans during Mardi Gras. In fact, the place where George himself used to kick back is still around . . . and it's still a pretty happening spot.

Day 1 / Morning

It's a 2½-hour (152-mile) drive from Philadelphia to Alexandria. Take the Schuylkill Expressway (I–76) to I–95; go south on I–95 for 95 miles to I–895. Take 895 through the Harbor Tunnel and continue for 12 miles until you come to I–295 (the Baltimore–Washington Expressway). Take the Expressway for 29 miles to the Anacostia Freeway and stay on that for 21 miles. Get on I–495 (the Capital Beltway) and drive south for 2 miles into Alexandria.

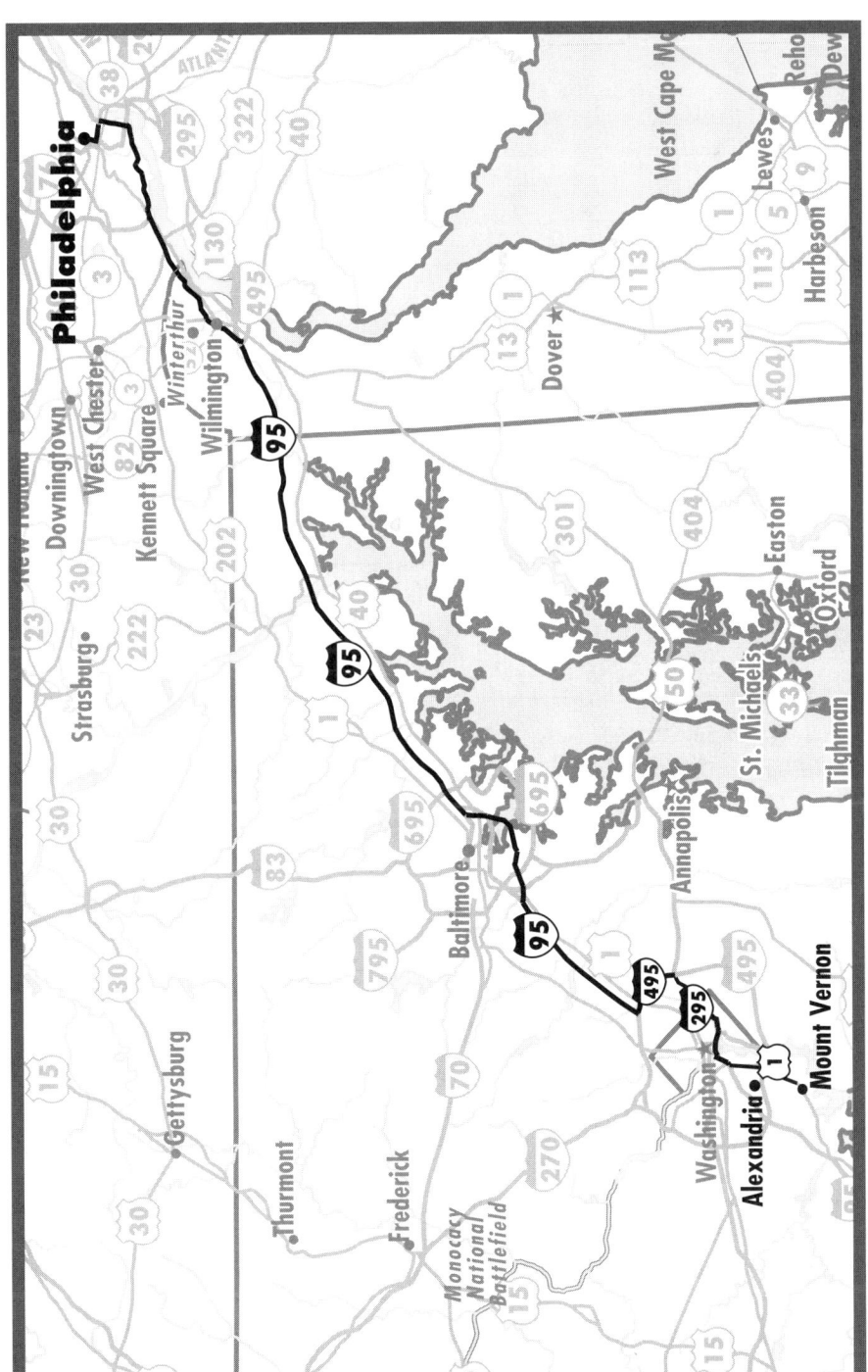

Afternoon

Stop at the **Ramsay House Visitor Center** (221 King Street, Alexandria, VA 22314; 800–388–9119 or 703–838–4200; open daily 9:00 A.M.–5:00 P.M.) and ask for a free twenty-four-hour guest pass that will allow you to park for free at any of the two-hour metered spots in Old Town (bring your license plate number). Also buy a Market Square Block Ticket ($9.00 for adults, $5.00 for children eleven to seventeen) for admission to three major attractions—Carlyle House, Gadsby's Tavern Museum, and Stabler-Leadbeater Apothecary Museum.

LUNCH: King Street Blues, 112 North St. Asaph Street, Alexandria, VA 22314; (703) 836–8800. This real Southern roadhouse tucked away just north of King Street in Old Town is a fun place with its whimsical murals and funky artwork, including a random pair of 3-D legs protruding from one wall. In a position of honor hangs a "reverent" stained-glass tribute to the restaurant's famous Wet Willie, a giant frankfurter with shredded pork barbecue, cheese, and other stuff. Also in residence (but not yet immortalized in stained glass) are its burger brother, the Wet Wimpy, and German sausage cousin, the Wet Wilhelm. The ribs are definitely worth a try, too. Generally moderate prices.

A few blocks east of St. Asaph Street and just north of King Street is **Carlyle House** (121 North Fairfax Street, Alexandria, VA 22314; 703–549–2997), one of the most important yet little-known buildings in American history. Completed in 1753 as a personal residence, it became the headquarters for British General Edward Braddock in 1755 and the place where the "revolutionary" idea of taxing the colonists was born. Guided tours 10:00 A.M.–4:30 P.M. Tuesday through Saturday; noon–5:00 P.M. Sunday.

The **Stabler–Leadbeater Apothecary Shop** (105–107 South Fairfax Street, Alexandria, VA 22314; 703–836–3713), opened in 1792, was the place where George and family, Daniel Webster, and Robert E. Lee bought everything from medicine to house paint. When the Depression caused the shop to close in 1933, the doors were simply locked and everything left as it was. Now this amazingly well preserved collection speaks volumes about the theories and tools that were the basis of medical care in early America. Open Monday through Saturday 10:00 A.M.–4:00 P.M., Sunday 1:00–5:00 P.M.

George Washington attended many balls and, in fact, held more than one of his own birthnight celebrations at what is now **Gadsby's Tavern**

Museum, 134 North Royal Street, Alexandria, VA 22314 (703–838–4242). Today Gadsby's has been restored to its eighteenth-century splendor as a museum furnished in period tavern style. Open April through October, Tuesday through Saturday 10:00 A.M.–5:00 P.M., Sunday and Monday 1:00–5:00 P.M.; November through March, Wednesday through Saturday 11:00 A.M.–4:00 P.M., Sunday 1:00–4:00 P.M.

A popular spot to river- and boat-watch is **Founders Park** (400 North Union Street, Alexandria, VA 22314; 703–838–4343), particularly at the **City Marina** at the park's southeast tip. The waterfront is also a favorite open-air stage for a variety of colorful street performers. And you never know when one of those magnificent tall ships will happen to dock nearby.

Evening

DINNER: Bilbo Baggins, 208 Queen Street, Alexandria, VA 22314; (703) 683–0300. If you are one of the many ardent fans of J. R. R. Tolkien's *The Hobbit* and the *Lord of the Rings* trilogy, you have to love this piece of the books' Middle Earth kingdom in Old Town Alexandria. The setting, with its literary-inspired murals and stained-glass windows, has the look of a charming old wood-and-brick cabin in the woods. There's also a lively bar that serves draft beer on tap. The menu shows imagination as well, from the tortellini with salmon, crabmeat, and fresh dill to citrus shrimp. Moderate.

In a town with as tumultuous a history as Alexandria, you can be sure there will still be some restless spirits from the past floating (flying? walking?) around. You can hear some of their stories—and perhaps even experience your own sighting—on the one-hour guided **Alexandria Colonial Tours Ghost and Graveyard Tour,** (703) 370–0185. $6.00 for ages thirteen and up, $4.00 for ages seven to twelve.

LODGING: Relais & Châteaux Morrison House Hotel, 116 South Alfred Street, Alexandria, VA 22314; (703) 838–8000. Designed and furnished in the style of a grand manor house of the late eighteenth–early nineteenth-century Federal period, this fine hotel reflects the character of Old Town Alexandria in the most charming of ways. Small and intimate, it is a bastion of elegance, from its comfortable parlor (the perfect place for daily afternoon tea and the popular piano sing-alongs that are held here every weekend) to its handsome mahogany-paneled library. Guest-room amenities include mahogany poster beds, brass chandeliers and sconces, decorated fireplaces, and Italian marble baths. Morrison House also has two distinctive restaurants—the laid-back, clublike Grille Room with its piano bar and the more upscale Elysium Room. Rates range from $175 to $400. Overnight parking is an additional $20 per day.

Day 2 / Morning

BREAKFAST: Alexandria Farmers' Market, Market Square in front of City Hall, King Street, Alexandria, VA 22314; (703) 838–4770. When in Alexandria, do as the colonials did—rise and shine early so that you can get the freshest breakfast fixings at this farmers' market held every Saturday from 5:00 to 9:00 A.M. George Washington was an early trustee of the market and would regularly send wagonloads of produce from Mount Vernon to be sold. Local farmers still bring their produce, meats, and plants to be sold here, and you can assemble a hearty morning meal from their fruits and fresh-squeezed juices, just-from-the-oven baked goods (including Southern ham biscuits), and tantalizing cinnamon-laced coffee. Look for real homemade crafts here as well.

Lee-Fendall House, 614 Oronoco Street, Alexandria, VA 22314; (703) 548–1789. In 1785 Alexandria lawyer Philip Fendall built this wood-frame house on land purchased from Revolutionary War hero "Light Horse" Harry Lee (father of Robert E. Lee). Four years later Fendall married Lee's sister, Mary, and subsequent generations of the Lee family lived here until 1903 (except for the period between 1863 to 1865 during the Civil War, when the site was used as a hospital for Union soldiers). From 1903 to 1937 renowned labor leader John L. Lewis came to live here and remained until he died in 1969. Guided tours offered Tuesday through Saturday 10:00 A.M.–4:00 P.M. and Sunday 1:00–4:00 P.M. focus on the lives of the residents during the early Victorian era (1850 to 1870) with family furnishings, records, and inventories. On the third floor is a permanent display of nineteenth- and twentieth-century dolls and dollhouses. Admission is $4.00 for adults, $2.00 for children eleven to seventeen, free for children under eleven.

Less than 4 blocks south on Cameron and North Washington Streets is **Christ Church** (703–549–1450), the house of worship regularly attended by George Washington (his pew has been preserved) and Robert E. Lee. Built between 1767 and 1773, this still-active Episcopal church welcomes visitors Monday through Saturday 9:00 A.M.–4:00 P.M., Sunday 2:00–4:00 P.M. Donations are welcome. Among the grave sites in the adjacent cemetery are those of eighteenth-century Yankee seamen and Confederate prisoners of war.

Afternoon

L U N C H : **Firehook Bakery & Coffeehouse** (main commissary), 214 North Fayette Street, Alexandria, VA 22314, corner of Fayette and Cameron Streets; (703) 519–8020. While you're picking up a sandwich and assorted goodies for your afternoon picnic, you can enjoy a great show watching the bakers mix, knead, shape, and bake traditional and exotic artisan breads in huge wood-burning ovens. Inexpensive sandwiches and giant cookies, including the award-winning Presidential Sweet (oatmeal with chocolate chips, dried cherries, pecans, and coconut). Firehook also has a retail outlet by the waterfront at 105 South Union Street; (703) 519–8021.

Take your picnic lunch to **Fort Ward Museum and Historic Site** (4301 West Braddock Road, Alexandria, VA 22304; 703–838–4848) located 2½ miles northwest of Old Town. To get there, follow King Street west to T. C. Williams High School. At the traffic light in front of the school, turn right onto Kenwood Street. At the next block, turn left onto West Braddock Road; follow it for ¾ mile. The entrance is on the right.

Immediately after Virginia's official secession in 1861, Union troops occupied Alexandria and nearby Arlington and began building a series of sixty-eight earthwork forts known as the Defenses of Washington. The best-preserved one, the restored Fort Ward, sits within a more than forty-five-acre park, which also includes picnic facilities and an open-air amphitheater where free twilight concerts are presented on Thursday evenings at 7:00 in summer. Adjacent are a museum (open Tuesday through Saturday 9:00 A.M.–5:00 P.M., Sunday noon–5:00 P.M.) and a reconstructed officers' hut that interpret the site's history and feature a broad-ranging display of Civil War artifacts. The park is open daily from 9:00 A.M. to sunset. Both the park and museum are free.

One of the things that makes Alexandria's waterfront so exciting is the fabulous art center known as the **Torpedo Factory,** 105 North Union Street, Alexandria, VA 22314; (703) 838–4565. Once used for the manufacture of weapons of war—such as the torpedo on display on the first floor—this huge building now houses studios for more than 160 artists. Although not all the work spaces are active at the same time, you can always find sculptors, painters, photographers, printmakers, jewelers, and other talented residents working in any number of media from paper and fibers to silver and gold. The center also showcases the works of over 1,500 more nonresident artists in its five cooperative galleries. On the third floor is the **Alexandria Archaeology Museum** (703–838–4399), a working laboratory where you can watch the pros piece together the city's past through rescued artifacts; there are hands-on activities for the kids. The Torpedo Factory is open daily 10:00 A.M.–5:00 P.M.; the Archaeology Museum is open Tuesday through Friday 10:00 A.M.–3:00 P.M., Saturday until 5:00 P.M., and Sunday 1:00–5:00 P.M. Both are free.

Evening

DINNER: The Fishmarket, 105 King Street, Alexandria, VA 22314; (703) 836–5676. The glistening seafood in the front display case should be your first clue that your catch of the day will be fresh. Built in 1765 and family-owned and -operated since 1950, the Fishmarket is indeed just what its name implies, as well as a restaurant where you can have your marine life prepared thirty different ways. Just about everything on the very moderately priced menu is available in lunch and dinner portions.

On weekend evenings when the museums close, Old Town shifts into party mode as the streets fill with revelers, and music from King Street pubs and clubs spills out onto the sidewalks. A number of the shops are open late, too, adding another dimension of entertainment to the evening. One of these is **Bird in the Cage Antiques** (110 King Street, Alexandria, VA 22314; 703–549–5114). Climb the stairs to a fantasyland of things past where little girls (and their mothers) have a ball trying on vintage prom dresses and feather boas and every antique and collectible has a story. For an international sampling of handmade crafts, art, and wearables from around the world, stop in at **Ten Thousand Villages** (824 King Street, Alexandria, VA 22314; 703–684–1435), which represents thirty developing countries, and **Women's Work** (1201 King Street, Alexandria, VA 22314; 703–684–7376), which represents fifty western Pacific islands.

Follow the long line to the **Scoop Grill and Homemade Ice Cream** (110 King Street, Alexandria, VA 22314; 703–549–4527) for a cone of Jack Daniel's, papaya, chocolate raspberry truffle, or other lick of heaven they've concocted today.

LODGING: Morrison House.

Day 3 / Morning

BREAKFAST: Two-Nineteen Restaurant, 219 King Street, Alexandria, VA 22314 (next to the visitor center); (703) 549–1141. If the weather is nice, you can sit outside and savor a traditional New Orleans brunch as you watch the weekend people-parade on King Street. You can

Mount Vernon, where George Washington slept whenever he could.

have your eggs perched atop fried Gulf fish with hollandaise, on artichoke bottoms over creamed spinach, or reclining on sautéed lump crabmeat and cloaked with brandied cream. Other Creole specialties include red beans, sausage, and rice; Louisiana fried oysters; and good old jambalaya. Moderate brunch and lunches, moderate to expensive dinners.

You couldn't possibly leave George Washington country without paying a visit to the place he cherished most, not only in Virginia but in the world—**Mount Vernon** (703–780–2000). The 8-mile trip south takes only about twenty minutes by car along the scenic George Washington Memorial Parkway, but an even more interesting way to travel there is by boat. On the *Miss Christin* (703–548–9000), which sails Tuesday through Sunday at 12:30 P.M. and returns at 4:00 P.M., the trip takes fifty minutes each way, but it's a relaxing sail along the Potomac with plenty of beautiful sights to see along the way. Tickets, which include admission to Mount Vernon, are $26 for adults, $15 for children ages six to ten, under three free.

During your 2½-hour layover at Mount Vernon, you'll have ample time to tour the mansion that Washington built between 1735 and 1787. Among the original furnishings are the bed where our first president died and his family's coat of arms. Recently opened at Mount Vernon is George Washington's personal study, filled with personal possessions that offer some interesting insight into the human side of this American legend. The more than 500-acre estate also features the working 4-acre Pioneer Farm; the slaves' living quarters, burial ground, and memorial; and the tombs of George, Martha, and other members of the family. Many special programs and exhibitions are held here throughout the year. Open daily April through August 8:00 A.M.–5:00 P.M.; March, September, and October 9:00 A.M.–5:00 P.M.; November through February 9:00 A.M.–4:00 P.M. Admission for adults is $11.00, $10.50 for senior citizens, and $5.00 for children.

LUNCH: Mount Vernon Inn, adjacent to the mansion; (703) 780–0011. I am always wary of dining establishments associated with major attractions because all too often they are merely bastions of mediocre food and so-so service hiding behind a stellar name. But this was an extra-delightful surprise. The dining rooms, of course, are pure colonial, complete with wood beams and fireplaces. However, instead of the usual cutesy theme menu (OK, so they do insist on calling one of their offerings a "pye"), the items reflect the chef's creativity as well as a true respect for old-time Southern cooking. You can start with a bowl of Virginia peanut and chestnut soup, then move on to salmon corn cakes, Southern pulled-pork barbeque, or colonial turkey "pye" with homemade buttermilk biscuit crust. The prices are surprisingly inexpensive to moderate.

If you took the early boat, you should arrive back in Alexandria at about 4:00 P.M. To return to Philadelphia, reverse the route from day one. The drive home should take about 2½ hours.

There's More

The Lyceum, 201 South Washington Street, Alexandria, VA 22314; (703) 838–4994. Built in 1839 as a community cultural center and library, this Greek Revival structure continues to fulfill its destiny as Alexandria's history museum. Here you can trace the story of this vital city from its founding in 1749 through archaeological finds, old photographs, maps, original art, and a wide variety of artifacts. Changing exhibits in the Coldsmith

Gallery focus on specific people, places, or events that have affected the course of Alexandria's history. Free.

George Washington Masonic National Memorial, King Street at Callahan Drive, Alexandria, VA 22314; (703) 683–2007. One of the most outstanding collections of Washington memorabilia in existence. Open daily 9:00 A.M.–5:00 P.M. Free.

Potomac Mills Mall, 2700 Potomac Mills Circle, Prince William, VA 22192; (703) 643–1770. A mecca for domestic and international travelers, this monster manufacturers' outlet and name-brand discounters' complex features 220 stores. Open year-round. Monday through Saturday 10:00 A.M.–9:30 P.M., Sunday 11:00 A.M.–7:00 P.M.

Special Events

February. Revolutionary War Encampment, Fort Ward Museum and Park; (703) 838–4848. Held the Sunday afternoon of Washington's Birthday weekend, this event features reenactors demonstrating camp life during the Revolution and a skirmish between British and colonial troops. Free.

February. George Washington Birthday Parade; (703) 991–4474. It is notoriously hard to be a hero in your own hometown ... unless you happen to be the first president of the United States. And George and Martha are always on hand to enjoy the festivities when marching bands, floats, military and reenactment units, Masonic groups, horses, and antique cars take to the street to honor Alexandria's favorite son.

May. Annual Memorial Day Jazz Festival; (703) 883–4686. Daylong extravaganza features a wide variety of jazz musicians and styles. Admission charge.

July. Annual Virginia Scottish Games and Festival, Episcopal High School, 3901 West Braddock Road, Alexandria, VA 22302; (703) 912–1943. Alexandria celebrates its Scottish roots with the U.S. National Highland Heptathlon, dancing competitions, bagpipe parades, and a British antique automobiles show. Admission charge.

September. Eighteenth Century Fair at Mount Vernon; (703) 780–2000. Take a peek into the past as more than seventy juried artisans demonstrate their crafts amid a colorful whirl of entertainers, including colonial musicians and fire-eaters. Food? Absolutely—and lots of it.

September. Annual Tour of Historic Alexandria Homes; (703) 683–5544. Owners of some of the city's most beautifully restored and decorated homes open their doors to the public. Admission.

Other Recommended Restaurants and Lodgings

Alexandria

Alexandria & Arlington Bed & Breakfast Network; (888) 549–3415 or (703) 549–3415. Hidden away on charming side streets throughout Alexandria are historic and just plain lovely private residences that offer guest accommodations. Finding them on your own would be a monumental task, but this one-stop-shopping service makes it easy to find just the right one to suit your taste and budget.

Ecco, 220 North Lee Street, Alexandria, VA 22314; (703) 684–0321. How could a restaurant that greets you with a life-size Charlie Chaplin shyly holding out a bouquet of silk flowers be anything but fun? This lively Italian spot makes delicious pastas and pizzas (there's even a sauceless white pie loaded with garlic, red peppers, and scallions if romance isn't on your day's menu). Portions are generous and prices quite moderate.

Fin & Hoof Restaurant, Sheraton Suites Alexandria, 801 North St. Asaph Street, Alexandria, VA 22314; (703) 836–4700. The daily breakfast buffet is a real bargain, featuring fresh fruit, made-to-order omelets and waffles; scrambled eggs, and all kinds of breakfast meats; assorted muffins, pastries, and cereals; juice and coffee—all for only $9.95. The restaurant also is known for its steak and seafood lunches and dinners.

Murphy's—A Grand Irish Pub, 713 King Street, Alexandria, VA 22314; (703) 548–1717. Traditional fare includes Irish stew, homemade Irish meat-and-potato pie, an "Irish Reuben," and, of course, corned beef and cabbage. There's also a wide variety of other pub grub, from potato skins and hot wings to burgers and club sandwiches to steaks, chops, and chicken. Inexpensive to moderate.

Gadsby's Tavern, 138 North Royal Street, Alexandria, VA 22314; (703) 548–1288. Quite good colonial American fare (yes, they serve "pye") including George Washington's Favorite Duck served in authentic surroundings. Period-style musical entertainment is offered in the evenings. Moderate lunches, moderate to expensive dinners, great Sunday brunch (rum French toast—yum!).

For More Information

Alexandria Convention & Visitors Association; (800) 838–4200 or (800) 388–9119; www.funside.com.

Alexandria Economic Development Partnership; (703) 739–3820.

Alexandria Chamber of Commerce; (703) 549–1000.

Virginia Tourism Corporation; (800) 932–5827 or (804) 786–2051; www.virginia.org.

Alexandria Transit Company's DASH system bus service; (703) 370–DASH.

INDEX

ABOUT THE AUTHOR

MARILYN ODESSER-TORPEY is a freelance travel and feature writer whose work has appeared in a number of publications, including *New England Travel & Life, Home & Garden, Main Line Today, Wine & Spirits Quarterly,* and *Elegant Wedding* magazines for the Philadelphia and Boston areas. A native Philadelphian, Marilyn only leaves home for quick—and, once in a blue moon, not-so-quick—escapes. She and her husband, Dan, their teenage daughter, Kristen, and three very rowdy birds are happy living in a lovely small town just west of the center of the universe. Twenty-something daughter, Dana, regularly checks in to make sure that the universe is just how she left it.